To be known, and to know others, is critical to all social relationships. The topic of "disclosure processes" pertains not only to people's disclosure of daily thoughts and emotions, but to their disclosure of many controversial problems in contemporary society, such as divorce, AIDS, and sexual abuse. The bulk of research has focused on disclosure processes in adults, and relatively little attention has been given to those phenomena in children and adolescents. The chapters in this book redress the balance by systematically examining disclosure processes in children and adolescents. They cover how, to whom, and the conditions under which children and adolescents reveal their personal thoughts and emotions. They include new research, extensive reviews of the research, and a focus on the contemporary issues of the role of disclosure processes in family therapy and sexual abuse. This book will be of interest to developmental psychologists, social psychologists, clinical psychologists, social workers, education specialists, and nurses.

Cambridge Studies in Social and Emotional Development

General Editor: Martin L. Hoffman, New York University

**Disclosure processes in children
and adolescents**

Published by the Press Syndicate of the University of Cambridge
The Pitt Building, Trumpington Street, Cambridge CB2 1RP
40 West 20th Street, New York, NY 10011-4211, USA
10 Stamford Road, Oakleigh, Melbourne 3166, Australia

© Cambridge University Press 1995

First published 1995

Printed in the United States of America

Library of Congress Cataloging-in-Publication Data

Disclosure processes in children and adolescents / edited by Ken J.
Rotenberg.

p.   cm. – (Cambridge studies in social and emotional
development)

ISBN 0-521-47098-6

1. Self-disclosure in children.   2. Self-disclosure in
adolescence.   I. Rotenberg, Ken J.   II. Series.
BF723.S26D57   1995
155.4'18 – dc20   94-22584
                                                                            CIP

A catalog record for this book is available from the British Library.

ISBN 0-521-47098-6 Hardback

Disclosure processes
in children and adolescents

Edited by

KEN J. ROTENBERG
Lakehead University

CAMBRIDGE
UNIVERSITY PRESS

Contents

v

Contributors

Jasmin Aquan-Assee, *Department of Psychology, Concordia University, 1455, de Maisonneuve Blvd. W., Montreal, Quebec H3G 1M8, Canada*

Thomas J. Berndt, *Department of Psychological Sciences, Purdue University, West Lafayette, Indiana 47907-1364*

Duane Buhrmester, *School of Human Development, University of Texas at Dallas, P.O. Box 830688, Richardson, Texas 75083-0688*

William M. Bukowski, *Department of Psychology, Concordia University, 1455, de Maisonneuve Blvd. W., Montreal, Quebec H3G 1M8, Canada*

Kay Bussey, *School of Behavioural Science, Macquarie University, North Ryde, Sydney NSW 2109, Australia*

Nancy Eisenberg, *Department of Psychology, Arizona State University, Tempe, Arizona 85287*

Richard A. Fabes, *Department of Family Resources and Human Development, Arizona State University, Tempe, Arizona 85287*

Beverly I. Fagot, *Oregon Social Learning Center, 207 East Fifth Avenue, Suite 202, Eugene, Oregon 97401*

Elizabeth J. Grimbeek, *School of Behavioral Science, Macquarie University, North Ryde, Sydney NSW 2109, Australia*

Nancy A. Hanna, *Department of Psychological Sciences, Purdue University, West Lafayette, Indiana 47907-1364*

Mona Holowatuik, *Department of Psychology, Lakehead University, Thunder Bay, Ontario P7B 5E1, Canada*

Nina Howe, *Department of Education, Concordia University, 1455, de Maisonneuve Blvd. W., Montreal, Quebec H3G 1M8, Canada*

Timothy U. Ketterson, *Department of Psychology, State University of New York at Albany, Albany, New York 12203*

Karen Luks, *Oregon Social Learning Center, 207 East Fifth Avenue, Suite 202, Eugene, Oregon 97401*

Christopher M. Manley, *Department of Psychology, University of Missouri at Columbia, Columbia, Missouri 65201*

Jovonna Poe, *Oregon Social Learning Center, 207 East Fifth Avenue, Suite 202, Eugene, Oregon 97401*

Karen Prager, *School of General Studies, University of Texas at Dallas, P.O. Box 830688, Richardson, Texas 75083-0688*

Ken J. Rotenberg, *Department of Psychology, Lakehead University, Thunder Bay, Ontario P7B 5E1, Canada*

H. Russell Searight, *Department of Family Medicine, Deaconess Hospital, and Departments of Community and Family Medicine and Psychology, Saint Louis University, Saint Louis, Missouri 63103*

Susan L. Thomas, *Department of Psychology, Southern Illinois University at Edwardsville, Edwardsville, Illinois 62026-1121*

1 Disclosure processes: an introduction

Ken J. Rotenberg

Revealing personal information to others, as well as the social perceptions of that act, have played a significant role in social relationships and society throughout history (see Rieber, 1980). Such acts and perceptions are an integral part of social relationships in modern society across a wide range of cultures (Altman & Taylor, 1973; Chelune, 1979; Goodwin, 1990; Ting-Tomey, 1991). Specifically, the revealing of personal information plays a crucial role in the major problems faced by men and women in modern times, such as AIDS (Maloney, 1988), abortion (Smith & Kronauge, 1990), rape (Koss, 1992), sexual preferences (Wells & Kline, 1987), and venereal disease (Inhorn, 1986). All involve persons revealing serious personal information that has significant social and health implications for themselves and often others. The contemporary importance attached to revealing personal information is reflected in the views held by various clinical psychologists that it is critical to mental health (Jourard, 1971; Raphael & Dohrenwend, 1987) and to the success of psychotherapy (Rogers, 1951; Truax & Carkhuff, 1967).

Revealing intimate information to others and perceptions of that act have been considered under the rubric of "disclosure processes." The fundamental assumption of the study of disclosure processes is that persons' verbal and nonverbal communications vary along a depth dimension, from very superficial to very personal or intimate (see Altman & Taylor, 1973). The focus of this book, as in the majority of studies on the topic, is on persons' verbal communications that are at the personal pole of this dimension (i.e., personal disclosure). Personal disclosure includes a person revealing his or her important thoughts, self-evaluations, intense feelings, or significant past experiences (see Altman & Taylor, 1973; Cozby, 1973). A distinction has been made between two aspects of personal disclosure: (1) descriptive, comprising the disclosure of factual information, and (2) eval-

1

uative, comprising the disclosure of feelings or judgments (Morton, 1978; Berg & Archer, 1982; Snell, Miller, & Belk, 1988).

Disclosure processes in *adults* have been investigated quite extensively. Books by Jourard (1971) and by Altman and Taylor (1973) were the original and significant contributions to the field. The bulk of the research on disclosure processes in adults has examined the role of personal disclosure in the intimate relationships that play a pivotal role in a person's social life. Personal disclosure has been found to play a significant role in the formation and maintenance of a range of adults' intimate relationships, such as same-sex friendships (e.g., Berg, 1984), heterosexual dating (e.g., Berg & McQuinn, 1986), and marriage (e.g., Hendrick, 1981; Prager, 1989). Furthermore, adults show the reciprocity of personal disclosure, whereby they match the personal level of others' disclosures, and adhere to that principal as a norm (Chaikin & Derlega, 1974; Miller & Kenny, 1986). The reciprocity of personal disclosure plays a significant role in adults' formation and maintenance of intimate relationships (Hendrick, 1981; Miller, 1990).

Considerable attention has been given to individual differences that affect patterns of personal disclosure and, as a consequence, shape or limit adults' intimate relationships. Researchers have investigated the affects on disclosure of loneliness (e.g., Chelune, Sultan, & Williams, 1980; Solano, Batten, & Parish, 1982), Eriksonian intimacy achievement (e.g., Prager, 1989), self-consciousness (e.g., Reno & Kenny, 1992), attachment (e.g., Mikulincer & Narchshon, 1991), sensation seeking (e.g., Franken, Gibson, & Mohan, 1990), and self-monitoring (e.g., Shaffer, Smith, & Tomarelli, 1982; Ludwig, Franco, & Malloy, 1986). One of the most extensive lines of investigation has been on sex differences in personal disclosure and intimate relationships. The majority of the studies indicate that females engage in more personal disclosure to same-sex peer friends than do males (e.g., Reisman, 1990; Dolgin, Meyer, & Schwartz, 1991). Finally, consistent with the position adopted by various clinical psychologists, personal disclosure promotes mental as well as physical health (e.g., Pennebaker, Hughes, & O'Heeron, 1987; Pennebaker, Colder, & Sharp, 1990) and plays a significant, albeit complex, role in psychotherapy (see Derlega, Margulis, & Winstead, 1987).

In contrast to the wealth of information about adults, little is known about disclosure processes in children and adolescents. There is, however, an increasing interest in this issue and a growing body of research. The existing research parallels that on disclosure processes in adults. I would like to point out that the works by Sullivan (1953) and Youniss (1980) have served as an important impetus for research on children's/adolescents' disclosure in intimate relationships and have provided valuable theoretical frameworks and insights. Some research has accumulated regarding children's/adolescents' personal disclosure in intimate relationships, such as with peer friends (Berndt & Bridgett, 1986; Buhrmester & Furman, 1987), siblings (Furman & Buhrmester, 1985), and parents (Hunter & Youniss, 1982). As in adults, researchers have documented the role of reciprocity of disclosure in children/adolescents and its role in the formation of intimate relationships (Cohn & Strassberg, 1983; Rotenberg & Mann, 1986; Rotenberg & Chase, 1992). Also, some attention has been given to sex differences in children's/adolescents' disclosure. The bulk of the research indicates that, as with adults, females provide more personal disclosures to same-sex peers than do males (Mulcahy, 1973; Papini, Farmer, Clark, & Snell, 1990), although this appears to be linked to feminine sex typing more than sex per se (Jones & Dembo, 1989). Finally, researchers have examined the individual differences in children's/adolescents' disclosure that limit their peer friendships, particularly loneliness (Franzio & Davis, 1985; Rotenberg & Whitney, 1992).

There are four major issues that stimulated the development of this book on disclosure processes in children and adolescents. First, it was apparent that there were limitations regarding the existing research on the role of personal disclosure in children's/adolescents' intimate relationships. The research has (a) been dispersed across a wide range of journals and other sources, (b) focused primarily on peer friendships, (c) with some exceptions, assessed self-reports of disclosure, and (d) given only limited attention to the role of individual differences in disclosure. These issues are addressed in this book.

In Chapter 2, Duanne Buhrmester and Karen Prager present an integrative review of research on children's/adolescents' disclosure to friends or other peers. In addition, these authors examine the functions of children's/adolescents' disclosure (social validation, social control, self-clarification, self-expression, and relationship development) and describe the role that personal disclosure plays in children's/adolescents' social development.

In Chapter 3, Thomas J. Berndt and Nancy A. Hanna describe their investigation of third- and seventh-grade children's personal disclosure to their peer friends and nonfriends. Rather interestingly, the study yielded no difference between the children's personal disclosure to friends and that to nonfriends. The authors attributed the lack of difference to the children's motivation to form intimate relationships with their nonfriend classmates.

In Chapter 4, Nina Howe, Jasmin Aquan-Assee, and William M. Bukowski describe the patterns of children's/adolescents' disclosure to their siblings, most likely one of their earliest experiences of intimacy. Howe and colleagues document the potential effects of the structural qualities of the sibling dyad (e.g., same-sex versus opposite-sex dyads) and qualities of the family (i.e., cohesion and adaptability) on disclosure between siblings across toddlerhood and early adolescence. It was found, for example, that there was greater personal disclosure between siblings when they were of the same sex and when they were part of the families characterized by flexibility in their relationships.

In Chapter 5, Ken J. Rotenberg and Mona Holowatuik describe their research on lonely preadolescents' disclosure behavior and related social perceptions (liking and familiarity). These researchers replicated earlier findings that lonely males displayed shy tendencies, whereas lonely females displayed an overeager orientation in their disclosure. In addition, though, lonely male preadolescents' disclosure was found to vary as a function of their partners' loneliness; greater personal disclosure was provided with nonlonely than with lonely partners.

A second thrust of the book is on children's/adolescents' personal disclosure to parents and adults in general. This has been the focus of some previous research (e.g., Hunter & Youniss, 1982; Hunter, 1985). Nevertheless, researchers have become increasingly aware that this is a complex phenomenon requiring further investigation. This issue is dealt with in five chapters of this book.

In Chapter 2, Buhrmester and Prager review the research on children's/adolescents' disclosure to parents versus peers. The review reveals that children's/adolescents' disclosures to parents as compared with those to peers differ in a complex fashion as a function of the age and sex of the children/adolescents and the interaction of the two factors. The authors describe in detail the different functions served by disclosure to parents as opposed to peers.

In Chapter 7, Ken J. Rotenberg deals with the issue of children's disclosure of negative moral behavior to adults as evidence of conscience development. He found in a study with kindergarten and second- and fourth-grade children that fourth-grade girls were most willing to disclose negative moral behavior to adults and hence displayed evidence of conscience development.

In Chapter 8, Beverley I. Fagot, Karen Luks, and Jovonna Poe describe a series of studies they undertook regarding the effectiveness of different types of parental strategies as a means of gaining information from children. In these studies, 3- to 7-year-old children were engaged in simple games, and later the mothers and fathers were asked to determine their children's feelings and experiences. In the third and final study, the researchers assessed the effects of parenting skills training on mothers' strategies of seeking information from their children. The authors found that the parents who were least successful in eliciting children's disclosure of their emotional states and experiences were those who used coercive styles of attempting to gain information (negative and intrusive). Parenting skills training decreased coercive styles in mothers and increased effectiveness in gaining information from their children.

In Chapter 10, H. Russell Searight, Susan L. Thomas, Christopher M. Manley, and Timothy U. Ketterson examine the preceding issue. These authors adopt a family systems approach to disclosure and argue that children's/adolescents' disclosure must be considered as part of the larger context of, and interrelations among, family members. This framework provides a useful means of describing the problems in disclosure of enmeshed and disengaged families. As previously indicated, Nina Howe and her colleagues in Chapter 4 identify the qualities of family interactions that affect children's/adolescents' disclosure to their siblings.

The third issue that served as an impetus for this book is the role that disclosure processes plays in our present knowledge of the social functioning of children/adolescents. Much of our knowledge about a variety of topics in developmental psychology (e.g., self-concept; see Damon & Hart, 1982) depends on children's/adolescents' disclosure of personal information to others. The most typical method of assessing children's/adolescents' self-concept is to require them to disclose their attributes to completely unfamiliar others (the experimenters) in a minimally intimate context (a group testing session in the school). Two outcomes of this procedure are quite possible. Such research may reveal a relatively "superficial" view of children's/adolescents' self-concepts, insofar as the subjects will likely provide little personal disclosures. Furthermore, disclosures provided under these conditions are likely linked to self-presentational skills, with children attempting to describe themselves in a socially desirable light (see Harter & Lee, 1989). A similar problem arises regarding other developmental topics, such as children's/adolescents' emotions and sexuality. For example with respect to the former topic, children acquire an understanding of a broad range of "display rules" – social rules prescribing how and when individuals regulate their verbal and nonverbal expression of emotion (Saarni, 1979; Gnepp & Hess, 1986). In some studies, children's/adolescents' reports of their emotions or even expression of emotions may reflect to a large extent their understanding of display rules rather than their veridical emotional states. By understanding disclosure processes in children/adolescents, researchers may devise methods that measure the various topics more adequately and at least allow identification of the *limits* of our existing knowledge of them.

Nancy Eisenberg and Richard Fabes's Chapter 6 is most relevant to the preceding issue. It focuses on the role of social desirability and broadly self-presentational effects on children's disclosure of vicariously induced negative emotion (sympathy or empathy). The authors hypothesized that girls acquire, through sex-role socialization, the expectation that they should display sympathetic reactions to the suffering of others. Consistent with that hypothesis, Eisenberg and Fabes found that girls reported greater distress reactions to others' distress than did boys when the children had high scores on a social desirability scale. By contrast, there were no sex differences in self-reported distress reactions when the children had low scores on a social desirability scale. The relation between self-presentation and disclosure is described further by Buhrmester and Prager in Chapter 2, as part of the social control function of disclosure.

The fourth and final impetus for this book is the current lack of attention given to the clinical and applied implications of disclosure processes of children/adolescents. Two chapters are dedicated to filling in this gap in our knowledge. In Chapter 9, Kay Bussey and Elizabeth J. Grimbeek deal with the controversial issue of children's disclosure of sexual abuse. These authors describe in considerable detail the cognitive and social factors that affect children's disclosure of being sexually abused. Included is a discussion of a less understood issue, that of the consequences of such disclosure for the children's psychological well-being and social functioning.

Searight and colleagues in Chapter 10 deal with the problems of disclosure by substance-abusing adolescents and the role of disclosure in family therapy. These authors discuss, for example, the potential for family therapy with drug-abusing adolescents to elicit misleading communication rather than honest personal disclosure.

At present, the research on disclosure processes in children and adolescents is scattered throughout the literature. This book is designed to integrate that information and provide it with a common focus. In addition, the book includes some new research from this rapidly expanding area. Such an undertaking should, by its very nature, serve a pivotal role in stimulating further investigation of the topic.

References

Altman, I., & Taylor, D. A. (1973). *Social penetration: The development of interpersonal relationships.* New York: Holt, Rinehart, & Winston.

Berg, J. H. (1984). Development of friendship between roommates. *Journal of Personality and Social Psychology, 46,* 346–56.

Berg, J. H., & Archer, R. L. (1982). Responses to self-disclosure and interaction goals. *Journal of Experimental Social Psychology, 18,* 501–12.

Berg, J. H., & McQuinn, R. D., (1986). Attraction and exchange in continuing and noncontinuing dating relationships. *Journal of Personality and Social Psychology,* *50,* 942–52.

Berndt, T. J., & Bridgett, P. T. (1986). Children's perceptions of friendships as supportive relationships. *Developmental Psychology, 22,* 640–8.

Buhrmester, D., & Furman, W. (1987). The development of companionship and intimacy. *Child Development, 58,* 1101–13.

Chaikin, A. L., & Derlega, V. J. (1974). Liking for the norm-breaker. *Journal of Personality, 42,* 117–29.

Chelune, G. J. (Ed.). (1979). *Self-disclosure: Origins, patterns and implications of openness in interpersonal relationships.* San Francisco: Jossey-Bass.

Chelune, G. J., Sultan, F. E., & Williams, C. L. (1980). Loneliness, self-disclosure and interpersonal effectiveness. *Journal of Counseling Psychology, 27,* 462–8.

Cohn, N., & Strassberg, D. (1983). Self-disclosure reciprocity among adolescents. *Personality and Social Psychology Bulletin, 9,* 97–102.

Cozby, P. C. (1973). Self-disclosure: A literature review. *Psychological Bulletin, 2,* 73–91.

Damon, W., & Hart, D. (1982). The development of self-understanding from infancy through adolescence. *Child Development, 53,* 841–64.

Derlega, V. J., Margulis, S. T., & Winstead, B. A. (1987). A social-psychological analysis of self-disclosure in psychotherapy. *Journal of Social and Clinical Psychology, 5,* 205–15.

Dolgin, K. G., Meyer, L., & Schwartz, J. (1991). Effects of gender, target's gender, topic and self-esteem on disclosure to best and middling friends. *Sex Roles, 25,* 311–29.

Franken, R. E., Gibson, K. J., & Mohan, P. (1990). Sensation seeking and disclosure to close and casual friends. *Personality and Individual Differences, 11,* 829–32.

Franzio, S. L., & Davis, M. H. (1985). Adolescent self-disclosure among preadolescents. *Personality and Social Psychology Bulletin, 9,* 97–102.

Furkman, W., & Buhrmester, D. (1985). Children's perceptions of the qualities of sibling relationships. *Child Development, 56,* 448–61.

Gnepp, J., & Hess, D. L. R. (1986). Children's understanding of verbal and facial display rules. *Developmental Psychology, 22,* 103–8.

Goodwin, R. (1990). Taboo topics among close friends: A factor-analytic investigation. *Journal of Social Psychology, 130,* 691–2.

Harter, S., & Lee, L. (1989). *Manifestations of true and false selves in early adolescence.* Paper presented at the biennial meeting of the Society for Research on Child Development, Kansas City, MO.

Hendrick, S. S. (1981). Self-disclosure and marital satisfaction. *Journal of Personality and Social Psychology, 40,* 1150–9.

Hunter, F. T. (1985). Adolescents' perceptions of discussions with parents and friends. *Developmental Psychology, 21,* 433–40.

Hunter, F. T., & Youniss, J. (1982). Changes in functions of three relations during adolescence. *Developmental Psychology, 18,* 806–11.

Inhorn, M. C. (1986). Genital herpes: An ethnographic inquiry into being discreditable in American society. *Medical Anthropology Quarterly, 17,* 59–63.

Jones, G. P., & Dembo, M. H. (1989). Age and sex role differences in intimate friendships during childhood and adolescence. *Merrill-Palmer Quarterly, 35,* 445–62.

Jourard, S. M. (1971). *Self-disclosure: An experimental analysis of the transparent self.* New York: Wiley-Interscience.

Koss, M. P. (1992). The underdetection of rape: Methodological choices influence incidence estimates. *Journal of Social Issues, 48,* 61–75.

Ludwig, D., Franco, J. N., & Malloy, T. E. (1986). Effects of reciprocity and self-monitoring on self-disclosure with a new acquaintance. *Journal of Personality and Social Psychology, 50,* 1077–82.

Maloney, B. D. (1988). The legacy of AIDS: Challenge for the next century. *Journal of Marital and Family Therapy, 14,* 143–50.

Mikulincer, M., & Narchshon, O. (1991). Attachment styles and patterns of self-disclosure. *Journal of Personality and Social Psychology, 61,* 321–31.

Miller, L. C. (1990). Intimacy and liking: Mutual influence and the role of unique relationships. *Journal of Personality and Social Psychology, 59,* 50–60.

Miller, L. C., & Kenny, D. A. (1986). Reciprocity of self-disclosure at the individual and dyadic levels: A social relations analysis. *Journal of Personality and Social Psychology, 50,* 713–19.

Morton, T. L. (1978). Intimacy and reciprocity of exchange: A comparison of spouses and strangers. *Journal of Personality and Social Psychology, 36,* 72–81.

Mulcahy, G. A. (1973). Sex differences in patterns of self-disclosure among adolescents: A developmental perspective. *Journal of Youth and Adolescence, 2,* 343–56.

Papini, D. R., Farmer, F. L., Clark, S. M., & Snell, W. E. (1990). Early adolescent age and gender differences in patterns of emotional self-disclosure to parents and friends. *Adolescence, 15,* 959–76.

Pennebaker, J. W., Colder, M., & Sharp, L. K. (1990). Accelerating the coping process. *Journal of Personality and Social Psychology, 58,* 528–37.

Pennebaker, J. W., Hughes, C. F., & O'Heeron, R. C. (1987). The psychophysiology of confession: Linking inhibitory and psychosomatic processes. *Journal of Personality and Social Psychology, 52,* 781–93.

Prager, K. J. (1989). Intimacy status and couple communication. *Journal of Social and Personal Relationships, 6,* 435–49.

Raphael, K. G., & Dohrenwend, B. P. (1987). Self-disclosure and mental health: A problem of confounded measurement. *Journal of Abnormal Psychology, 96,* 214–17.

Reisman, J. M. (1990). Intimacy in same-sex friendships. *Sex Roles, 23,* 65–82.

Reno, R. R., & Kenny, D. A. (1992). Effects of self-consciousness and social anxiety on self-disclosure among unacquainted individuals: An application of the Social Relations Model. *Journal of Personality, 60,* 79–94.

Rieber, R. W. (Ed.). (1980). *Psychology of language and thought: Essays on the theory and history of psycholinguistics.* New York: Plenum.

Rogers, C. (1951). *Client-centered therapy: Its current practice, implications, and theory.* Boston: Houghton Mifflin.

Rotenberg, K. J., & Chase, N. (1992). Development of the reciprocity of self-disclosure. *Journal of Genetic Psychology, 153,* 75–86.

Rotenberg, K. J., & Mann, L. (1986). The development of the norm of the reciprocity of self-disclosure and its function in children's attraction to peers. *Child Development, 57,* 1349–57.

Rotenberg, K. J., & Whitney, P. (1992). Loneliness and disclosure processes in preadolescence. *Merrill-Palmer Quarterly, 38,* 401–16.

Saarni, C. (1979). Children's understanding of display rules of expressive behavior. *Developmental Psychology, 15,* 424–9.

Shaffer, D. R., Smith, J. E., & Tomarelli, M. (1982). Self-monitoring as a determinant of self-disclosure reciprocity during the acquaintance process. *Journal of Personality and Social Psychology, 43,* 163–75.

Snell, W. E., Jr., Miller, R. S., & Belk, S. S. (1988). Development of the emotional self-disclosure scale. *Sex Roles, 18,* 59–73.

Smith, H. W., & Kronauge, C. (1990). The politics of abortion: Husband notification legislation, self-disclosure, and marital bargaining. *Sociology Quarterly, 31,* 585–98.

Solano, C. H., Batten, P. G., & Parish, E. A. (1982). Loneliness and patterns of self-disclosure. *Journal of Personality and Social Psychology, 43,* 524–31.

Sullivan, H. S. (1953). *The interpersonal theory of psychiatry.* New York: Norton.

Ting-Tomey, S. (1991). Intimacy expression in three cultures: France, Japan, and the United States. *International Journal of Intercultural Relations, 15,* 29–46.

Truax, C. B., & Carkhuff, R. R. (1967). *Toward effective counseling and psychotherapy: Training and practice.* Chicago: Aldine.

Wells, J. W., & Kline, W. B. (1987). Self-disclosure of homosexual orientation. *Journal of Social Psychology, 127,* 191–7.

Youniss, J. (1980). *Parents and peers in social development.* Chicago: University of Chicago Press.

2 Patterns and functions of self-disclosure during childhood and adolescence

Duane Buhrmester and Karen Prager

As the eyes are the "window of the soul," so too is self-disclosure a window to people's pressing feelings, thoughts, and concerns. In this chapter, we view the complex interplay between individual development and interpersonal experiences through the window of self-disclosure. We begin with an overview of our conceptual assumptions about the role that self-disclosure plays in the larger processes of individual development and interpersonal relationships. Next we summarize the current literature on developmental changes in patterns of self-disclosure. This summary provides a jumping-off point for the final sections in which we explore possible links between changing patterns of disclosure and concurrent changes in individual development.

Self-disclosure and development

In this chapter, self-disclosure is seen as part of a larger process in which social interactions shape, and are shaped by, the development of the individual child. Our thinking about these processes represents a marriage of ideas drawn from H. S. Sullivan's (1953) "interpersonal theory" of social development and Erik Erikson's (1968) "psychosocial" theory of personality and identity development. (A full discussion of the specific ways that Sullivan's and Erikson's ideas are reflected in our thinking is beyond the scope of this chapter. Suffice it to say that our notion of "needed social input and provisions" is similar to Sullivan's notion of social needs, whereas our notion of "developmental issues and concerns" is, in spirit, similar to Erikson's notions of "crises" and "preoccupations.") Figure 2.1 depicts what we view as the major components in this process.

The *issues and concerns* that occupy youth's attention exert a central organizing influence on self-disclosure. We assume that at any point in time, youngsters are concerned about a number of issues and outcomes

10

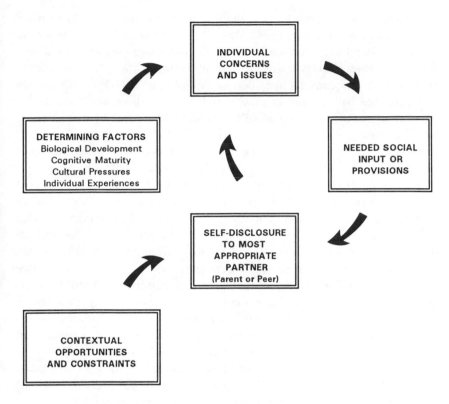

Figure 2.1. Self-disclosure and individual development.

that organize their thoughts, needs, and goals (Parker & Gottman, 1989). These issues/concerns are shaped by a diverse set of *determining factors,* including biological developments, cognitive maturity, cultural pressures, and individual life experiences. For example, a pubescent male may be preoccupied with issues of sexuality and moral character as they bear on his relationship with his girlfriend. Several determining factors set the stage for these concerns, including pubertal maturity, self-reflective cognitive capabilities, cultural mores about teenage sexuality, and personal involvement in a romantic relationship. Concerns about this issue pervade the teenager's thinking, feeling, and planning.

Salient issues and concerns in turn create *needs* for particular types of *social input* or *social provisions* that youngsters seek through social relationships. Social input/provisions are "needed" in the sense that they supply some type of beneficial information, feedback, or interactional forum that assists youngsters in their efforts to deal with their concerns (Weiss, 1974).

Self-disclosure, then, has an instrumental function: It is a means by which youngsters gain social input/provisions that address underlying issues and concerns. By telling a confidant about his lustful impulses and moral anxieties, our pubescent boy opens the door to a conversation that could generate feedback and constructive dialogue, helping him to deal with his concerns. As we will discuss in greater detail later, there are a number of different types of social inputs and provisions that can be gained through self-disclosure.

Two general factors appear to determine the types of relationship partners that are targeted as the *recipients of disclosure*. First, the specific type of social input/provisions that is needed partially dictates the type of partner that will be best able to supply that input. For example, a male friend may be in a better position than either a parent or a female peer to understand our pubescent boy's sexual impulses and moral concerns. Second, the structure of the social environment creates different *constraints on,* and *opportunities for,* disclosure to different partners. Although a male friend may understand our pubescent male's sexual impulses and anxieties, the social norms governing adolescent male–male friendship may place restrictions on self-disclosure. That is, the norms of male–male interactions may allow discussion of lustful desires (with appropriate bravado) but may inhibit disclosure that would expose the young man's vulnerabilities.

Finally, experiences with interaction partners affect, for good or ill, how issues and concerns are played out and resolved by the individual adolescent. For example, after talking it over with his friend, our teenager may decide that sexual activity is acceptable between partners that are emotionally committed to each other. As this example illustrates, self-disclosing interactions are not only prompted by underlying concerns, but also actively contribute to how concerns are resolved.

Our primary aim in this chapter is to explore how self-disclosure processes influence and are influenced by basic developmental processes. The account presented in Figure 2.1 helps us to identify mechanisms involved in developmental change. Starting with the determining factors, it is clear that there are a number of predictable developmental changes in the biological, cognitive, and cultural factors that shape the issues and concerns that are most salient to children and adolescents of different ages. Changing concerns in turn bring about changes in the types of social input/provisions that are sought to address these concerns. Changes in the types of input that are sought may lead to changes in the types of relationship partners who are the most frequent targets of self-disclosure. As such, developmental changes in the types of social input desired by young people may help explain developmental changes in the frequency of their disclosure to different relationship partners.

Research on changing patterns of self-disclosure

Ideally, the existing literature on children's and adolescents' self-disclosure would provide empirical accounts of developmental changes in each of the components of the process described in Figure 2.1. Although many studies have examined children's and adolescents' self-disclosure, the vast majority have concentrated on one component of the account: normative developmental changes in the recipients of disclosure, specifically parents and friends. Less is known, for example, about links between issues/concerns and the types of social input/provisions that are sought through self-disclosure, or about links between needed input/provisions and the choice of self-disclosure recipient.

In light of the current state of research, we attempt to accomplish two aims in this chapter. The first (which is addressed in this section) is to summarize the major findings about the one issue that has been studied most: age-related changes in recipients of disclosure. The second aim is to use these findings as the jumping-off point for a speculative discussion (in the final sections of the chapter) of developmental changes in the other components in Figure 2.1.

Descriptions of studies

Over the past 20 years, an increasing number of studies have either directly examined age-related patterns in naturally occurring self-disclosure or examined closely related aspects of interpersonal relationships (e.g., intimacy). These studies emerge from diverse theoretical concerns, starting with early work examining self-disclosure and its relationship to personal adjustment (Rivenbark, 1971; Jourard, 1979) and moving more recently to investigations examining (a) H. S. Sullivan's (1953) theory of friendship and social relationships during childhood and adolescence (e.g., Buhrmester & Furman, 1987), (b) children's constructions of relationships with parents and peers (e.g., Youniss & Smollar, 1985), (c) family communication patterns (e.g., Noller & Callan, 1990), and (d) patterns of social-support seeking (e.g., Hirsch & Rapkin, 1987). Although each of these approaches has yielded information about changing patterns of self-disclosure, this information is dispersed across several literatures. Our goal was to draw together and summarize these diverse perspectives about developmental changes in the targets or recipients of self-disclosure.

We limited our review to 50 studies that met three criteria: (a) A construct closely resembling self-disclosure was assessed, including preference for a target person as a confidant, receipt of emotional support from a specific person, time spent in conversation with a target person, or level of intimacy achieved in a specific relationship; (b) the study was designed to assess self-disclosure in at least two types of relationships (e.g., with same-sex friend and mother) or for at least two different age groups of subjects; and (c) the subjects were between 6 and 20 years of age (see Table 2.1). Notable studies that were not included in the review were those examining age differences in children's conceptions of relationships (e.g., Bigelow & La Gaipa, 1975) and those in which levels of self-disclosure were experimentally manipulated.

Forty-three of the 50 studies used retrospective self-report ratings to assess self-disclosure. A small handful of studies (5 out of 50) involved direct behavioral observation, 1 study used daily diary techniques, and another assessed objective intimate knowledge about the partner. Obviously, our current knowledge is limited by the heavy reliance on self-report questionnaires. Little empirical attention has been given to evaluating the effects of self-report biases, although some authors have speculated that gender differences may be partially due to the greater willingness of females to report self-disclosure (Berndt, 1982; Reis, Senchak, & Solomon, 1985). As such, the conclusions that are drawn from this body of research are largely limited to an understanding of youth's *perceptions of self-disclosure experiences*. Although subjective perceptions are certainly crucial to understand (Hinde & Stevenson-Hinde, 1987), they cannot provide, by themselves, a complete account of self-disclosing exchanges. Further progress in the area will depend on investigators using other methodologies that provide different types of information about self-disclosure processes (Olson, 1977).

The vast majority of these studies were conducted with middle- to upper-middle-class predominantly white samples. Only 3 studies were specifically designed to investigate Afro- or Hispanic-American samples. A total of 10 studies were conducted outside the United States, 6 of which were in Canada, Australia, and the United Kingdom, 2 in Israel, and 1 each in Costa Rica, Turkey, and the former USSR. In most instances the patterns of findings are quite similar across different ethnic and cultural samples, but there are provocative exceptions. For example, findings from 2 studies suggest that parents play more important roles as targets of disclosure among youth of Hispanic, as compared with Anglo, cultural backgrounds (Serrano, 1984; DeRosier & Kupersmidt, 1991). Further work is needed to identify the specific cultural pressures that influence patterns of self-disclosure. Because of the limited information available on other cultural and ethnic populations, this review's conclusions are explicitly confined to middle-class white Americans.

Table 2.1. *Summary of studies examining self-disclosure in children and adolescents*

Investigation	Sample	Measure/construct	Peer relationship effects	Family relationship effects	Peer–family comparisons
Balswick & Balkwell, 1977 (U.S.)	991 high school Afro-Amer. & Anglo-Amer.	S-R extent of topic disclosure to Mom & Dad		F: Mom > Dad M: Dad > Mom	
Berg-Cross, Kidd, & Carr, 1990 (Black American)	60 14–16 yr	S-R Y/N Choice of Mom, Dad & frd as target of topic disclosure		Mom > Dad for six of nine topics	Mom > Frd for 7/9 topics Dad > Frd for 3/9 topics Frd > Dad for 2/9 topics
Berndt & Perry, 1986 (U.S.)	32 8 yr 41 10 yr 26 12 yr 23 14 yr	I-R extent of intimacy w/SSF	SSF: Linear increase from 7–14 yr SSF: No gender differences		
Blyth & Foster-Clark, 1987 (U.S.)	2,403 12–16 yr	S-R extent of intimacy w/Mom, Dad, & SSF	SSF: F > M; OSF: F = M M: SSF = OSF F: SSF > OSF	Mom: F = M; Dad: M > F M: Mom = Dad F: Mom = Dad	M: Mom & Dad > SSF > OSF F: SSF > Mom > Dad > OSF
Blyth & Traeger, 1988 (U.S.)	1,617 12–16 yr	S-R extent of intimacy w/Mom, Dad, SSF, & OSF	SSF M's: 12–14 yr < 15 yr[a] SSF F's: 12 yr < 13–15 yr[a] OSF M's: 12 yrs < 13–14 yr < 15 yr[a] OSF F's: 12 yr < 13 yr < 14 yr < 15 yr[a] SSF & OSF: F > M M & F: SSF > OSF	Mom & Dad M: no age differences Mom F: no age differences Dad F: 12 yr > 13–15 yr Dad F: M > F; Mom F: M = F M: Mom = Dad; F: Mom > Dad	12- to 14-yr M: Mom = Dad > SSF > OSF 12 yr F: SSF > OSF M: Mom = Dad = SSF > OSF 12 yr F: SSF = Mom = Dad > OSF 13- to 14-yr F: SSF > Mom > Dad > OSF 15-yr F: SSF = Mom > OSF = Dad
Buhrmester, 1990 (U.S.)	133 10–12 yr 100 13–15 yr	S-R extent of intimacy w/SSF	SSF: no age differences SSF: F > M		

Table 2.1. (*cont.*)

Investigation	Sample	Measure/construct	Peer relationship effects	Family relationship effects	Peer–family comparisons
Buhrmester & Carbery, 1992 (U.S.)	132 13–16 yr	Daily interaction record of disclosure w/ Mom, Dad, SS peers, & OS peers	SS peers: F > M / OS peers: F = M / M: SS peers = OS peers / F: SS peers > OS peers	Mom: F > M / Dad: F = M / M: Dad > Mom / F: Mom > Dad	M: Dad = OS peer > Mom > SS peer / F: SS peer = Mom > OS peer = Dad
Buhrmester & Furman, 1987 (U.S.)	129 7 yr / 153 10 yr / 133 13 yr	S-R extent intimate disclosure w/Mom, Dad, SSF, OSF, RP	SSF M's: No age differences. / SSF F's: 7 yr < 11 yr < 13 yr / SSF: F > M for 13 yr but not 7 yr / OSF: 7 & 11 yr < 13 yr; F = M / RP: 11 < 13; F = M	Mom: 7 yrs & 11 yr > 13 yrs; F = M / Dad: 7 yrs & 11 yr > 13 yrs; F = M	7 yr: Mom & Dad > Frd / 10 yr: Mom & Dad > Frd / 12 yr: frd > Mom & Dad
Burke & Weir, 1978 (Canada)	274 13–20 yr	S-R extent of disclosure and problems discussed w/ Mom, Dad, & peers	Peers: F > M / No analysis for age effect	Mom & Dad: F = M / F: Mom > Dad / M: Mom = Dad / No analysis for age effects	M: Peers = Mom = Dad / F: Peers > Mom > Dad
Camarena, Sarigiani, & Peterson, 1990 (U.S.)	335 13 yr	S-R extent of self-disclosure w/SSF	SSF: F > M		
Cramer, 1987 (U.K.)	309 13–31 yr / Mean = 19 yr / (72% F)	S-R extent of empathy (understanding) w/Frd	Frd: F > M		
Cramer, 1989 (U.K.)	194 16 yr / (84% F)	S-R extent of empathy (understanding) w/SSF, OSF, Mom & Dad	SSF = OSF / SSF & OSF: no analysis for gender differences	Mom > Dad / Mom & Dad: no analysis of gender differences	SSF = OSF > Mom > Dad
Crockett, Losoff, & Petersen, 1984 (U.S.) Measure 1	335 assessed at 11, 12, & 13 yr	S-R time talking on phone with SSF	SSF F: 11 yr < 12 yr < 13 yr[a] / SSF M: 11 yr < 13 yr; 12 yr = 11 & 13 yr[a] / SSF: F > M at all ages		

Study	N / ages	Measure	Results	Comments
Crocket, Losoff, & Petersen, 1984 (U.S.) Measure 2	335 assessed at 11, 12, & 13 yr	S-R Y/N choice of SSF as target to talk about problems	SSF F: 11 yr < 12 yr = 13 yr[a] SSF M: 11 yr < 12 yr < 13 yrs[a] SSF: F > M at all ages	Based on comparison with data from Richardson et al., 1984 M: Mom > Dad > SSF[a] 11 & 12 F: Mom > SSF > Dad[a] 13-yr F: Mom = SSF > Dad[a]
Crocket, Losoff, & Petersen, 1984 (U.S.) Measure 3	335 assessed at 12 & 13 yr	S-R forced choice among SSF, Mom, or Dad as to who understands best	SSF M's: 12 yr < 13 yr[a] SSF F's: 12 yr = 13 yr[a] SSF: F > M at both ages	Based on comparison with data from Richardson et al., 1984 12-yr M: Mom > SSF > Dad[a] 13-yr M: Mom = SSF > Dad[a] 12- & 13-yr F: SSF > Mom > Dad
DeRosier & Kupersmidt, 1991 (Costa Rican)	60 9 yr 82 11 yr	S-R extent of intimate disclosure w/SSF	SSF: 9 yr < 11 yr SSF: No gender differences	Mom: 9 yr = 11 yr; Dad: 9 yr > 11 yr Mom & Dad: no gender differences Mom > Dad
Diaz & Berndt, 1982	40 10 yr 40 14 yr	Objective intimate knowledge of SSF	SSF: 10 yr < 14 yr for intimate knowledge SSF: 10 yr = 14 yr for external knowledge SSF: F > M for external knowledge	
Dorval, Brannan, Duckworth, & Smith, 1987 (U.S.)	20 7 yr 20 11 yr 20 17 yr 20 22 yr 20 25 yr	Observed relatedness of conversation turns w/SSF	SSF: increase w/age in factual and perspective relatedness and inferring SSF: no analysis of gender differences	
East, 1991 (U.S.)	450 11 yr withdrawn, aggressive, & sociable	S-R extent of warm-closeness w/Mom & Dad Parent-R of warm/close w/ child		Child ratings of Mom: F > M Child ratings of Dad: F = M Mom ratings of child: F > M Dad ratings of child: F = M

Table 2.1. (*cont.*)

Investigation	Sample	Measure/construct	Peer relationship effects	Family relationship effects	Peer–family comparisons
Furman & Buhrmester, 1985 (U.S.)	199 11–13 yr	S-R extent of intimate disclosure w/ Mom, Dad, & SSF	SSF: F > M	Mom: F > M Dad: F = M F: Mom > Dad M: Mom = Dad	M: SSF = Mom = Dad F: SSF = Mom > Dad
Furman & Buhrmester, 1992 (U.S.)	107 9 yr 119 12 yr 112 15 yr 216 19 yr	S-R extent of intimate disclosure w/ Mom, Dad, SSF, & RP (not reported separately from support in publication)	SSF: 9 yr < 12, 15, & 19 yr SSF: F > M at all ages RP: 9 yr < 12; 15 yr < 19 yrs RP: F > M	Mom F's: 9 yr > 12; 15 yr < 19 yr Mom M's: 9 yr > 12 yr > 15 & 19 yr Mom: F > M at 15 & 19 yrs Dad: 9 & 12 yr > 15 yr < 19 yr Dad: M > F	9 yr: Mom = Dad > SSF > RP 12 yr: Mom = Dad = SSF > RP 15 yr: SSF > Mom = RP > Dad 19 yr: SSF = Mom = RP > Dad
Giordano, Cernkovich, & Pugh, 1986 (U.S.)	942 12–19 yr delinquents/ nondelinquent, & black/white	S-R extent of disclosure to Frd	Frd: F > M Frd: Black = white Frd: Delinquent > nonoffender		
Gottman & Mettetal, 1986 (U.S.)	10 6–7 yr 10 11–12 yr 10 16–17 yr Mostly F	Observed conversation codes w/SSF	Gossip: 6 yr < 11 yr < 16 yr Disclosure: 6 yr = 11 yr < 16 yr No analysis of gender differences		
Hirsch & Rapkin, 1987 (U.S.)	159 assessed at 11 & 12 yr	S-R extent of intimate disclosure w/Frds	Frds: 11 yr < 12 yrs Frds: no analysis of gender differences		
Hortacsu, 1989 (Turkish)	648 12–18 yr	S-R Y/N choice of Mom, Dad, & frd as conversation partner	Frd: 12 yr < 15–18 yr[a] Frd: F > M Frd: no analysis of gender differences	Mom: 12 yr > 15–17 yr > 18 yr[a] Dad: no age differences[a] Mom: F > M; Dad: F < M M: Mom = Dad; F: Mom > Dad	12 yr: Mom > Frd; Dad = Mom & Frd 15–18 yr: Frd > Mom & Dad

18

Study	N, age	Measure	Gender/Age effect	Age/Gender effect	Target comparison
Hunter & Youniss, 1982 (U.S.)	30 9 yr 30 12 yr 30 15 yr 30 19 yr	S-R frequency of intimacy w/ Frd, Mom, & Dad	SSF: 9 yr < 12 yr < 15 yr < 18 yr SSF: F > M at 12–19 yr; F = M at 9 yr	Mom: no age differences Mom: F = M Dad: 9 yr < 12 yr > 15–19 yr Dad: F = M	9 yr: Mom > Frd & Dad 12 yr: Frd = Mom = Dad 15–19 yr: Frd > Mom > Dad
Johnson & Aires, 1983 (U.S.)	176 18–23 yr	S-R frequency of topic disclosure to SSF	SSF: F > M for family activities, family problems, doubts and fears, intimate relationships and secrets about the past		
Jones & Dembo, 1989 (U.S.)	42 9–10 yr 90 11–12 yr 85 13–14 yr	S-R frequency of frankness/spontaneity and sensitivity/knowledge w/SSF	SSF F: 9 yr < 11 yr = 13 yr[a] SSF M: 9 yr = 11yr = 13 yr[a] SSF: F = M at 9 yr; F > M at 11–14 yr[a]		
Kneisel, 1987 (U.S.)	47 12 yr 71 14 yr 89 17 yr	S-R likelihood of seeking support from Mom, Dad, SSF, & OSF	SSF & OSF: Increase from 12–17 yr SSF & OSF: no analysis of gender differences	Mom & Dad: no age differences Mom > Dad No analysis of gender differences	Female Frd > Mom > Dad & Male Frd No analysis of age interactions
Kon, Losenkov, De Lissovoy, & De Lissovoy, 1978 (U.S.S.R.)[a]	223 14 yr 212 15 yr 265 16 yr 235 17 yr 372 20 yr	S-R extent of confidentiality w/ Frd, Mom, & Dad	Frd: no age differences Frd: F = M	Mom: linear decrease from 14 to 16 yr Mom: F = M Dad M's: linear decrease from 14 to 16 yr Dad F's: no age differences Dad: M > F	14–15 yr: SSF & Mom > Dad 16–20 yr: SSF > Mom > Dad
Mulcahy, 1973 (Canada)	97 15–20 yr	S-R extent of topic disclosure to SSF & OSF	SSF: F > M OSF: F = M M: SSF = OSF F: SSF > OSF		
Noller & Callan, 1990 (Australia)	54 13 yr 65 14 yr 43 15 yr 63 16 yr 71 17 yr	S-R extent of topic disclosure to Mom & Dad		Mom: F > M; Dad: M = F F: Mom > Dad; M: Mom = Dad No analysis of age effects	

Table 2.1. *(cont.)*

Investigation	Sample	Measure/construct	Peer relationship effects	Family relationship effects	Peer–family comparisons
Papini, Farmer, Clark, Micka, & Barnett, 1990 (U.S.)	26 12 yr 57 13 yr 58 14 yr 33 15 yr	S-R frequency of emotional disclosure to Frd & parents	Frd: 12 yr < 15 yr Frd: F > M at all ages	Parents: no age differences Parents: F > M at all ages	12 yr: parents > Frds 13–14 yr: parents = Frds 15 yr: Frds > parents
Papini, Farmer, Clark, & Snell, 1988 (U.S.)	47 15 yr 59 16 yr 63 17 yr	S-R frequency of sexual disclosure to Mom, Dad, SSF, & OSF	SSF: F = M OSF: F = M M: SSF > OSF F: SSF > OSF SSF & OSF: no analysis of age differences	Mom: F > M Dad: M > F M: Mom = Dad F: Mom > Dad Mom & Dad: No analysis of age differences	M: SSF > OSF > Mom & Dad F: SSF > OSF > Mom > Dad No analysis of age interactions
Raffaelli & Duckett, 1989 (U.S.)[a]	160 10–11 yr 168 12–13 yr 73 14 yr	S-R time spent talking to family & Frds	Frds F's: 10 yr < 12–13 yr < 14 yr[a] Frds M's: 10 yr < 12–14 yr[a] Frds: F > M at all ages	Family: no age or gender differences	10 yr: Frd = family 12–14 yr: Frds > family
Reid, Landesman, Treder, & Jaccard, 1989 (U.S.)	249 6–12 yr	S-R satisfaction w/ emotional support from Mom, Dad, & Frd	Frds: no analysis of gender or age differences	Mom & Dad: no analyses of gender or age differences Mom = Dad	Mom = Dad > frd
Richardson, Galambos, Schulenberg, & Petersen, 1984 (U.S.) Measure 1	334 assessed at 12 & 13 yr	S-R forced choice among Mom or Dad as who understands best		Mom: M = F Dad: M > F M & F: Mom > Dad Mom & Dad: no age differences	Based on comparison with data from Crockett et al., 1984 12-yr M: Mom > SSF > Dad[a] 13-yr M: Mom = SSF > Dad[a] 12- & 13-yr F: SSF > Mom > Dad[a]
Richardson, Galambos, Schulenberg, & Petersen, 1984 (U.S.) Measure 2	334 assessed at 11, 12, & 13 yr	S-R Y/N choice of Mom & Dad as targets of talk about problems		Mom: M = F Dad: M > F M & F: Mom > Dad Mom & Dad: no age differences	Based on comparison with data from Crockett et al., 1984 M: Mom > Dad > SSF[a] 11 & 12 F: Mom > SSF > Dad[a] 13-yr F: Mom = SSF > Dad[a]

Study	Sample	Measure	Age differences	Gender differences	Target differences
Rivenbark, 1971 (U.S.)	25 9 yr 36 11 yr 34 13 yr 28 15 yr 26 17 yr	S-R extent of topic disclosure to Mom, Dad, SSF, & OSF	SSF M's: no age differences SSF F's: 9 & 11 yr < 13, 15, & 17 yr SSF: F > M at 13–17 yr; F = M at 9–11 OSF: 11 & 13 yr < 15 & 17 yr OSF: F > M at 11–15; F + M at 9 & 19	Mom & Dad: no reliable age differences F: Mom > Dad M: Mom = Dad Mom: F > M Dad: F = M	F's: Mom > Dad = SSF > OSF at 9–13 yr; F's: Mom = SSF > OSF > Dad at 15 yr; F's: SSF > Mom > OSF > Dad at 17 yr M's: Mom = Dad > SSF > OSF at 9–11 yr M's: Mom = Dad = SSF > OSF at 13–15; M's: SSF = OSF > Mom = Dad at 17 yr
Rosenberg, Hertz-Lazarowitz, & Guttman, 1985 (Israel)	208 10–11 yr divorced vs. intact families	S-R frequency of frank/spontaneity & sensitivity/knowledge w/ Mom, Dad, Frd	Frd: no analysis of gender differences	Intact: Mom = Dad Divorced Mom > Dad Mom & Dad: no analysis of gender differences	Intact: Mom = Dad > Frd Divorced: Mom > Frd = Dad
Rotenberg & Sliz, 1988 (Canada)	16 5 yr 16 7 yr 16 9 yr	Experimental low and high personal topic disclosure via recording to SSF	SSF: 5 yr < 7 yr = 9 yr No gender differences		
Serrano, 1984 (Anglo-Amer. & Mex.-Amer.)	88 14 yr	S-R extent of topic disclosure to Mom, Dad, & Frd	Frd: no gender or ethnic difference reported	Mom: no gender or ethnic difference reported Dad: M > F	Anglo M: Mom > Frd = Dad Anglo F: Frd > Mom > Dad Mex./Amer. M: Mom > Frd = Dad Mex./Amer. F: Mom > Frd = Dad
Sharabany, Gershoni, & Hofman, 1981 (Israel)[a]	120 11 yr 120 13 yr 120 14 yr 120 17 yr	S-R extent of intimacy w/ SSF & OSF	SSF: no age differences SSF: F > M at all ages OSF M's: 10 yr < 12–14 yr < 17 yr OSF F's: 10 yr < 12 yr < 14 yr < 17 yr OSF: F > M for 14–17 yrs but not 10–12 yr		

Table 2.1. *(cont.)*

Investigation	Sample	Measure/construct	Peer relationship effects	Family relationship effects	Peer–family comparisons
Slavin, 1991 (U.S.)	378 14 yr 455 15 yr 403 16 yr	S-R extent of emotional support from family & Frds	Frds: no age differences Frds: F > M	Family: 14 & 15 yr > 16 yr	F: Frds > family M: Frds = family
Slavin & Raimer, 1990 (U.S.)	104 14 yr 66 15 yr 107 16 yr 7 mo. long	S-R extent of emotional support from parents and Frds	Frd: No age differences Frd: F > M	Parents: no age or gender differences	F: Frd > Parents M: Frd = Parents
Smollar & Youniss, 1982 (U.S.) Study no. 1	40 10–11 yr 38 13–14 yr 47 16–17 yr	S-R extent of obligation to provide emotional support to Frds	Frd: F > M Frd: 10–11 yr < 13–14 yr < 16–17 yr[a]		
Smollar & Youniss, 1982 (U.S.) Study no. 2	20 10–11 yr 20 14–16 yr 20 18–19 yr 20 22–24 yr	S-R extent of talk about personal problems to Frds	Frds M's: 10 & 14 yr < 18 & 22 yr Frds F's: 10 yr < 14 yr < 18 & 22 yr F = M at 10 yr: F > M at 14–22 yr		
Tan & Berndt, 1991 (U.S.)	106 8 & 12 yr	Observed conversation of Frds & classmates	12 yr > 8 yrs in whispering, self-focused comments, gossip about peers, & talk about experimental setting; no analysis of gender differences		
Tanne, 1990a (U.S.)	20 7 yr 20 11 yr 20 15 yr	Observed topical coherence of conversations between SSF	Females talked at more length and depth about a smaller number of topics related to troubles than males; topics were more personal in older groups		

Citation	N and age	Measure	Peer/friend effects	Parent/adult effects	Relationship comparison
West & Zingle, 1969 (U.S.)	296 14 yr	S-R extent of topic disclosure to Mom, Dad, SSF, & OSF	M & F: SSF > OSF; SSF: F > M; OSF: F = M	Mom: F > M; Dad: F = M; M & F: Mom > Dad	M & F: SSF > Mom > Dad > OSF
Wintre, Hicks, McVey, & Fox, 1987 (U.S.)[a]	48 8 yr, 48 11 yr, 48 14 yr, 48 17 yr	S-R Y/N choice of peer and adults as confidants for personal problems	Peers: 8 yr < 11 yr < 14 & 17 yr[a]; Peers: F > M	Adults: 8 & 11 yr > 14 & 17 yr[a]; Adults: F = M	8 & 11 yr: Adults > peers[a]; 14 & 17 yr: Peers > adults[a]
Youniss & Ketterlinus, 1987 (U.S. Catholic)	352 14 yr, 253 16 yr	S-R extent that Mom & Dad know youth		No age differences; F: Mom > Dad; M: Mom = Dad; Mom: F = M; Dad: M > F	
Youniss & Smolar, 1985 (U.S.)	180 12–20 yr	S-R extent of topic disclosure to parents & Frds	No analysis of gender differences	Dad: M > F; Mom: No analysis of gender differences; M: Mom > Dad; F: Mom > Dad	Parents = Frds for school issues & future issues; Frds > parents for dating, sexuality, & marriage

Note: M denotes males; F, females; SSF, same-sex friends; OSF, opposite-sex friends; S-R, self-report; I-R, interviewer report; Y/N, yes/no response; Frd, friend; Parent-R, parent report; RP, romantic partner. In some studies, parents, adults, or peers were targets instead of specific dyadic relationships.

[a] Because statistical comparisons were not reported for the effects of interest, the first author informally estimated age, gender, and/or relationship-type effects based on information about means, standard deviations, sample size, etc. that was presented in the report.

23

Summary of research findings

Our summary of findings roughly follows the organization of a hierarchical ANOVA model: We first consider the findings for main effects, then consider interactions among factors. Although our first interest lay in effects related to age and partners who are recipients of self-disclosure (i.e., parents or peers), we were also interested in the extent to which patterns of findings varied systematically according to the gender of both subjects and recipients. The framework for our review, then, included four factors: age of child, sex of child, type of recipient (parents vs. peers), and sex of recipient. The conjunction of the latter two factors resulted in four categories of targets being considered: female friends, male friends, mothers, and fathers. In keeping with the convention used in most of the literature, friend-recipients were referred to as "same-sex" and "opposite-sex" friends.

The relevant findings from the studies reviewed are summarized in Table 2.1. Each row summarizes, for a single study, the sample populations studied, the relevant measures used, and the results concerning significant age and gender differences in self-disclosure to peers, mothers, and fathers, and comparisons between self-disclosure to parents and peers. In a few cases where the original report did not provide significance tests of specific comparisons of interest, the first author informally estimated age, gender, and relationship-type effects, based on other information in the report, for example, tables of means, standard deviations, and sample sizes.

Table 2.2 presents a summary of the number of studies reporting particular findings during each of our age periods: 9 to 11 years (preadolescence), 12 to 14 years (early adolescence), 15 to 17 years (middle adolescence), and 18 to 20 years (late adolescence). Within each cell of the table is a "box score" ratio [i.e., the ratio of findings reflecting significant differences (numerator) to the total number of findings bearing on a particular effect (denominator: significant findings + null findings)]. When a study included subjects from multiple age groups, its findings were tallied under more than one age period. When studies used different age groupings than we did (e.g., 10 to 12 years instead of our 9 to 11 years and 12 to 14 years), we tallied results under the older age period (e.g., in the 12- to 14-years column).

When attempting to summarize these results, it quickly became apparent that only a few meaningful conclusions could be drawn about main effects because they were almost always substantially qualified by two-, three-, and even four-way interactions. Rather than discuss separately all possible higher-order interactions, we limited our discussion to those that seemed to be of greatest conceptual interest.

Table 2.2. *Tabulation of significant differences in self-disclosure*

Relationship/effect	Sex	Age period (years)				
		6–8	9–11	12–14	15–17	18–20
Same-sex friend						
Increase with age	M	1/1	7/11	15/23	10/17	1/5
	F	1/1	9/12	17/23	10/17	1/5
Female > male		0/3	10/17	25/28	15/17	7/8
Opposite-sex friend						
Increase with age	M	0/1	1/2	3/4	3/3	1/1
	F	0/1	1/2	4/4	3/3	1/1
Female > male			1/3	3/6	4/6	1/3
Mother						
Decrease with age	M		0/3	3/11	4/13	1/3
	F		0/3	3/11	5/13	2/3
Female > male		0/1	3/8	6/17	7/12	2/5
Father						
Decrease with age	M		0/3	3/11	4/13	1/4
	F		0/3	4/11	3/13	1/4
Male > female			1/5	9/16	8/13	4/6
Mother vs. father						
Mother > father	M		3/8	6/18	4/13	4/8
	F		5/8	15/19	13/13	8/8
Mother vs. friend						
Mother > friend	M	2/2	6/10	10/19	3/16	0/5
Mother = friend	M	0/2	4/10	6/19	4/16	0/5
Friend > mother	M	0/2	0/10	3/19	9/16	5/5
Mother > friend	F	2/2	6/9	4/20	0/13	0/5
Mother = friend	F	0/2	3/9	8/20	0/13	0/5
Friend > mother	F	0/2	0/9	8/20	13/13	5/5
Father vs. friend						
Father > friend	M	2/2	4/9	5/18	2/16	0/5
Father = friend	M	0/2	3/9	8/18	5/16	0/5
Friend > father	M	0/2	2/9	5/18	9/16	5/5
Father > friend	F	2/2	4/9	1/20	0/13	0/5
Father = friend	F	0/2	5/9	7/20	0/13	0/5
Friend > father	F	0/2	0/9	14/20	13/13	5/5

Note: Ratios represent the number of studies finding an effect for an age period (numerator) over the total number of studies examining the effect for that age period.

1. *Is there an overall increase in self-disclosure with age?* Overall age trends in frequency of disclosure were clearly dependent on who the recipient of disclosure was. There is a robust increase with age in disclosure to peers that is not paralleled by an equally robust decrease in disclosure to parents (see items 4 and 5). Therefore, we suspect that there may be an overall net increase in self-disclosure during adolescence that is due to increases in self-disclosure to friends.

2. *Do females self-disclose more than males?* When comparisons were summed across age periods and recipients, 49% of the comparisons revealed that females disclosed more than males, and 13% of the comparisons found that males disclosed more than females; for 38% of the comparisons, there were no significant gender differences. Thus, there was a ubiquitous trend for females to self-disclose more than males. The only consistent exception to this finding occurred in the case of disclosure to fathers: In 59% of the comparisons, males disclosed more than females to their fathers, and in no instance were females found to disclose more to fathers than did males (see item 5).

3. *Do youngsters self-disclose more to parents or peers?* Overall, when comparisons were summed across age periods, gender of parent, and gender of subject, 46% of the comparisons found greater disclosure to same-sex friends than to parents, whereas 24% of the comparisons found more disclosure to parents than friends; for 30% of the comparisons, disclosure to parents and friends did not significantly differ. The review indicates that this "main effect" for target (parents vs. peers) interacts significantly with the age of the adolescent and the gender of both the adolescent and the parent. For this reason, the next two points consider the effects of age and gender *separately* for each target (parents, then peers).

4. *How does self-disclosure to parents change across childhood and adolescence?* There was mixed evidence of an age-related decrease in self-disclosure to parents. Beginning in the early adolescent period, roughly 30% of the comparisons revealed decreases in self-disclosure to parents, while 70% of comparisons found no significant age differences. There were no comparisons that revealed significant increases in self-disclosure to parents during childhood and adolescence. This pattern of findings generally held true for both males and females, and for relationships with mothers and fathers.

There was reliable evidence of an interaction between sex of child and sex of parent that was generally invariant across age periods. In 42% of the comparisons, daughters disclosed more to their mothers than did sons, whereas in no case did sons disclose more to mothers than did daughters. By contrast, in 59% of the comparisons, sons disclosed more to their fathers than did daughters, whereas in no case did daughters disclose more to fathers than did sons.

Overall, the evidence indicates that there is no increase in self-disclosure to parents during early and middle adolescence, with suggestive evidence of a modest decrease (e.g., Furman & Buhrmester, 1992). There is much stronger evidence of gender-related differences in self-disclosure. Within the family, the most disclosure occurs between daughters and mothers, whereas the least disclosure occurs between daughters and fathers; sons' disclosures to mothers and fathers fall midway between the two extremes shown by daughters, with a slight trend toward sons disclosing more to mothers than fathers.

5. *How does self-disclosure to same-sex friends change across childhood and adolescence?* The findings revealed a robust age-related increase in self-disclosure to same-sex friends during middle childhood and early adolescence, which appears to reach an asymptote during middle and late adolescence. When we looked for changes with age in the 6- to 14-year age period, we found that 70% of the comparisons revealed significant age-related increases in disclosure to same-sex friends. In the 15- to 17-year age period, 59% of the comparisons revealed age-related increases, whereas in the 18- to 20-year age period only 20% of the comparisons showed increases. In the few studies that reported age by gender interactions (e.g., Rivenbark, 1971; Smollar & Youniss, 1982; Blyth & Foster-Clark, 1987; Buhrmester & Furman, 1987) the evidence suggested that the developmental increase may be less marked for boys than girls, and that the increase may begin earlier for girls (around age 10 or 11) than for boys (around age 13 or 14).

There was consistent evidence of gender differences in self-disclosure to same-sex friends, with the difference becoming more robust in the older age periods. Comparisons for children in the 6- to 8-year age period revealed no gender differences, whereas 59% of the comparisons in the 9- to 11-year age period showed greater disclosure by girls than boys. For the age periods between 12 and 20 years, 89% of the comparisons indicated more self-disclosure by females than males. These findings indicate that a robust gender difference emerges at about the same time in development that girls begin to increase disclosure to friends (i.e., 10 or 11 years).

6. *How does self-disclosure to opposite-sex peers change across childhood and adolescence?* Although only a handful of studies have examined disclosure to opposite-sex peers, the available evidence reliably documents a rapid increase in disclosure to opposite-sex peers during early and middle adolescence: 93% of the comparisons in the 12- to 17-year age period revealed significant age-related increases. Almost no studies have examined self-

disclosure to opposite-sex peers in children younger than 11 years, largely because cross-sex interactions are rare during childhood (Maccoby, 1988) and few children report having meaningful relationships with opposite-sex peers (Buhrmester & Furman, 1987).

The evidence is mixed as to whether the gender difference found for same-sex friendships carries over into opposite-sex relationships. Roughly 50% of the comparisons found girls disclosing more than boys. There are a few findings hinting that this gender difference emerges in early and middle adolescence and then disappears in late adolescence and young adulthood (e.g., Rivenbark, 1971).

7. *How does the relative extent of self-disclosure to parents versus peers change across childhood and adolescence?* There was consistent evidence of a shift toward greater disclosure to friends than to parents that occurs during early adolescence. For children younger than 11 years, 95% of the comparisons indicated that there was greater or equal disclosure to parents compared with friends. Early adolescence (12 to 14 years) appears to be a period of transition, with 36% of the comparisons showing greater disclosure to parents than friends, and 28% showing greater disclosure to friends than parents. By the 15- to 20-year age period, only 12% of comparisons found more disclosure to parents than friends, whereas 88% of comparisons found more disclosure to friends than parents.

Interestingly, there was evidence of a gender difference in the timing of the shift to greater disclosure to friends compared with parents, with the shift occurring later for males than females. For males, it was not until the 15- to 17-year age period that over 50% of the comparisons favored friends over parents. By contrast, females surpassed this 50% mark in the 12- to 14-year age period, with fully 100% of the comparisons favoring friends over parents in the 15- to 17-year age period.

In sum, the strongest findings from the review indicate that (1) girls disclose more than boys to all targets except fathers, beginning around age 11, (2) self-disclosure to friends increases during early and middle adolescence, (3) disclosure to friends surpasses disclosure to parents beginning in early adolescence for girls and in middle adolescence for boys, and (4) boys and girls disclose more to same-sex friends than to opposite-sex peers through late adolescence, and more to mothers than to fathers.

Exploring the role of self-disclosure in development

The foregoing review provides an account of one component in the larger interpersonal process described in Figure 2.1: age-related changes in the partners who are recipients of children's self-disclosure. Our aim in this section is to explore the ways in which changes in recipients are related to changes in the other components of this process. We address such questions as: How do the types of social input that youth need change with age, and how are changes in desired inputs related to changes in the underlying issues and concerns that are most salient to youth? In addition, what are the determining factors that lead to the developmental emergence of new issues and concerns? Moreover, how might the changes that take place in the other components of this process help explain the documented changes in the recipients of disclosure? Finally, how do constraints and opportunities in the environment interact with concerns and needs in shaping recipient choice?

Before moving on to discuss these questions, it seems prudent to consider how the pervasive effects of gender that were revealed in our review might be understood in terms of the processes described in Figure 2.1. Gender influences are likely to be evident for each component of Figure 2.1. Although a detailed discussion of all of the ways that gender influences these interpersonal processes is beyond the scope of this chapter, we discuss a few possibilities here.

Briefly, beginning with the determining factors, there is ample evidence that biological and cultural factors have different effects on boys and girls. For instance, boys and girls must come to terms with different biological reproductive capacities and with different cultural norms, roles, and expectations that define "appropriate" male and female behavior (e.g., Bardwick & Douvan, 1971; Hill & Lynch, 1983). Gender-related determining factors in turn give rise to differences in which issues/concerns are most salient to boys and girls, and when they are likely to emerge in development. For example, if the pubescent teenager discussed earlier were a girl rather than a boy, then her issues and concerns could be different than those of a boy. Although she may, like her male counterpart, also be grappling with decisions about sexual behavior, her concerns may have a different focus: What if I get pregnant? Will he respect me in the morning? How will this affect my reputation among my peers?

Gender differences in issues and concerns may affect priorities placed on obtaining different types of social input and provisions. Although the girl in our example, like the boy, might need help with clarifying her values and coping with her feelings, she may feel most pressed to receive reassurance that her boyfriend will not talk behind her back and feel a stronger need than the boy to get advice about preventing pregnancy. These needs for input, plus constraints and opportunities present in the social environment, influence gender differences in the selection of recipients of self-disclosure. Our teenaged girl's need for reassurance of confidentiality may prompt her to self-disclose her concerns to her boyfriend in order to get reassurance of his trustworthiness. Environmental constraints, however, may prevent her from finding a likely recipient with whom to discuss her concerns about birth control. The probability of a disapproving response from adults and an uniformed one from peers may leave her with no choice of recipient, despite a felt need.

When faced with the task of discussing all of the components of Figure 2.1, we had several choices about where to begin. Our choice was guided by our primary goal in writing this chapter: to understand how developmental changes in issues and concerns help explain findings about age-related changes in the recipients of self-disclosure. Therefore, we began by considering the component that most immediately affects choice of recipients: the types of social input/provisions that youngsters seek. By first identifying the types of input/provisions gained through disclosure, we felt that we could then work "backward" through Figure 2.1, discussing, in turn, the issues/concerns that give rise to the need for different types of social input, as well as the determining factors that give rise to those issues/concerns. In addition, we could also move "forward" through Figure 2.1 to explain selection of partners as recipients of disclosure, within the confines of environmental opportunities and constraints. Thus, we began by asking the question What are the different types of social input or exchanges that youth seek through self-disclosure?

We found Derlega and Grzelak's (1979) list of five broad "functions" of self-disclosure to be a useful taxonomy for organizing our thinking and discussion about social inputs. According to Derlega and Grzelak's reasoning, self-disclosure serves a function to the extent that it accrues some benefit to, or addresses some basic concern of, the discloser. The five broad functions are (a) receiving social validation, (b) gaining social control, (c) achieving self-clarification, (d) exercising self-expression, and (e) enhancing relationship development. Derlega and Grzelak's list of five functions appears to represent five different types of desired social inputs or provisions that address basic concerns of the discloser.

Each of the next five subsections discusses one type of these functional inputs that can be gained through self-disclosure. In each subsection, we (a) discuss the specific nature of the social input or exchange that is gained through self-disclosure, (b) consider the issues and concerns that seem to give rise to the need for this social input/provision, (c) discuss the developmental time table of the determining factors that seem to prompt changes in youth's salient issues/concerns, and (d) consider how all of these factors might, in conjunction with environmental constraints and opportunities, explain documented developmental changes in the recipients of self-disclosure. Gender-related considerations were most evident when considering how self-disclosure is used to gain social control, achieve self-expression, and enhance relationship development; therefore, our discussion of gender-related issues is concentrated in those subsections.

Social validation

Derlega and Grzelak contend that one reason people self-disclose is to gain feedback that "may help an individual to define the appropriateness and correctness of his or her attitudes, beliefs, and values" (1979 p. 157). Similarly, H. S. Sullivan (1953) argued that people feel better when they gain "consensual validation," wherein they discover that others share their thoughts, opinions, and insecurities.

At least two interrelated issues/concerns can give rise to a need to gain social validation through self-disclosure (Berg & Archer, 1982). The first is concern about *social approval*. By disclosing information about themselves, youth invite evaluative reactions from the listener that can provide a gauge of social acceptance and value. Social approval obviously affects self-esteem; Cooley's (1902) notion of the "looking-glass self" suggests that people come to view and value themselves in terms of how they are viewed and valued by others. Second, concern about *self-acceptance* can motivate people to seek social feedback that reassures them that they are not alone in their thoughts, feelings, and experiences. Consensual validation thus relieves their fear about being different or abnormal (Elkind, 1967).

A number of determining factors may contribute to developmental changes in the nature of children's concerns about social approval and self-evalaution. The need for social approval evolves through well-documented developmental changes. During early childhood, gaining the approval (and avoiding the disapproval) of parents and other adults upon whom children are physically and emotionally dependent is of paramount concern (Harter, 1989). As children move into middle childhood and adolescence, their concerns about approval focus more on peer-group acceptance and conformity (Berndt, 1979). This shift in sources of approval is likely to be an outgrowth of a number of determining factors, including cultural conventions that dictate that youth spend much of their time in age-segregated school settings, and basic maturational factors that lead youth to want to form interdependent relationships with age-mates who share their interests and concerns.

Somewhat different factors appear to be involved in developmental changes in self-evaluative concerns. In early childhood, cognitive abilities limit children to perceiving and evaluting themselves in terms of concrete characteristics and their here-and-now personal experiences (Montemayor & Eisen, 1977). During middle childhood, the emergence of the ability to make social comparisons awakens concerns about evaluating onself in relation to others (Ruble & Frey, 1987). Finally, with the growth of formal operational abilities, adolescents become preoccupied with reflecting upon abstract and hypothetical conceptions of themselves (Damon & Hart, 1982). These latter cognitive advances converge with a number of maturational and cultural factors to make early adolescence a time of heightened insecurities about self-evaluation, as is evidenced by the adolescent "dip" in self-esteem that has been found in a number of studies (Simmons, Burgeson, Carlton-Ford, & Blyth, 1987).

These developmental changes in the concerns that motivate children to seek social validation may help explain one of the major findings from our literature review: Disclosure to peers increases during early adolescence, while disclosure to parents does not. Whereas young children (under age 6 to 7) see personal value or worth as emanating from adult approval (Piaget, 1932; Harter, 1989), beginning in the elementary school years (ages 8 to 12) the situation begins to change. Social comparisons increasingly become the means by which worth is judged. Because of their similar developmental level and their propinquity, peers become salient points of reference for comparison, and peer approval becomes increasingly predictive of self-worth (Rosenberg, 1979; Harter, 1987). Interestingly, at the same time that concerns with social comparison become salient, negative gossip becomes a dominant conversational theme among preadolescent friends (Parker & Gottman, 1989). Although negative gossip seldom involves disclosure about oneself per se, it does involve youth revealing their attitudes and opinions about other peers. The process of sharing negative attitudes about others is a form of social comparison that can indirectly bestow approval on children: Implicit in the disparaging remarks about others is the tacit acknowledgment that "present company" is excepted from these criticisms. The disclosure partners can gain approval from one another for being different, even better, than the peers who are the objects of the gossip. Negative gossip with peers also provides the opportunity for youth to explore the standards of worth used for social comparisons in the peer society (Brown & Gilligan, 1992). Through gossip, youth gain a fuller understanding of the peer society's values that are used to judge others and themselves.

Parents are not good partners for this sort of gossip. They do not have the inside track on peers about whom youth like to gossip, and most adults cannot tolerate, without interdicting, the vicious disparagement that preadolescents sometimes express. In addition, parents are not immersed in the peer culture and do not experience teenage peer-group pressures.

Thus, the approving or disapproving reactions of friends to self-disclosures are sought as more meaningful than those of parents because friends are plugged into the values of peer culture. Parents' opinions and approval are respected in certain domains (Kon, 1981), but in the areas of most pressing concern in young teens' daily lives – dress, social status, and romance – peer values and reactions are of utmost importance (Wilks, 1986).

Finally, the observed increases in self-disclosure to friends during early adolescence may be linked to heightened insecurities about self-worth that are known to emerge during that period (Simmons et al., 1987). Through reciprocal self-disclosing interactions, teenagers discover that they are not alone in their thoughts, feelings, and experiences, and they relieve their fears about being abnormal. Because they are at the same life stage and are experiencing many of the same insecurities, friends are in the best position to mitigate such feelings of aloneness and uniqueness. By late adolescence, validation by peers and friends is more strongly related to self-worth than parental approval (Harter, 1987), and self-disclosure to friends is a frequent means of gaining social validation (Prager, Fuller, & Gonzales, 1989). Parents are not in as good a position as peers to relieve adolescent insecurities. At best, parents may disclose previous experiences in which they felt similar feelings, but these occurred many years ago and may seem remote to both the parent and the adolescent.

Social control

Derlega and Grzelak (1979) assert that people can also use self-disclosure as a form of strategic self-presentation to bring about desired social outcomes. In some instances, people disclose selected information in order to manage other people's impressions and to gain social approval (Jones & Pittman, 1982). Conversely, people can also withhold personal disclosure (Derlega & Chaikin, 1977) so as to conceal aspects of themselves that do not conform to the image they wish to present. Thus, when viewed from the framework adopted in this chapter, underlying *self-presentational concerns* give rise to a desire to regulate self-disclosing interactions in ways that control one's social image.

There appear to be important developmental changes in concerns about self-presentation. Studies in a number of areas suggest that a combination of cognitive and sociocultural determinants lead to a heightened concern about impression management during early adolescence (Ruble & Frey, 1987; Parker & Gottman, 1989; Buhrmester, Goldfarb, & Cantrell, 1992). Cognitively, advances in perspective-taking ability allow adolescents to contemplate how they are viewed from the perspective of the "generalized other" and to evaluate themselves via broader systems of social conventions (Selman, 1980). This sets the stage for an intensely self-conscious concern among young adolescents that others are evaluating their every word and action (Harter, 1989). At the same time, the reality of the peer society justifies young adolescents' self-conscious concerns. Many conversations among peers are, in fact, devoted to scrutinizing and evaluating the characteristics of peers (Gottman & Mettetal, 1986; Brown & Gilligan, 1992). To be accepted by members of the "right crowd," teenagers must often conform to the crowd's standards and norms. This combination of cognitive and sociocultural factors leads young adolescents to be highly concerned about projecting the right or "cool" image of themselves in public interactions; thus, they are very careful about what they disclose when they are in the public eye of peer society.

The increase in concern about self-presentation during preadolescence and adolescence may help explain several findings from the literature review. Work by Harter and Lee (1989) sheds light on who is likely to be the audience for adolescent self-presentational efforts. In their study, young teenagers reported that they were more likely to act "phony" with parents than with close friends. Self-presentational concerns may lead adolescents to limit how much, and what, they disclose to parents, and may help explain the finding that adolescents disclose more to friends than parents. Reluctance to "tell all" to parents probably stems from a continuing concern for parental approval, as well as a fear of reprimand. If youth were to disclose to parents their involvements with alcohol, drugs, sexuality, and other forms of forbidden behavior, they would likely confront parental constraints on their behavior. On the other hand, adolescents may be willing to selectively disclose to parents about success in school or athletics in order to strategically cultivate a certain image in parents' eyes.

Interestingly, Harter and Lee (1989) found that adolescents reported acting even more phony with groups of peers than with either close friends or parents. It may seem ironic that teenagers report being most concerned about self-presentation with a group of peers, but least of all with close friends, who are presumably also members of the peer group. The fact that close friendships are viewed as havens from many self-presentational concerns highlights an important distinction between peer-group relationships and close dyadic friendships (Buhrmester et al., 1992). Close friendships have certain characteristics that are conspicuously absent from other adolescent peer relationships. During adolescence, "true friends" are defined as trusted confidants who will not make fun of you and who will loyally keep disclosures secret (Rawlins & Holl, 1987; Rotenberg, 1991). Without reassurance of a friend's loyalty and confidentiality, adolescents face possible humiliation if other peers hear that they have said or done something that fails to conform to peer-group standards (Brown & Gilligan, 1992). Fears of humiliation, then, lead adolescents to carefully monitor and censor what information is disseminated to the peer group at large; the opportunity to discuss embarrassing things only exists if the teenager has friends who can be trusted not to "spread things around" (Rotenberg, 1991). Interestingly, it is a testimony to the strength of adolescents' need to gain social valida-tion through self-disclosure that they confide in friends as much as they do; after all, they are risking one of their most valued commodities – their reputations in the peer group – in order to gain the benefits of self-disclosure with a close friend (Rawlins & Holl, 1987).

Self-presentational concerns also seem to play an important role in deter-mining gender differences in frequency of self-disclosure to same-sex friends. Recall from our review that girls were found to disclose more to their same-sex friends than boys do. Youths' efforts to present themselves in a manner consistent with cultural norms of proper "masculine" and "feminine" behavior may in part explain this gender difference (Doyle, 1989).

Recent work suggests that gender socialization pressures may be particu-larly intense in peer-group relationships (Maccoby, 1990; Tannen, 1990a; Brown & Gilligan, 1992). Maccoby (1990) notes that, during childhood, peer relationships are overwhelmingly segregated by gender. The sex-segregated nature of peer relations in childhood creates unique male and female cultures, each of which has strongly enforced conversational rules and norms (Tannen, 1990b). The rules and norms pertaining to self-disclosure appear to be quite different for boys and girls. Indeed, they appear to make boys' friendships less of a haven from self-presentational concerns than do girls' friendships. In male–male interactions, dominance and status are major concerns, resulting in a *status-oriented* style character-ized by interrupting, contradicting, boasting, or engaging in other forms of self-display. This status-oriented style serves to limit self-disclosure among boys by motivating them to conceal weaknesses and to keep their self-presentational guard up even with close friends (Wright & Keple, 1981).

In contrast, norms for female–female interactions emphasize social har-mony, resulting in an *enabling* style characterized by expressions of agree-ment, polite turn taking, and acknowledgments of one another's points of view (Maccoby, 1990). These norms encourage girls to disclose their con-cerns and vulnerabilities openly to one another. Tannen (1990b) argues that there is a fundamental difference in how self-disclosures of personal insecu-rities are interpreted in male–male versus female–female interactions. Fe-males view such disclosures as a means of building interpersonal connectedness and gaining social support, whereas males are more inclined to view them as an admission of weakness that may undermine respect and stature. Adolescent boys can engage in notoriously brutal teasing and physical assault of peers who are perceived as "girlish" or vulnerable. Thus, the potential risks resulting from the larger peer group learning about a confided weakness may be greater for boys than girls.

Self-clarification

Derlega and Grzelak also argue that, through self-disclosure, people can gain self-clarification of opinions, beliefs, attitudes, values, and standards. In addition to gaining direct feedback from listeners about their ideas, disclosers are often forced to formulate their thoughts more clearly in the process of communicating them to the listener (Jourard, 1971). Moreover, self-disclosure can generate a co-constructive dialogue between two people, in which each person's evolving ideas feed off the other's, resulting in deeper clarification of the issues than either might achieve alone.

At least two sets of underlying issues and concerns may prompt youth to use self-disclosure as a means to gain self-clarification. The first are concerns about having guiding sets of *standards of conduct and moral values*. By sharing attitudes and discussing opinions, youth can explore and clarify their stances on pressing moral issues. The second set of issues concern *self-understanding and identity*. Through self-disclosing interactions, youth engage in self-reflective discussions that help them better understand who they are and what they will become in the future.

Both of these sets of concerns undergo important transformations during childhood and adolescence. In early childhood, cognitive and social constraints lead children to believe that standards of "good" and "bad" are set down by adult authorities (Piaget, 1932). As children's cognitive abilities mature and their social experiences broaden, they come to be more concerned about the wider systems of social and cultural conventions that bear on standards of conduct and moral values (Kohlberg & Gilligan, 1972). Still later, some youth are thought to actively evolve their own standards and moral principals that are somewhat autonomous of the prevailing cultural prescriptions (Kohlberg & Gilligan, 1972). Both Piaget (1932) and Kohlberg (1969) argue that interactions involving the reciprocal exchange of perspective play an important role in the development of more autonomous standards and values.

The development of concerns about self-understanding (Damon & Hart, 1982) and a coherent sense of identity (Erikson, 1968) also undergo major developmental changes. The achievement of formal operations in early adolescence enables teenagers to construct more abstract self-portraits, to distinguish between their real and ideal selves, and to begin the process of resolving discrepancies between multiple aspects of themselves (Harter, 1990). In late adolescence, teens' focus shifts to impending adulthood, and they feel pressure to make decisions and choices about personal occupational goals, religious and political ideologies, and standards for interpersonal behavior (Marcia, 1966; Schenkel & Marcia, 1972). Erikson (1968) saw this as a period of "moratorium," a time of active preoccupation with questions like "Who am I?" and "Who will I become?" Self-disclosing conversations then become an important forum in which teens' beliefs, values, and self-perceptions are explored.

The developmental changes that occur in needs for self-clarification may help explain the finding of age-related increases in self-disclosure to friends, relative to parents, during adolescence. Friends may be the preferred targets of self-clarifying self-disclosure because of basic structural differences between adolescents' relationships with peers and with parents. Youniss (1980) has noted that the egalitarian authority structure of friendship allows adolescents to construct their understanding of values and of themselves in a context in which each partner is equally free to challenge the ideas of the other. The open forum created by friendship's egalitarian authority structure allows equal weight to be given to each participant's views (Hartup, 1983). As a result, conclusions that are reached as a result of dialogue are experienced as self-chosen.

In contrast, the unilateral authority structure of parent–child relationships is less conducive to such co-constructive interactions (Youniss, 1980; Hunter, 1985). The parents' standards are likely those that the adolescent had identified with as a child. These are the very standards the adolescent may need most strongly to question and reevaluate. Since parents' standards carry the weight of authority, a dialogue with parents may actually discourage the adolescent from experiencing those standards as freely self-chosen. Thus, the different authority structures of parent–child and peer relationships may lead adolescents to choose friends rather than parents as recipients of self-clarifying self-disclosure.

Although adolescents may less frequently engage in self-clarifying dialogues with parents, the exchanges they do have with parents may nonetheless be instrumental in fostering identity exploration. A number of studies suggest that adolescents' opportunities to engage in identity exploration are dependent in part on the quality of parent–adolescent relationships (Campbell, Adams, & Dobson, 1984; Grotevant & Cooper, 1986; Papini, Sebby, & Clark, 1989). Adolescents whose relationships with their parents have achieved a balance between warmth and connectedness, on the one hand,

and the free expression of differences and separateness, on the other, are those most likely to engage in identity exploration. Grotevant and Cooper (1986) found that self-exploring adolescents were more able than their nonexploring peers to articulate to their parents the ways in which they viewed the world differently than their parents did, while at the same time expressing openness to their parents' ideas.

The importance of separateness and distinctiveness in parent–adolescent communication serves to highlight what appears to be is a fundamental difference in the contributions that interactions with parents and peers make to identity development. The central identity issue with regard to parents involves clarifying how one's own values, ideologies, career goals, and so forth are going to be different from or similar to those of parents. In contrast, the issue in peer relationships involves sorting through which, among the broad array of identifications offered by peer culture (e.g., jocks, druggies, brains), one chooses to adopt. Frequent and extended self-clarifying dialogues with parents may create pressure for adolescents to embrace their parents' views. After all, from the adolescent's perspective, parents' views are often seen as fixed, and it is "hopeless" to get parents to see things another way (Brown & Gilligan, 1992). As we will discuss later, briefer dialogues that allow for adolescent "self-assertive disclosure" may be optimum for encouraging adolescent identity development within the context of the parent–adolescent relationship.

Self-expression

Derlega and Grzelak (1979) argue that, through self-disclosure, people can gain an expressive or cathartic release of pent-up feelings. More generally, expressive self-disclosure can act to mobilize coping assistance and social support (Thoits, 1986; Eckenrode & Wethington, 1990). By discussing their problems and feelings of distress, disclosers implicitly invite their listeners to offer emotional support and advice and to act as a sounding board to help them talk through a problem (Albrecht & Adelman, 1987; Cutrona, Suhr, & MacFarlane, 1990).

Two different sets of determining factors seem to influence the extent to which self-expressive disclosure is employed as a means of gaining coping assistance: (a) the extent to which discussion of problems is utilized as a coping mechanism, and (b) the types of stressors youth face. Use of discussion as a coping mechanism appears to increase during adolescence. Adolescence is accompanied by an increased capacity for self-reflective thought and a concomitant increase in the use of internalized coping strategies, such as cognitive restructuring and intellectualization (Cramer, 1987). Several authors have suggested that adolescents use and refine these newly developed strategies in self-disclosing interactions as they explore different ways of handling their thoughts and feelings (Harter, 1989; Parker & Gottman, 1989). Thus, adolescents may come to rely more heavily than younger children on self-disclosing conversations as a means of coping with stress.

There are a large variety of life stressors that can motivate youth to engage in expressive self-disclosure (Stiles, 1987). Whereas many types of stress occur on an irregular basis (e.g., accidents, loss, divorce), other types occur according to a predictable developmental timetable (e.g., entrance to school). One of the most far-reaching of the developmentally predictable stressors is puberty. Pubertal changes take place relatively rapidly and are accompanied by a number of stress-inducing concerns about bodily appearance, sexual impulses, and reproductive roles (Peterson, 1983; Adams & Gullota, 1989). These stressful concerns can prompt adolescents to engage in self-expressive disclosure.

Needs for cathartic release and coping assistance may be greater in girls than in boys (Hill, Holmbeck, Maslow, Green, & Lynch, 1985), which may partly explain why girls disclose to their friends more than boys do. Girls not only experience earlier pubertal maturation than boys, but pubertal changes are often more stress-inducing for girls (Ruble & Brooks-Gunn, 1982). For girls who live in a culture that touts thinness as a necessary requirement for female physical attractiveness, physical maturity has become linked to dissatisfaction with body weight (Dornbusch et al., 1984; Striegel-Moore, Silberstein, & Rodin, 1986; Crockett & Peterson, 1987). No comparable linkage has been found for boys. In addition, menarche is an intensely important and ambivalent event for girls (Peterson, 1983). Menarche is a positive event in that it signifies maturity, yet menstruation is viewed negatively by males and females alike in this culture (Ernster, 1975; Brooks-Gunn & Ruble, 1983). Thus, the stress accompanying puberty may be a stronger motivator for girls than boys to use self-disclosure as an avenue of coping, and the earlier onset of puberty for girls may partially explain the tendency of girls to increase levels of self-disclosure (to friends) at a younger age.

The nature of these puberty-related concerns may also help explain the tendency of girls to prefer same-sex friends as targets of self-disclosure. Menstruation is still a topic shrouded in secrecy (Patterson & Hale, 1985). Girls say clearly that it is not a subject to discuss with any male (Brooks-Gunn & Ruble, 1983). Communication with mothers is also often difficult at this time, as menarche appears to accompany a time of significant mother–daughter conflict (Hill & Holmbeck, 1987; Steinberg, 1988). Thus, female friends may frequently turn to each other to express their feelings and obtain support.

The social environment also offers more opportunities for girls than boys to engage in self-expressive self-disclosure with friends. The practice of disclosing personal problems and vulnerabilities is more consistent with feminine connectedness-oriented interaction norms than with masculine status-protecting norms (Rawlins, 1992). Females, therefore, are less likely to be ostracized when they use self-disclosure as a coping strategy.

A different aspect of the onset of puberty may explain increases in self-disclosure to same-sex friends for both boys and girls. For all teens, the onset of puberty brings with it sexual feelings and impulses of greater intensity than had been experienced previously. In early adolescence, self-disclosure between same-sex friends allows for the expression of excitement and anxiety associated with sexual fantasies and romantic crushes. These conversations may assist both sexes in managing the strong, unfamiliar feelings that accompany this stage of development.

Finally, self-disclosure serves as a catharsis for positive as well as negative emotions in adolescence (Mitchell, 1976). Self-disclosure allows adolescents to intensify the experience of positive emotions in two ways. First, adolescents get to relive the positive experience while telling the story of what took place. Second, their emotional experiences are intensified via contagion when a confidant expresses the same positive emotions upon hearing the story. Much of adolescent self-disclosure to their friends may well consist of sharing humorous or positive stories of daily experiences.

Relationship development

The fifth of Derlega and Grzelak's self-disclosure functions is the promotion of closeness and intimacy in relationships. At a relatively superficial level, disclosure of similarities establishes the initial connections between people (Duck, 1973). Revelations of more personal and private aspects of the self create experiences of intimacy in developing relationships (Altman & Taylor, 1973) and maintain intimacy in well-established relationships (Prager, 1989).

Derlega and Grzelak's focus was primarily on the role that self-disclosure plays in fostering intimacy. We believe that self-disclosure *regulates several aspects of interdependence* (Kelley, 1979), with intimacy being one of those aspects. We address three aspects of interdependence: intimacy, autonomy, and individuation. First, as Derlega and Grzelak noted, self-disclosure can be used to regulate intimacy and distance in relationships. *Sharing confidences* engenders closeness and intimacy, while *withholding confidences* limits or undermines intimacy and creates distance. Second, the regulation of self-disclosure affects autonomy (or self-determination and control) in relationships. For example, by withholding information about daily activities and plans, a person can eliminate the opportunity for the partner to control or shape those activities. Finally, certain types of self-disclosures can serve to enhance individuation (i.e., foster the perception that the discloser's identity is independent of and distinct from the partner's). When people disclose that they hold an oppposing stance on an important moral or political issue, or when they disclose that they have interests or tastes that differ from those of the partner, they emphasize how they are distinct as individuals.

All three aspects of interdependence evolve over the course of development. There are at least two periods in development when the regulation of autonomy and individuation are of paramount concern. The first period of "separation and individuation" occurs during infancy and toddlerhood (Erikson, 1968; Stern, 1973; Mahler & McDevitt, 1980), while the second occurs during adolescence (Blos, 1979; Grotevant & Cooper, 1986). In both cases, a combination of physical maturation, emergent cognitive abilities, and social pressures set the stage for increased concern about behavioral autonomy and self-definition. For our purposes here, we focus on the adolescent period, during which concerns with intimacy, autonomy, and individuation are all prominent. In particular, adolescence seems to be marked by increased concern with forming intimate connections with friends and romantic partners outside the family, and with heightened concern about establishing autonomy and individuality in the context of parent–adolescent relationships.

Beginning in early adolescence, concerns about intimacy in same-sex friendships increase in intensity and salience (Sullivan, 1953; Buhrmester & Furman, 1986). Blos (1967) contended that, at least initially, the increased desire for attachment to friends is an outgrowth of teenagers' efforts to reduce their emotional dependence on parents: Because teens continue to have strong dependency needs, yet have a desire to separate themselves from dependence on parents, they transfer these needs to peers. In addition to this compensatory motivation, there are at least three other reasons why adolescents seek increased intimacy in relationships with peers. First, peer relationships become more rewarding; they provide fun and excitement, and as an result of peers' more mature interpersonal sensitivity, friends become more capable sources of affection, love, and intimacy (Sullivan, 1953; Buhrmester, 1990). Second, intimate friendships take on an instrumental role in helping adolescents work through age-related issues and concerns; close friends serve as confidants and as sources of social provisions that address the emergent concerns that we discussed in the previous sections. Third, sexual maturity and sociocultural norms about dating combine to intensify concern about establishing intimate romantic relationships during middle and late adolescence.

Developmental changes in concerns about extrafamilial intimacy help explain several of the findings from our literature review. The increased desire to forge intimate friendships during early adolescence undoubtedly underlies the observed increase in the frequency of self-disclosure to friends during this period. Self-disclosure of common interests and experiences is an important means by which friendships are formed (Altman & Taylor, 1973). Indeed, adolescents cite the mutual disclosure of secrets and personal feelings as the defining feature of friendships (Savin-Williams & Berndt, 1990) and one of friendships highest rewards (Kon, 1981; Hortacsu, 1989).

Gender differences in self-disclosure to friends may be understood in part as a function of boys' and girls' different levels of concern about, and opportunities for, intimacy and individuation in relationships with friends. Our review found that girls more frequently self-disclosed to same-sex friends than did boys. While sociocultural definitions of the masculine role constrain boys from seeking intimacy from same-sex friendships (Jourard, 1971; Lewis, 1978; Jones & Dembo, 1989), definitions of femininity do not present obstacles to intimacy between girls. Self-disclosure, then, becomes part of the gender-appropriate way of making and keeping intimate friendships for girls (Maccoby, 1990). Furthermore, the norms of girls' friendships not only foster the appetite for self-disclosure, but also create the opportunity for girls to self-disclose: Female friends expect and encourage self-disclosure from each other. In contrast, the norms of boys' friendships are less encouraging of self-disclosure, and boys' friendships do not provide the same opportunities for self-disclosure. Boys who self-disclose vulnerabilities may be viewed as behaving inappropriately and be judged as poorly adjusted by their peers (Catalbiano & Smithson, 1983).

Both boys and girls increase their disclosure to opposite-sex peers during adolescence, most likely because of their increased interest in romantic and sexually charged encounters. Again, self-disclosure is a crucial tool in establishing, deepening, and maintaining intimate romantic relationships. Interestingly, although pubertal maturity brings with it heightened interest in romantic relationships, the data we reviewed show that few self-disclosing interactions occur between opposite-sex peers at the time of puberty (e.g., Sharabany, Gershoni, & Hoffman, 1981). Rather, during the early teenage years, romantically charged interaction occurs in mixed-sex groups where young teens' same-sex friends are also present (Dunphy, 1963). Same-sex friends are crucial collaborators in young teens' initial forays to learn how to behave in romantically charged interactions (Rubenstein, Watson, Drolette, & Rubenstein, 1976; Dickinson, 1978). It is not until middle adolescence that self-disclosure increases in opposite-sex relationships. Perhaps intimate relationships become possible only after adolescents have had some practice managing erotic feelings in interactions with peers, and after older adolescents are allotted the freedom to spend time alone with romantic partners.

In contrast to the increased interest adolescents express in self-disclosure to peers, our review found no evidence of increased self-disclosure to parents, with about a third of the studies finding a decrease in self-disclosure to parents during adolescence. We suspect that emergent concerns about autonomy and individuality help explain adolescents' patterns of self-disclosure to parents. Adolescents' increasingly adult-like stature and secondary sex characteristics increase the salience of their impending adult status and lead teenagers to expect more adult-like privileges. The emergence of formal operational cognitive abilities, along with the previously mentioned prospect of imminent adult status, contribute to increased concern with constructing a provisional, individuated identity as well (Erikson, 1968; Damon & Hart, 1982; Youniss & Smollar, 1985).

There appear to be at least three general ways that the regulation of self-disclosure is involved in the transformation of parent–adolescent relationships. First, by withholding disclosure about their daily activities, adolescents create arenas of privacy and protect themselves from parental interference and unwanted supervision (Derlega & Chaikin, 1977; Hill & Holmbeck, 1986). Second, by concealing important aspects of their true feelings, adolescents reduce dependency on their parents for support and nurturance regarding their daily dilemmas. This disengagement from parents may support adolescent strivings for emotional autonomy by assisting them in shedding childhood dependencies (Douvan & Adelson, 1966).

Third, adolescents use a particular class of self-disclosure – self-assertive disclosure – to establish their individuality in the context of their relationship with their parents. Several studies have found that disagreements and conflict between children and their parents increase during early adolescence (e.g., Montemayor, 1983). Although not typically studied as a form of self-disclosure, disagreements most certainly involve a type of self-assertive disclosure in which adolescents reveal how their opinions and desires differ from those of their parents. Traditional psychodynamic theory viewed such disagreement and conflict as an inevitable outgrowth of adolescents' efforts to disengage or detach themselves from their parents, thereby severing their childhood dependency ties (Freud, 1958). Within the psychodynamic view, autonomy and individuality were seen as being achieved at the direct expense of connectedness and intimacy in parent–adolescent relationships.

More recent theoretical work has challenged the psychodynamic view that disengagement from parents is a necessary or even desirable step toward the development of autonomy and individuality. Theorists such as Blos (1979), Grotevant and Cooper (1986), and Youniss (1980) see the adolescent quest for autonomy as existing alongside, rather than in opposition to, a desire to maintain emotional connections with parents. Grotevant and Cooper (1986) acknowledge that self-assertive disclosures to parents play an important role in fostering adolescent autonomy and individuality. But they also contend that such self-assertion need not result in diminishing intimacy in parent–adolescent relationships. Rather, if self-assertions are made in a family atmosphere of respect, acceptance, and warmth, then both autonomy and connectedness are enhanced. Indeed, empirical findings suggest that adolescent autonomy and individuation are most strongly correlated with a pattern of family interactions in which differing viewpoints and disagreements are openly acknowledged and accepted (Cooper, Grotevant, & Condon, 1983). Interestingly, self-assertive disclosure predicts adolescent development only when it is accompanied by expressions of warmth and mutual respect (Campbell et al., 1984). Self-assertive disclosures without the accompanying messages of connectedness may lead to adolescent disengagement because of the antagonism and conflict that are generated.

Finally, gender differences in concerns with, and in opportunities for, intimacy on the part of both adolescents and parents may underlie gender differences in boys' and girls' disclosure to mothers and fathers. Our review revealed that both boys and girls disclose more to mothers than fathers. This difference can be best understood if we recall that mothers and fathers are subject to the same gender-specific socialization pressures as their children. These pressures affect parents' own levels of concern about intimacy and individuality, as well as their interaction styles (Tannen, 1990b). Socialization for the mothering role predisposes women to expect close relationships with their children (Unger & Crawford, 1992), while at the same time, as discussed earlier, female socialization in peer relationships encourages women to develop an enabling interaction style (Maccoby, 1990). Thus, adolescents probably disclose more to mothers than to fathers because they have a lifetime of closeness with mothers as the primary caregivers, and because the female enabling interaction style is more apt to elicit children's self-disclosures.

Differences in adolescent disclosure patterns with fathers, relative to mothers, may stem from gender-related constraints on self-disclosure within the father–child relationship. The father's "breadwinner" role traditionally involves extended time away from the home (Giveans & Robinson, 1985; Doyle, 1989), and fathers, as a result, are less often physically available to hear adolescents' self-disclosures (Buhrmester & Carberry, 1992). In addition, socialization for male roles may not predispose fathers to expect, or be comfortable with, intimate conversations with their adolescent children. In fact, the fathers' male socialization may result in a "constricting" interaction style that is less likely to facilitate children's self-disclosures (Maccoby, 1990).

Although both sons and daughters disclose less to their fathers than to their mothers, our review revealed that only daughters evidence a precipitous decline in self-disclosure to fathers across adolescence. Indeed, many adolescent daughters describe their relationships with their fathers as "nonrelationships," lacking in personal or emotional involvement (Wright & Keple, 1981; Youniss & Smollar, 1985). More than sons, daughters may particularly lack opportunities to disclose to fathers. During adolescence, daughters become less involved in the masculine sex-typed activities that provide opportunities for father–adolescent interactions, such as sports, camping, and household projects (Youniss & Smollar, 1985). There may also be incompatibility between fathers' and daughters' social interaction styles. Fathers' status-oriented communication style may especially inhibit, or at least not encourage, self-disclosure by daughters. Finally, fathers appear to take a particularly authoritarian and controlling role with their daughters during adolescence (Martin, 1985; Youniss & Smollar, 1985). The asymmetry created by this intrusion on the daughters' needs for self-determination and autonomy may especially encourage daughters to withhold disclosures to avoid fathers' limits and constraints.

Conclusions

We have tried to accomplish three goals in this chapter. First, we developed a conceptual account that views self-disclosure as a means of gaining social inputs that address the changing concerns and needs of developing children. Next, we reviewed existing research on patterns of self-disclosure and arrived at a set of generalizations about age and gender differences in the social partners who are the most frequent recipients of self-disclosure. Finally, we discussed how age and gender differences in five basic categories of concerns might help explain age and gender differences in patterns of self-disclosure.

Our conceptual account of the determinants of self-disclosure argues that it is important to distinguish between the proximal and distal factors that influence self-disclosure. Within the proximal level of determinants, there appear to be two distinguishable sets of influences: (a) intraindividual factors, which we described in terms of concerns/needs, and (b) contextual factors, which we described in terms of the opportunities and constraints created by the immediate sociocultural environment. Unlike other approaches that tend to attribute changes in self-disclosure patterns primarily to either internal maturational processes (e.g., Sullivan, 1953) or to changes in social-contextual pressures (e.g., Blieszner & Adams, 1992; Nardi, 1992), this framework encourages simultaneous consideration of both intrapersonal and situational influences.

Developmental changes in the proximal determinants of self-disclosure are viewed as taking place on these two fronts. At the intraindividual level, there are normative developmental changes in the issues and concerns that preoccupy children's attention (both consciously and unconsciously). These concerns in turn give rise to needs for certain types of social input, or social provisions; many of these social inputs are sought through self-disclosing interactions. Thus, when considered from the perspective of intraindividual processes, developmental changes in patterns of self-disclosure are integrally linked to fundamental changes in the issues and tasks involved in personality development.

At the same time, there are normative changes in the proximal social contexts of development. Different network members are more or less available as recipients of disclosure, and the qualities of partners – as well as the structure of the relationships with them – make them more or less appropriate providers of needed types of social input. Furthermore, age-related changes in peer and family social norms and expectations, as well as gender-related norms of appropriate behavior for males and females, create pressures that affect the perceived appropriateness of self-disclosure in different interactional contexts. For example, in the area of gender-related contextual pressures, research has examined the ways in which public contexts seem to exaggerate gender differences in social behavior, while private contexts tend to minimize these differences (Kidder, Belletirie, & Cohn, 1977; Eagly, Wood, & Fishbaugh, 1981).

By itself, an account of the proximal determinants of self-disclosure describes but does not explain developmental changes. That is, in order to explain why there are developmental changes in concerns/needs and contexts, we must identify the distal factors that cause changes in the proximal factors. Distal determinants are those not immediately present in the self-disclosing situation that nevertheless have an impact on the individual's concerns/needs, as well as the opportunities and constraints, that exist in the immediate social context. We have suggested, albeit in general terms, that these distal determinants include aspects of physical maturation, cognitive development, age- and gender-related social norms, and individual life histories. Further, sociocultural economic systems, religious traditions, and reproductive functions may represent forces that shape the proximal factors that in turn determine patterns of self-disclosure (Bronfenbrenner, 1986). As such, explanations at the distal level cannot be confined to an individual-psychological level of analysis.

Our conceptual account identifies several avenues for further research. First, research is needed that specifies more clearly the concerns/needs that preoccupy the attention of children at different ages. For the purposes of this chapter, we explored the concerns/needs that underlay the five "functions" of self-disclosure that Derlega and Grzelak (1979) identified through conceptual analysis. We hope our discussion of these concerns/needs illustrates the usefulness of our approach in understanding developmental changes in self-disclosure; however, our discussion was not meant to be a definitive account of the changing concerns/needs of children. Empirical documentation of normative developmental changes in children's concerns is needed. In-depth interviews with children, parents, and teachers might be a useful starting point for studying children's conscious preoccupations. Analyses of the thematic content of children's conversations with parents and peers is also likely to yield insight into children's concerns and needs (Parker & Gottman, 1989). Thought-sampling techniques such as the Experience Sampling Method (Csikszentmihalyi & Larson, 1984) and the Thematic Apperception Test (Murray, 1943) might also provide useful information about concerns that are less accessible to conscious introspection. In addition to documenting normative developmental trends, more fine-grained assessment of individual differences in concerns and needs among children at a particular age should illuminate reasons why some children self-disclose more than others.

Second, research is needed on age-related changes in the contextual opportunities and constraints that children face. Who are the people that are most (and least) available for children of different ages and genders to disclose to? How do the norms and expectations that bear on self-disclosure in different relationship and social contexts change as children grow older? We suspect that the nature of these contextual forces vary considerably from one culture to another, and even from one family or peer group to another within a culture. For example, a family or peer group that adopts a stoic approach to coping with stress might have norms and expectations that actively discourage self-expressive self-disclosure, whereas another family or peer group may openly encourage the expression of stress-related emotions. Thus, researchers need to be sensitive to the "local" nature of contextual forces and not begin by assuming they will find a universal set of social constraints and opportunities that affect self-disclosure. Various methods might be used to assess contextual forces, including ethnographic methods to infer social norms from observed behavior, or interviews with children asking them to describe their conscious perceptions of social norms.

Third, we need to establish empirically the ways in which concerns/needs interact with contextual factors to determine why children self-disclose and whom they disclose to. Although in this chapter we have asserted that self-disclosing behavior is proximally determined by underlying concerns and contextual forces, in reality this is a working hypothesis that requires empirical evaluation. Correlational studies, supplemented by controlled experiments, are needed to verify that specific concerns/needs and contextual forces are systematically linked to particular patterns of self-disclosure. Furthermore, whereas we have principally talked about issues and concerns as separate from the social contexts, in reality, the social context is likely to influence conscious concerns. For example, the presence of an all-male group heightens a young man's concern about status and self-presentation, whereas a dyadic interaction with a female romantic partner might diminish self-presentational concerns and simultaneously increase concerns with establishing intimate contact. Moreover, in addition to evidence bearing on the general hypothesis that there are links among concerns, contextual norms, and self-disclosure, more specific mappings are needed. For example, given that a child is especially concerned about self-worth, what is the particular form that self-disclosure will take in one social context versus another context?

Fourth, research is needed to evaluate the impact that self-disclosure has on individual development. If it is true, as we have suggested, that children use self-disclosure as a means of gaining social input that addresses developmental issues/concerns, then there ought to be some detectable impact of self-disclosure on how individual issues/concerns are resolved. Links between self-disclosure processes and individual development might be evident at a purely quantitative level: Children who lack the opportunity for self-disclosure may fail to gain needed social input and, as a consequence, evidence more difficulties in individual development. These links may also be manifest at a more qualitative level: The type of social input children receive in response their self-disclosures (i.e., facilitative vs. destructive) may determine what impact that self-disclosure has on their development. These two possibilities are not, of course, mutually exclusive of one another, and both should be explored in future research.

Finally, once we gain a clearer understanding of the proximal factors that shape self-disclosure, we then can turn to the task of identifying the distal factors that account for changes in proximal influences. Research is needed to identify the distal determining factors, such as cognitive maturation of age-graded cultural norms, that explain age-related changes in concerns/needs and contextual forces. In this chapter we have only begun to speculate about what these distal factors might be. More attention will need to be given to specifying the distal determinants of both normative developmental changes and individual differences in the proximal variables affecting self-disclosure.

References

Adams, G. R., & Gullotta, T. (1989). *Adolescent life experiences.* Pacific Grove, CA: Brooks/Cole.

Albrecht, T. L., & Adelman, M. B. (1987). Dilemmas of supportive communication. In T. L. Albrecht & M. B. Adelman (and associates), *Communicating social support* (pp. 240–54). Newbury Park, CA: Sage.

Altman, I., & Taylor, D. A. (1973). *Social penetration: The development of interpersonal relationships.* New York: Holt, Rinehart, & Winston.

Balswick, J. O., & Balkwell, J. W. (1977). Self-disclosure to same- and opposite-sex parents: An empirical test of insights from role theory. *Sociometry, 40,* 282–6.

Bardwick, J., & Douvan, E. (1971). Ambivalence: The socialization of women. In V. Gornick & B. K. Moran (Eds.), *Woman in sexist society* (pp. 147–59). New York: Basic.

Berg, J. H., & Archer, R. L. (1982). Responses to self-disclosure and interaction goals. *Journal of Experimental Social Psychology, 18,* 245–57.

Berg-Cross, L., Kidd, F., & Carr, P. (1990). Cohesion, affect, and self-disclosure in African-American adolescent families. *Journal of Family Psychology, 4,* 235–50.

Berndt, T. J. (1979). Developmental changes in conformity to peers and parents. *Developmental Psychology, 15,* 608–16.

Berndt, T. J. (1982). The features and effects of friendship in early adolescence. *Child Development, 53,* 1447–60.

Berndt, T. J., & Perry, T. B. (1986). Children's perceptions of friendships as supportive relationships. *Developmental Psychology, 22,* 640–8.

Bigelow, B. J., & LaGaipa, J. J. (1975). Children's written descriptions of friendship: A multidimensional analysis. *Developmental Psychology, 11,* 857–8.

Blieszner, R., & Adams, R. G. (1992). *Adult friendships.* London: Sage.

Blos, P. (1967). The second individuation process of adolescence. In R. S. Essler et al. (Eds.), *Psychoanalytic study of the child* (Vol. 22, pp. 162–86). New York: International Universities Press.

Blos, P. (1979). *The adolescent passage.* New York: International Universities Press.

Blyth, D. A., & Foster-Clark, F. (1987). Gender differences in perceived intimacy with different members of adolescent's social networks. *Sex Roles, 17,* 687–718.

Blyth, D. A., & Traeger, C. (1988). Adolescent self-esteem and perceived relationships with parents and peers. In S. Salzinger, J. Antrobers, & M. Hammer (Eds.), *Social networks of children, adolescents, and college students* (pp. 171–94). Hillsdale, NJ: Erlbaum.

Bronfenbrenner, U. (1986). Ecology of the family as a context for human development: Research perspectives. *Developmental Psychology, 22,* 723–42.

Brooks-Gunn, J., & Ruble, D. N. (1983). Dysmenorrhea in adolescence. In S.
Golub (Ed.), *Menarche: The transition from girl to woman* (pp. 251–61). Lexington, MA: Lexington Books.

Brown, L. M., & Gilligan, C. (1992). *Meeting at the crossroads: Women's psychology and girls' development.* Cambridge, MA: Harvard University Press.

Buhrmester, D. (1990). Intimacy of friendship, interpersonal competence, and
adjustment during preadolescence and adolescence. *Child Development, 61,*
1101–11.

Buhrmester, D., & Carbery, J. (1992, March). *Daily patterns of self-disclosure and
adolescent adjustment.* Paper presented at the biennial meeting of the Society for
Research on Adolescence, Washington, DC.

Buhrmester, D., & Furman, W. (1986). The changing functions of friendship in
childhood: A neo-Sullivanian perspective. In V. J. Derlega & B. A. Winstead
(Eds.), *Friendship and social interaction* (pp. 43–62). New York: Springer-Verlag.

Buhrmester, D., & Furman, W. (1987). The development of companionship and
intimacy. *Child Development, 58,* 1101–13.

Buhrmester, D., Goldfarb, J., & Cantrell, D. (1992). Self-presentation when sharing with friends and non-friends. *Journal of Early Adolescence, 12,* 61–79.

Burke, R. J., & Weir, T. (1978). Sex differences in adolescent life stress, social
support, and well-being. *Journal of Psychology, 98,* 277–88.

Camarena, P. M., Sarigiani, P. A., & Petersen, A. C. (1990). Gender-specific
pathways to intimacy in early adolescence. *Journal of Youth and Adolescence, 19,*
19–32.

Campbell, E., Adams, G., & Dobson, W. R. (1984). Familial correlations of identity
formation in late adolescence: A study of the predictive utility of connectedness
and individuality in family relations. *Journal of Youth and Adolescence, 13,* 509–25.

Catalbiano, M. L., & Smithson, M. (1983). Variables affecting the perception of
self-disclosure appropriateness. *Journal of Social Psychology, 120,* 119–28.

Cooley, C. H. (1902). *Human nature and the social order.* New York: Scribner.

Cooper, C. R., Grotevant, H. D., & Condon, S. M. (1983). Methodological challenges of selectivity in family interaction. Assessing temporal patterns of individuation. *Journal of Marriage and the Family,* 749–54.

Cramer, D. (1987). Self-esteem, advice-giving and the facilitative nature of close
personal relationships. *Person-Centered Review, 2,* 99–110.

Cramer, D. (1989). Self-esteem and the facilitative nature of parents and close
friends. *Person-Centered Review, 4,* 61–76.

Cramer, P. (1987). The development of defense mechanisms. *Journal of Personality,*
55, 597–614.

Crockett, L. J., Losoff, M., & Petersen, A. C. (1984). Perceptions of the peer group
and friendship in early adolescence. *Journal of Early Adolescence, 4,* 155–81.

Crockett, L. J., & Peterson, A. C. (1987). Pubertal status and psychosocial develop-
ment: Findings from the early adolescent study. In R. M. Lerner & T. T. Foch
(Eds.), *Biological–psychosocial interactions in early adolescence* (pp. 173–88).
Hillsdale, NJ: Erlbaum.

Csikszentmihalyi, M., & Larson, R. (1984). *Being adolescent.* New York: Basic.

Cutrona, C. E., Suhr, J. A., & MacFarlane, R. (1990). Interpersonal transactions
and the psychological sense of support. In S. Duck (Ed.), *Personal relationships
and social support* (pp. 30–45). London: Sage.

Damon, W., & Hart, D. (1982). The development of self-understanding from infancy through adolescence. *Child Development, 53,* 841–64.

Derlega, V. J., & Chaikin, A. L. (1977). Privacy and self-disclosure in social relationships. *Journal of Social Issues, 33,* 102–15.

Derlega, V. J., & Grzelak, J. (1979). Appropriateness of self-disclosure. In G. J. Chelune (Ed.), *Self-Disclosure: Origins, patterns, and implications of openness in interpersonal relationships* (pp. 151–76). San Francisco: Jossey-Bass.

DeRosier, M. E., & Kupersmidt, J. B. (1991). Costa Rican children's perceptions of their social networks. *Developmental Psychology, 27,* 656–62.

Diaz, R. M., & Berndt, T. J. (1982). Children's knowledge of a best friend: Fact or fancy? *Developmental Psychology, 18,* 787–94.

Dickinson, G. (1978). Adolescent sex information sources: 1964–1974. *Adolescence, 13,* 653–8.

Dorval, B., Brannan, J., Duckworth, M., & Smith, P. (1987, April). *Developmental trends in conceptions of friendship in comparisons to the quality of friends' talk and commentary on it.* Paper presented at the biennial meeting of the Society for Research in Child Development, Baltimore, MD.

Douvan, E., & Adelson, J. (1966). *The adolescent experience.* New York: Wiley.

Doyle, J. A. (1989). *The male experience.* Dubuque, IA: Brown.

Duck, S. (1973). *Personal relationships and personal constructs: A study of friendship formation.* Chichester, UK: Wiley.

Dunphy, D. C. (1963). The social structure of urban adolescent peer groups. *Sociometry, 26,* 230–46.

Eagly, A. H., Wood, W., & Fishbaugh, L. (1981). Sex differences in conformity: Surveillance by the group as a determinant of male nonconformity. *Journal of Personality and Social Psychology, 40,* 384–94.

East, P. L. (1991). The parent–child relationships of withdrawn, aggressive, and sociable children: Child and parent perspectives. *Merrill-Palmer Quarterly, 37,* 425–44.

Eckenrode, J., & Wethington, E. (1990). The process and outcome of mobilizing social support. In S. Duck (Ed.), *Personal relationships and social support* (pp. 83–104). London: Sage.

Elkind, D. (1967). Egocentrism in adolescence. *Child Development, 38,* 1025–34.

Erikson, E. (1968). *Identity: Youth and crisis.* New York: Norton.

Ernster, V. L. (1975). American menstrual expressions. *Sex Roles, 1,* 3–13.

Freud, A. (1958). Adolescence. *Psychoanalytic Study of the Child, 13,* 255–78.

Furman, W., & Buhrmester, D. (1985). Children's perceptions of the personal relationships in their social networks. *Developmental Psychology, 21,* 1016–24.

Furman, W., & Buhrmester, D. (1992). Age and sex differences in perceptions of networks of personal relationships. *Child Development, 63,* 103–15.

Giordano, P. C., Cernkovich, S. A., & Pugh, M. D. (1986). Friendships and delinquency. *American Journal of Sociology, 91,* 1170–1202.

Giveans, D. L., & Robinson, M. K. (1985). Fathers and the preschool-age child. In S. H. H. Hanson, & F. W. Bozett (Eds.), *Dimensions of fatherhood* (pp. 115–40). Beverly Hills, CA: Sage.

Gottman, J. M., & Mettetal, G. (1986). Speculations about social and affective development: Friendship and acquaintanceship through adolescence. In J. M. Gottman and J. G. Parker (Eds.), *Conversations of friends: Speculations on affective development* (pp. 192–240). Cambridge University Press.

Grotevant, H., & Cooper, C. (1986). Individuation in family relationships: A perspective on individual differences in the development of identity and role-taking skill in adolescence. *Human Development, 29,* 82–100.

Harter, S. (1987). The determinants and mediational role of global self-worth in children. In N. Eisenberg (Ed.), *Contemporary issues in developmental psychology.* New York: Wiley.

Harter, S. (1989). Processes underlying adolescent self-concept formation. In R. Montemayor, G. R. Adams, & T. P. Gullotta (Eds.), *From childhood to adolescence: A transitional period?* (pp. 205–39). London: Sage.

Harter, S. (1990). Self and identity development. In S. S. Feldman & G. R. Elliot (Eds.), *At the threshold: The developing adolescent* (pp. 352–87). Cambridge, MA: Harvard University Press.

Harter, S., & Lee, L. (1989). *Manifestations of true and false selves in early adolescence.* Paper presented at the biennial meeting of the Society for Research on Child Development, Kansas City, MO.

Hartup, W. W. (1983). The peer system. In E. M. Heatherington (Ed.), P. H. Mussen (Series Ed.), *Handbook of child psychology: Vol. 4. Socialization, personality, and social development* (pp. 103–96). New York: Wiley.

Hill, J. P., & Holmbeck, G. N. (1986). Attachment and autonomy during adolescence. *Annals of Child Development, 3,* 145–89.

Hill, J. P., & Holmbeck, G. N. (1987). Familial adaptation to biological change during adolescence. In R. M. Lerner & T. T. Foch (Eds.), *Biological–psychosocial interactions in early adolescence* (pp. 207–23). Hillsdale, NJ: Erlbaum.

Hill, J. P., Holmbeck, G. N., Maslow, L., Green, T. M., & Lynch, M. E. (1985). Pubertal status and parent–child relations in families of seventh-grade boys. *Journal of Early Adolescence, 5,* 31–44.

Hill, J. P., & Lynch, M. E. (1983). The intensification of gender-related role expectations during early adolescence. In J. Brooks-Gunn & A. C. Peterson (Eds.), *Girls at puberty* (pp. 201–28). New York: Plenum.

Hinde, R. A., & Stevenson-Hinde, J. (1987). Interpersonal relationships and child development. *Developmental Review, 7,* 1–21.

Hirsch, B. J., & Rapkin, B. D. (1987). The transition to junior high school: A longitudinal study of self-esteem, psychological symptomatology, school life, and social support. *Child Development, 58,* 1235–43.

Hortacsu, N. (1989). Targets of communication during adolescence. *Journal of Adolescence, 12,* 253–63.

Hunter, F. T., & Youniss, J. (1982). Changing functions of three relationships during adolescence. *Developmental Psychology, 18,* 806–11.

Hunter, F. T. (1985). Adolescents' perceptions of discussions with parents and friends. *Developmental Psychology, 21,* 433–40.

Johnson, F. L., & Aries, E. J. (1983). Conversational patterns among same-sex pairs of late-adolescent close friends. *Journal of Genetic Psychology, 142,* 225–38.

Jones, E. E., & Pittman, T. S. (1982). Toward a general theory of strategic self-presentation. In J. Suls (Ed.), *Psychological perspectives on the self* (Vol. 1, pp. 231–62). Hillsdale, NJ: Erlbaum.

Jones, G. P., & Dembo, M. H. (1989). Age and sex role differences in intimate friendships during childhood and adolescence. *Merrill-Palmer Quarterly, 35,* 445–62.

Jourard, S. M. (1971). *The transparent self.* New York: Van Nostrand.

Jourard, S. M. (1979). *Self-disclosure: An experimental analysis of the transparent self.* New York: Kruiger.

Kelley, H. H. (1979). *Personal relationships: Their structures and process.* Hillsdale, NJ: Erlbaum.

Kidder, L. M., Belletirie, G., & Cohn E. S. (1977). Secret ambitions and public performance: The effect of anonymity on reward allocations made by men and women. *Journal of Experimental Social Psychology, 13,* 70–80.

Kneisel, P. J. (1987, April). *Social support preferences of female adolescents in the context of interpersonal stress.* Paper presented at the biennial meeting of the Society for Research in Child Development, Baltimore, MD.

Kohlberg, L. (1969). Stage and sequence: The cognitive developmental approach to socialization. In D. Goslin (Ed.), *Handbook of socialization theory and research* (pp. 347–404). Chicago: Rand McNally.

Kohlberg, L., & Gilligan, C. (1972). The adolescent as philosopher: The discovery of the self in a post-conventional world. In J. Kagan & R. Coles (Eds.), *Twelve to sixteen: Early adolescence* (pp. 39–57). New York: Norton.

Kon, I. S. (1981). Adolescent friendship: Some unanswered questions for future research. In S. Duck & R. Gilmour (Eds.), *Personal relationships: Vol 2. Developing personal relationships* (pp. 187–204). London: Academic.

Kon, I. S., Losenkov, V. A., De Lissovoy, C., & De Lissovoy, V. (1978). Friendship in adolescence: Values and behavior. *Journal of Marriage and the Family, 40,* 143–55.

Lewis, R. A. (1978). Emotional intimacy among men. *Journal of Social Issues, 34,* 108–21.

Maccoby, E. E. (1988). Gender as a social category. *Developmental Psychology, 26,* 755–65.

Maccoby, E. E. (1990). Gender and relationships: A developmental account. *American Psychologist, 45,* 513–20.

Mahler, M. S., & McDevitt, J. B. (1980). The separation-individuation process and identity formation. In S. I. Greenspan & G. H. Pollack (Eds.), *The course of life: Psychoanalytic contributions toward understanding personality development.* Adelphi, MD: Mental Health Study Center.

Marcia, J. (1966). Development and validation of ego identity status. *Journal of Personality, 36,* 118–33.

Martin, D. H. (1985). Fathers and adolescents. In S. M. H. Hanson & F. W. Bozett (Eds.), *Dimensions of fatherhood* (pp. 170–95). Beverly Hills, CA: Sage.

Mitchell, J. J. (1976). Adoelscent intimacy. *Adolescence, 11,* 275–80.

Montemayor, R. (1983). Parents and adolescents in conflict: All families some of the time and some families most of the time. *Journal of Early Adolescence, 3,* 83–103.

Montemayor, R., & Eisen, M. (1977). The development of self-conceptions from childhood to adolescence. *Developmental Psychology, 13,* 314–19.

Mulcahy, G. A. (1973). Sex differences in patterns of self-disclosure among adolescents: A developmental perspective. *Journal of Youth and Adolescence, 2,* 343–56.

Murray, H. A. (1943). *The Thematic Apperception Test: Manual.* Cambridge, MA: Harvard University Press.

Nardi, P. M. (1992). "Seamless souls": An introduction to mens' friendships. In P. M. Nardi (Ed.), *Men's friendships* (pp. 1–14). London: Sage.

Noller, P., & Callan, V. J. (1990). Adolescents' perceptions of the nature of their communication with parents. *Journal of Youth and Adolescence, 19,* 349–62.

Olson, D. H. (1977). Insiders' and outsiders' views of relationships: Research studies. In G. Levinger & H. L. Raush (Eds.), *Close relationships: Perspectives on the meaning of intimacy* (pp. 115–35). Amherst: University of Massachusetts Press.

Papini, D. R., Farmer, F. F., Clark, S. M., Micka, J. C., & Barnett, J. K. (1990). Early adolescent age and gender differences in patterns of emotional self-disclosure to parents and friends. *Adolescence, 15,* 959–76.

Papini, D. R., Farmer, F. L., Clark, S. M., & Snell, W. E. (1988). An evaluation of adolescent patterns of sexual self-disclosure to parents and friends. *Journal of Adolescent Research, 3,* 387–401.

Papini, D. R., Sebby, R. A., & Clark, S. (1989). Affective quality of family relations and adolescent identity exploration. *Adolescence, 24,* 457–66.

Parker, J., & Gottman, J. M. (1989). Social and emotional development in relational context: Friendship interaction from early childhood to adolescence. In T. J. Berndt & G. W. Ladd (Eds.), *Peer relationships in child development* (pp. 95–131). New York: Wiley.

Patterson, E. T., & Hale, E. S. (1985). Making sure: Integrating menstrual care practices into activities of daily living. *Advances in Nursing Science, 7,* 18–31.

Peterson, A. C. (1983). The nature of biological–psychosocial interactions: The sample case of early adolescence. In R. M. Lerner & T. T. Fock (Eds.), *Biological–psychosocial interactions in early adolescence* (pp. 35–61). Hillsdale, NJ: Erlbaum.

Piaget, J. (1932). *The moral judgment of the child.* New York: Harcourt.

Prager, K. J. (1989). Intimacy status and couple communication. *Journal of Social and Personal Relationships, 6,* 435–49.

Prager, K. J., Fuller, D. O., & Gonzalez, A. S. (1989). The function of self-disclosure in social interaction. *Journal of Social Behavior and Personality, 4,* 563–80.

Raffaelli, M., & Duckett, E. (1989). "We were just talking . . .": Conversations in early adolescence. *Journal of Youth and Adolescence, 18,* 567–82.

Rawlins, W. K. (1992). *Friendship matters: Communication, dialectics and the life course.* New York: De Gruyter.

Rawlins, W. K., & Holl, M. (1987). The communicative achievement of friendship during adolescence: Predicaments of trust and violation. *Western Journal of Speech Communication, 51,* 345–63.

Reid, M., Landesman, S., Treder, R., & Jaccard, J. (1989). "My family and friends": Six- to twelve-year-old children's perceptions of social support. *Child Development, 60,* 896–910.

Reis, H. T., Senchak, M., & Solomon, B. (1985). Sex differences in the intimacy of social interaction: Further examination of potential explanations. *Journal of Personality and Social Psychology, 48,* 1204–17.

Richardson, R. A., Galambos, N. L., Schulenberg, J. E., & Petersen, A. C. (1984). Young adolescents' perceptions of the family environment. *Journal of Early Adolescence, 4,* 131–53.

Rivenbark, W. H. (1971). Self-disclosure patterns among adolescents. *Psychological Reports, 28,* 35–42.

Rosenberg, M. (1965). *Society and the adolescent self-image.* Princeton, NJ: Princeton University Press.

Rosenberg, M. (1979). *Conceiving the self.* New York: Basic.

Rosenberg, M., Hertz-Lazarowitz, R., & Guttmann, J. (1985, July). *Children of divorce and their intimate relationship with parents and peers.* Paper presented at the eighth biennial meeting of the International Society for the Study of Behavioural Development, Tours, France.

Rotenberg, K. J. (1991). The trust-value basis of children's friendships. In K. J. Rotenberg (Ed.), *Children's interpersonal trust: Sensitivity to lying, deception and promise violation* (pp. 160–72). New York: Springer-Verlag.

Rotenberg, K. J., & Sliz, D. (1988). Children's restrictive disclosure to friends. *Merrill-Palmer Quarterly, 34,* 203–15.

Rubenstein, J., Watson, F., Drolette, M., & Rubenstein, H. (1976). Young adolescents' sexual interests. *Adolescence, 12,* 54–71.

Ruble, D. N., & Brooks-Gunn, J. (1982). The experience of menarche. *Child Development, 53,* 1557–66.

Ruble, D. N., & Frey, K. S. (1987). Social comparison and self-evaluation in the classroom: Developmental changes in knowledge and function. In J. C. Masters & W. S. Smith (Eds.), *Social comparison, social justice, and relative deprivation* (pp. 81–104). Hillsdale, NJ: Erlbaum.

Savin-Williams, R. C., & Berndt, T. J. (1990). Friendship and peer relations. In S. S. Feldman & G. R. Elliot (Eds.), *At the threshold: The developing adolescent.* Cambridge, MA: Harvard University Press.

Schenkel, S., & Marcia, J. E. (1972). Attitudes toward premarital intercourse in determining ego identity status in college women. *Journal of Personality, 3,* 472–82.

Selman, R. L. (1980). *The growth of interpersonal understanding: Developmental and clinical analysis.* New York: Academic.

Serrano, R. G. (1984). Mexican-American adolescent self-disclosure in friendship formation. *Adolescence, 19,* 539–49.

Sharabany, R., Gershoni, R., & Hoffman, J. (1981). Girlfriend, boyfriend: Age and sex differences in intimate friendships. *Developmental Psychology, 17,* 800–808.

Simmons, R., Burgeson, R., Carlton-Ford, S., & Blyth, D. (1987). The impact of cumulative change in early adolescence. *Child Development, 58,* 1220–34.

Slavin, L. A. (1991). Validation studies of the PEPSS, a measure of perceived emotional support for use with adolescents. *Journal of Adolescent Research, 6,* 316–35.

Slavin, L. A., & Raimer, K. L. (1990). Gender differences in emotional support and depressive symptoms among adolescents: A perspective analysis. *American Journal of Community Psychology, 18,* 407–21.

Smollar, J., & Youniss, J. (1982). Social development through friendship. In K. H. Rubin & H. S. Ross (Eds.), *Peer relations and social skills in childhood* (pp. 279–98). New York: Springer-Verlag.

Steinberg, L. (1988). Reciprocal relation between parent–child distance and pubertal maturation. *Developmental Psychology, 24,* 122–8.

Stern, D. N. (1973). *The Interpersonal world of the infant.* New York: Basic.

Stiles, W. B. (1987). "I have to talk to somebody": A fever model of disclosure. In V. J. Derlega & J. H. Berg (Eds.), *Self-disclosure: Theory, research and therapy* (pp. 257–82). New York: Plenum.

Striegel-Moore, R. H., Silberstein, L. R., & Rodin, J. (1986). Toward an understanding of risk factors for bulimia. *American Psychologist, 41,* 246–63.

Sullivan, H. S. (1953). *The interpersonal theory of psychiatry.* New York: Norton.

Tan, S., & Berndt, T. J. (1991, May). *Friendly conversations and the conversations of friends.* Paper presented at the meeting of the Midwestern Psychological Association, Chicago.

Tannen, D. (1990a). Gender differences in topical coherence: Creating involvement in best friends' talk. *Discourse Processes, 13,* 73–90.

Tannen, D. (1990b). *You just don't understand: Women and men in conversation.* New York: Ballantine.

Thoits, P. A. (1986). Social support and coping assistance. *Journal of Consulting and Clinical Psychology, 54,* 416–23.

Unger, R., & Crawford, M. (1992). *Women and gender.* New York: McGraw-Hill.

Weiss, R. S. (1974). The provisions of social relationships. In Z. Rubin (Ed.)., *Doing unto others* (pp. 17–26). Englewood Cliffs, NJ: Prentice-Hall.

West, L. W., & Zingle, H. W. (1969). A self-disclosure inventory for adolescents. *Psychological Reports, 24,* 439–45.

Wilks, J. (1986). The relative importance of parents and friends in adolescent decision-making. *Journal of Youth and Adolescence, 15,* 323–34.

Wintre, M. G., Hicks, R., McVey, G., & Fox, J. (1987, April). *Age and sex differences in choice of consultant for various types of problems.* Paper presented at the biennial meeting of the Society for Research in Child Development, Baltimore, MD.

Wright, H., & Keple, W. (1981). Friends and parents of a sample of high school juniors: An explanatory study of relationship intensity and interpersonal rewards. *Journal of Marriage & the Family, 43,* 559–70.

Youniss, J. (1980). *Parents and peers in social development. A Sullivan–Piaget perspective.* Chicago: University of Chicago Press.

Youniss, J., & Ketterlinus, R. D. (1987). Communication and connectedness in mother– and father–adolescent relationships. *Journal of Youth and Adolescence, 3,* 265–80.

Youniss, J., & Smollar, J. (1985). *Adolescent relationships with mothers, fathers, and friends.* Chicago: University of Chicago Press.

3 Intimacy and self-disclosure in friendships

Thomas J. Berndt and Nancy A. Hanna

Intimacy and self-disclosure are important features of friendships in childhood and adolescence. Most theorists and researchers have considered the two features to be highly related, if not synonymous. Sullivan (1953), one of the first theorists to emphasize the importance of intimate friendships, argued that the emergence of such friendships during later childhood has a powerful influence on personality development. He defined intimacy as "closeness, without specifying that which is close other than the persons" (1953, p. 246). Sullivan further suggested that intimacy was partly the result of self-disclosure. Also, he argued that self-disclosure to friends has positive effects on children's personalities. For example, he proposed that conversations with friends help children gain a better understanding of themselves and other people. More generally, Sullivan assumed that intimate friendships involving frequent self-disclosure have positive effects on children's social development.

Most researchers who explore adults' relationships agree with Sullivan that intimacy and self-disclosure are closely related and have positive effects on individuals. Clark and Reis (1988), for example, defined intimacy as "a process in which one person expresses important self-relevant feelings and information to another, and as a result of the other's response comes to feel known, validated (i.e., obtains confirmation of his or her world view and personal worth), and cared for" (1988, p. 628). In this definition, self-disclosure is taken both as a sign that two persons have an intimate relationship and as a contributor to the intimacy of their relationship. Clark and Reis cautioned that intimate self-disclosure does not always have positive effects on individuals and their relationships, but they cited more evidence on the benefits than the risks of intimacy.

The research by the authors reported in this chapter was supported in part by a grant from the National Institute of Mental Health.

In this chapter, we examine the nature and effects of intimacy and self-disclosure in children's and adolescents' friendships. We focus on three questions. First, how should we define intimacy, self-disclosure, and the relation between the two? When considering this question, we also review the operational definitions of these constructs in previous research. Second, does current evidence support Sullivan's (1953) hypotheses about the developmental changes in the intimacy of friendships and the frequency of intimate self-disclosure between friends? We argue that the answer to this question depends on the measures of intimacy and self-disclosure that researchers use. Finally, does current evidence support hypotheses about the benefits of intimacy and self-disclosure between friends? We conclude that many studies provide data consistent with the hypotheses, but some studies suggest negative effects of intimate self-disclosure. Also, few studies clearly show whether intimacy and self-disclosure between friends affect children's social adjustment or vice versa.

Self-disclosure and intimacy: overlapping but distinct constructs

Several researchers have adopted the position of Clark and Reis (1988) that self-disclosure is one sign of an intimate relationship. For example, one measure of the intimacy of adolescents' friendships includes a scale for *frankness* with items like "I feel free to talk with him (her) about almost everything" (Sharabany, Gershoni, & Hofman, 1981). Other researchers have proposed definitions of intimacy that match the core meaning of the term as Sullivan (1953) defined it: a feeling of closeness in a relationship (see Reisman, 1990). Still others distinguish between self-disclosure as a process or pattern of interaction and intimacy as a quality of a relationship (Camarena, Sarigiani, & Petersen, 1990). These researchers argue that self-disclosure may contribute to intimacy in a relationship but does not always do so.

The assumptions that researchers make about the relations between intimacy and self-disclosure depend on how they define self-disclosure. As many researchers have pointed out, not all self-disclosure (i.e., comments about oneself to another person) is highly intimate (Gottman & Mettetal, 1986; Papini, Farmer, Clark, Micka, & Barnett, 1990). People often disclose some types of information about themselves (e.g., "I was born in Iowa") to people who are acquaintances or strangers. Conversely, a person may develop an intimate relationship with another person (i.e., one that is very close) before either of them has directly disclosed much information about him- or herself.

We view intimacy and self-disclosure as distinct but overlapping constructs. When applied to friendship, intimacy refers to a quality that can be defined most accurately, as Sullivan argued, as the closeness of the positive relationship between friends. Intimacy is related to self-disclosure because friends who have an intimate relationship typically are eager to learn about each other and willing to disclose private information to each other.

Self-disclosure is not a quality of a relationship but a type of behavior, typically verbal behavior, in which a person tells another person about him- or herself. Although the information disclosed may be highly intimate, the kind normally revealed only to a close friend, this need not be the case. Providing any information about oneself to another person, regardless of how intimate or mundane the information, counts as self-disclosure.

Our definitions of intimacy and self-disclosure have implications for the measurement of these constructs. To measure the intimacy of a friendship, researchers have several options. One option is to assess people's perceptions of the closeness of their friendships. A few researchers have done so (e.g., Berscheid, Snyder, & Omoto, 1989), but they have seldom labeled these as measures of intimacy. Another option that has been chosen more often is to derive measures of intimacy from people's reports about their willingness to disclose personal information to a friend, or their reports that they have done so previously (e.g., Sharabany et al., 1981; Berndt & Perry, 1986). These measures are appropriately labeled, in our opinion, because a willingness to disclose such information is one indication that people believe they have a close friendship with another person. Stated differently, these measures assess people's perceptions of the intimacy of their friendships. We would emphasize, however, that such measures assess people's reports of intimate self-disclosure to friends, not their actual self-disclosure.

Still another option chosen by a few researchers is to directly observe interactions between friends and code instances of self-disclosure during the friends' conversations (e.g., Gottman & Mettetal, 1986; Berndt, Perry, & Miller, 1988). Because self-disclosures can vary in their intimacy, researchers have sometimes distinguished between disclosures low and high in intimacy (Gottman & Mettetal, 1986). However, highly intimate disclosures are rare in research settings, so researchers have often used a single code for all instances of self-disclosure. Later, we will describe another study in which this procedure was used.

Few studies involving observations of actual self-disclosure have been done. One reason is that arranging interactions between pairs of friends and then coding the resulting conversations is difficult and time-consuming. To avoid these problems, some researchers have tried to assess friends' self-disclosures from their reports about recent conversations with friends (e.g., Mazur, 1989). Unfortunately, researchers rarely collect data that would make it possible to judge the validity of these reports. At best, retrospective reports provide an outline of the sequence of topics in a conversation and a record of a few comments that were salient and therefore memorable. Such reports are not likely to provide adequate measures of the type and frequency of self-disclosure between friends.

Finally, a few researchers have devised creative alternatives to the methods most commonly used. Hornstein and Truesdell (1988) asked women for permission to record their telephone conversations during a short period and then coded their intimate disclosures with friends, acquaintances, and strangers. This method does not allow researchers to assess the nonverbal cues present in face-to-face interaction (and in videotape records of those interactions). Also, the method is not suitable for research with young children, who spend little time talking with friends on the telephone. On the other hand, an important advantage of the method is that recording takes place in a natural setting, the participant's home, instead of the laboratory settings used in some other studies (e.g., Gottman & Mettetal, 1986).

Rotenberg and Sliz (1988) assessed children's self-disclosure to friends by asking them to prepare a message for a friend and then record that message on an audiotape recorder. The children were asked to talk about specified topics that varied in their intimacy. For example, messages in which children told good or bad things about themselves were considered highly personal, or high in intimacy. Messages in which children told what their house looked like or said whether they had brothers or sisters were considered not very personal, or low in intimacy. Then the researchers coded the number and type of statements in the children's messages. This method does not capture the interchange of actual conversations, but it does provide samples of actual self-disclosure by children.

Obtaining people's reports about their friendships is qualitatively different from observing two friends' interactions. Neither method is inherently better than the other. Each is ideal for assessing specific types of constructs. To repeat briefly, we have endorsed the common practice of judging the intimacy of children's friendships from their reported willingness to disclose intimate information to friends. In addition, we have argued that direct observations of self-disclosure during conversations are valuable in showing what friends actually say to each other about themselves. Not all self-disclosures involve intimate information, however.

We conclude that hypotheses about intimacy in friendship should be distinguished from hypotheses about friends' self-disclosure, despite the tendency of Sullivan (1953) and later writers to take the two as synonymous. The two sets of hypotheses must be distinguished not only because intimacy and self-disclosure are distinct constructs, but also because the usual methods of assessing the two constructs differ greatly. Given the difference in methods, we should not be surprised if the research data suggest different conclusions about the two. We turn, next, to the data on developmental changes in the reported intimacy of friendships and in actual self-disclosure to friends.

Developments in friendship: reported intimacy and actual self-disclosure

Sullivan (1953) did not state an explicit rationale for his hypothesis that intimacy first becomes an important feature of friendship in later childhood. By contrast, Douvan and Adelson (1966) suggested that intimacy becomes an important feature of friendships only during adolescence. They also suggested several reasons for the emergence of intimate friendships during that period. First, adolescents are in the process of loosening and restructuring their relationships with parents, and they need the support and security of friends to complete this process. Second, adolescents are confronted with the physical changes of puberty and are in the midst of a search for their own identity. They need friends as advisers, models, and sounding boards for ideas. Third, adolescents in the United States are given free time for interactions with friends and settings in which they can meet friends with minimal interference from adults. According to Douvan and Adelson (1966), these circumstances give friendships a special intensity during adolescence.

Like previous writers, Douvan and Adelson (1966) assumed that the developmental changes in friends' interactions paralleled the changes in adolescents' perceptions of their friendships. Indeed, Douvan and Adelson used interviews with adolescents as the basis for their judgments about the content and psychological functions of self-disclosure between friends. Yet later researchers have shown different patterns of age changes in reports about the intimacy of friendships and in actual self-disclosure during friends' conversations.

Increases in the reported intimacy of friendships

Many researchers have replicated Douvan and Adelson's (1966) findings that adolescents perceive intimacy as a more important feature of friendship than do younger children. In some studies (e.g., Bigelow, 1977; Berndt, 1981; Selman, 1981), children and adolescents were asked to define a best friendship or to say what they expected from a best friend.

Children under 12 years of age rarely said that they shared their thoughts and feelings with friends, discussed personal problems with friends, or had other kinds of interactions that typify an intimate relationship. In other studies (Sharabany et al., 1981; Berndt & Perry, 1986; Reisman, 1990), children and adolescents described the features of their own friendships. Again, children under 12 years rarely mentioned sharing personal confidences and the discussion of personal issues that are part of an intimate friendship.

In one study, the differentiation between close friendships and other peer relationships increased during adolescence (Berndt & Perry, 1986). Students in the second, fourth, sixth, and eighth grades reported on the intimacy of a close friendship by responding to questions about their discussion of personal feelings and problems with the friend (e.g., "When you have a problem at home or at school, do you talk to this friend about it?"). The students responded to the same questions about their relationship with a classmate who was not a close friend.

Between second and eighth grade, affirmative answers to the questions about friends increased with age, indicating an increase in the intimacy of friendship. Affirmative answers to the questions about other classmates decreased with age. These findings and other research (Furman & Bierman, 1984) establish that the development of more intimate friendships during adolescence is accompanied by a decrease in the intimacy of relationships with nonfriends. Moreover, friendships seem to grow in importance at the expense of parent–child relationships. While reports of conversations about thoughts and feelings with friends increase between childhood and adolescence, reports about comparable conversations with parents decrease (Papini et al., 1990).

However, the consistency of the research data should not be exaggerated. Not all researchers have found significant increases between childhood and adolescence or during the adolescent years in the reported intimacy of friendships (Buhrmester, 1990). Sometimes the age change is significant for one measure of intimacy but not others (Berndt, Hawkins, & Hoyle, 1986). Still, the weight of the evidence supports the conclusion that adolescents view their friendships as more intimate than do younger children.

A more controversial issue is whether the developmental change toward more intimate friendships is equally great for boys and girls. Youniss and Smollar (1985) argued that about one-third of adolescent boys do not have an intimate relationship with a same-sex friend. This estimate is hard to interpret because it is based on the boys' responses to several questions in which they ranked the quality of their relationships with their mother, their father, a same-sex friend, and an opposite-sex friend. Youniss and Smollar suggested that boys who ranked their same-sex friend last on several questions lacked an intimate same-sex friendship. Yet another interpretation of the data is that these boys had fairly intimate relationships with same-sex friends but viewed these friendships as less intimate than their relationships with their parents and girlfriends.

In many studies, boys reported that they shared their thoughts, feelings, and problems with friends less often than girls did (Sharabany et al., 1981; Berndt et al., 1986; Buhrmester, 1990; Papini et al., 1990). The sex difference seems to increase during adolescence (e.g., Jones & Dembo, 1989). Some researchers, however, have not found a significant sex difference between boys' and girls' reports about the intimacy of their friendships (Furman & Buhrmester, 1985; Berndt & Perry, 1986). In adulthood, too, sex differences in the intimacy of friendship are not consistent across studies and, when significant, are not large (Wright, 1982).

Some researchers have suggested that adolescents' reports about the intimacy of their friendships are less related to their sex than to their sex-role orientation. Many popular and scholarly writers have suggested that the traditional masculine sex role discourages intimate self-disclosure, and some evidence supports this suggestion (e.g., Snell, Miller, Belk, Garcia-Falconi, & Hernandez-Sanchez, 1989). Other studies suggest a somewhat different conclusion. In one study of college students (Buhrmester, Furman, Wittenberg, & Reis, 1988), a measure of masculinity was unrelated to students' reports of their competence in self-disclosure to friends and romantic partners. By contrast, self-reported disclosure competence was strongly related to a measure of students' femininity.

Research with children and adolescents has also yielded mixed results. In a study with 8- to 14-year-olds (Jones & Dembo, 1989), boys who were traditionally sex typed – high in masculinity and low in femininity – rated their friendships lower in intimacy than did other boys. However, boys who were rated high in masculinity and also high in femininity had friendships as intimate as those of girls. In another study (Townsend, McCracken, & Wilton, 1988), adolescent boys with highly intimate friendships had higher masculinity scores than boys with less intimate friendships, and the same effect held for girls. Boys with highly intimate friendships had higher femininity scores than those with less intimate friendships, but this effect was not found for girls. The inconsistent findings make it difficult to draw conclusions about the relation of sex-role orientations to the reported intimacy of friendships. Still, the findings imply that feminine traits may promote intimate self-disclosure to friends more than masculine traits hinder it. More careful tests of this hypothesis are needed.

Taken together, we believe that previous research provides an adequate basis for conclusions about developmental changes in children's and adolescents' perceptions of their friendships. More often than young children, adolescents perceive their friends as people with whom they can share personal information. Adolescents more often perceive friends as people who can help them solve personal problems. A developmental change toward more intimate friendships does occur, as Sullivan (1953) assumed. But the change occurs later than Sullivan believed, during the adolescent years rather than before puberty.

Self-disclosure by friends: no change with age?

The evidence for a developmental change in friends' self-disclosure during actual conversations is weak. The available data provide modest support for the commonsense hypothesis that friends engage in more intimate self-disclosure during their conversations than do acquaintances or strangers. As mentioned earlier, the women in one study agreed to have their telephone conversations with friends, acquaintances, and strangers recorded and analyzed (Hornstein & Truesdell, 1988). Each comment during these conversations was coded for its descriptive intimacy and its evaluative intimacy. Comments were coded as high in descriptive intimacy when they involved highly personal issues (e.g., "I was once a heroin addict"). Comments were coded as high in evaluative intimacy when they were expressed with strong affect or indicated extreme opinions (e.g., "I absolutely detest rock music").

When women were talking with their friends, they made more comments high in descriptive and evaluative intimacy than when talking with acquaintances or strangers. Comments to strangers were lower in descriptive and evaluative intimacy than comments to friends and acquaintances. Most intriguing were comments to acquaintances, which were similar to those of friends in their evaluative intimacy, but similar to those of strangers in their descriptive intimacy. So acquaintances were prone to express their feelings openly when talking about nonintimate topics, but only friends disclosed intimate or personal information about themselves frequently.

Another study (Gottman & Mettetal, 1986) included two groups of adolescent girls: 11- to 12-year-olds and 16- to 17-year-olds. Pairs of girls who were either close friends, acquaintances, or strangers came to a laboratory room that was furnished like a typical living room. They were asked to talk about whatever they wanted for 30 minutes. Videotaped records of their conversations were coded for many types of comments. Especially common were episodes of gossip – positive or negative comments about other people (see also Eckert, 1990). Less often, the girls disclosed personal information about themselves. If this information involved what the researchers considered threatening facts, opinions, and feelings, they coded it as high in intimacy. Otherwise, they coded it as low in intimacy.

Friends and acquaintances did not differ in how often they engaged in low-intimate self-disclosure. Friends disclosed more highly intimate information to each other than acquaintances did, but only about 4% of the topics of friends' conversations were highly intimate. About 1% of the topics of acquaintances' conversations were highly intimate. Also, the proportion of highly intimate topics in friends' conversations was not significantly greater at 11 to 12 years of age than at 16 to 17 years. These findings do not suggest an increase in the intimacy of friendships during adolescence, and so do not match those from the studies of adolescents' self-reports.

Rotenberg and Sliz (1988) concluded that intimate self-disclosure occurs between friends as early as 6 years of age and does not change markedly between 6 and 10 years. As mentioned earlier, these researchers asked kindergarteners and second and fourth graders to prepare taped messages on specified topics for friends and nonfriends. Children in all three grades prepared longer messages on personal topics when they thought the messages would be given to friends rather than nonfriends. The friend–nonfriend difference was equally great at all three grades.

By contrast, the friend–nonfriend difference was larger at fourth grade than at the earlier grades when children were talking about their achievements or other positive characteristics that they had. However, the researchers did not attribute this result to an increase with age in the intimacy of children's friendships. They argued that fourth graders had learned the norm that people should not brag about themselves, especially when talking to people who are not close friends.

In sum, the few researchers who have observed and recorded friends' conversations have not found dramatic increases with age in the intimacy of friends' self-disclosure (see also Berndt et al., 1988). Still, the findings are difficult to compare with those in which children and adolescents reported on the intimacy of their friendships, because no study included a definitely preadolescent group and a definitely adolescent group. The samples in previous studies were either adults (Hornstein & Truesdell, 1988), children (Rotenberg & Sliz, 1988), or adolescents (Gottman & Mettetal, 1986). Although Gottman and Mettetal labeled their 11- to 12-year-olds as a middle-childhood group, most other researchers would consider them as early adolescents because the adolescent growth spurt and the development of secondary sex characteristics begin around 11 years of age (Tanner,

1978). Therefore, these studies are not directly relevant to hypotheses about the emergence of intimate self-disclosure between friends in early adolescence.

Self-disclosure by children and adolescents in a natural setting

Along with Bridgett Perry, we observed relatively unstructured conversations of children and adolescents with a friend or other classmate (T. J. Berndt, T. B. Perry, & N. A. Hanna, unpublished data). We also wanted to examine other features of friends' conversations, such as their frequency of agreements and disagreements with each other. Although some researchers found that friends have more positive interactions than nonfriends do (e.g., Newcomb & Brady, 1982), others found that friends disagree with or criticize each other more than nonfriends do (Gottman, 1983; Nelson & Aboud, 1985).

In addition, we wanted to observe friends' conversations not in a laboratory, but in the schools where they normally spend their days. We had to assure that conversations with friends and nonfriends occurred under comparable conditions, but we wanted the conversations to take place in a comfortable and familiar setting. In sum, we tried to identify the distinctive features of children's and adolescents' conversations with friends in a natural setting. Our strategy in reaching this goal was to record conversations in schools and compare the conversations of close friends with those of other classmates who were not close friends.

Method. The study included 106 third and seventh graders whose mean ages were 9 and 13 years, respectively. Approximately the same number of girls and boys were in the sample.

All students named their best friends and then used a 5-point scale to indicate how much they liked each of the same-sex classmates participating in the study. On the scale, ratings of 5 were labeled *like very much, as much as a best friend.* Ratings of 1 were labeled *don't like.* Students could also rate a classmate 0, meaning they didn't know the classmate. Pairs of students were considered close friends if either one or both of them named the other as a best friend and they gave each other ratings of 4 or 5. Pairs of students were considered merely as classmates if neither named the other as a best friend and they rated each other either 2 or 3 on the response scale.

Then each student was randomly paired either with a close friend or with another classmate. No pairs included children who disliked each other, that is, who had rated each other as 1. No pairs included strangers, students who had rated each other as 0. Thus, our two types of pairs contrast close friends with other classmates who are well-acquainted with each other and neither strongly like nor dislike each other.

Each pair of students was brought to a private room or unused area away from their regular classroom. Each student was asked to read a list of possible vacation places and then independently to rank his or her top four choices from the list: Next each student read lists of after-school activities, experiences that make children angry, and experiences that make children proud of themselves. The students also ranked the top four items on these lists to indicate their preferences or the items that best applied to themselves.

After completing their self-rankings, each student read the lists a second time and ranked the items as they thought their partner would rank them. Then the pair of students was given a new list of possible vacation places and asked to talk about them together. They were encouraged to begin their conversation by saying how they had ranked the vacation places. Next they were asked to try to agree on how most students their age would rank them. Students were given 4 minutes to discuss the list and make their rankings. This task gave both friends and other classmates topics to talk about without totally structuring their conversations. Most pairs spent part of the time on the assigned task and then engaged in free conversation. Such a balance of task-centered and unstructured conversation is also typical in natural settings.

After discussing the vacation places, the pairs of friends or other classmates discussed the lists of after-school activities and experiences that make children angry and proud. The conversations were videotaped with the students' knowledge and consent. Later, the videotapes were coded using two sets of codes. The first set of codes was for the topic of each statement during the conversations. Many statements were related to the ranking task students were given, but other statements reflected self-disclosure, gossip about peers, comments about the partner, or other topics. The second set of codes was for other verbal behaviors that coordinate a conversation or express a speaker's emotions. This set included agreements or acknowledgments, disagreements or verbal aggression, commands, questions, and whispers. It also included "we-directs," statements like "Let's make Disneyworld number 1," which represent a suggestion or a polite form of a directive.

The reliability of coding was assessed before final codes were assigned to any videotapes. Reliability was assessed again on a sample of tapes halfway through the coding process and a third time near the end of the process. The repeated assessments allowed us to determine whether reliability decreased over time. In fact, reliability remained high or improved during the

Table 3.1. *Mean frequencies of conversation topics and other verbal behaviors*

	Third grade		Seventh grade	
	Friends	Classmates	Friends	Classmates
Conversation topics				
Task-related	7.76	6.18	8.24	7.76
Self-disclosure	1.64	1.28	1.53	2.09
Family	0.77	0.96	0.67	0.97
Gossip	0.57	0.39	1.81	1.16
Partner	0.97	0.88	1.15	1.20
Research setting	0.56	0.68	1.86	1.10
Small talk	1.26	1.93	2.26	1.95
Other verbal behaviors				
Agreements/acknowledgments	3.95	3.28	3.15	4.79
Disagreements/verbal aggression	1.73	0.76	1.52	0.95
We-directs	0.87	0.82	0.88	0.65
Commands	0.85	0.83	0.68	0.38
Whispering	0.47	1.53	0.68	0.18
Questions	2.99	2.80	2.99	3.31

coding process. For example, the correlations between two observers' scores for each of the verbal codes were above .90 before coding began and above .95 near the end of coding.

Results and discussion. Table 3.1 shows the mean scores for each category of verbal behavior for friends and other classmates in each grade. To our surprise, friends did not engage in more self-disclosure than nonfriends did. None of the categories of conversation topics showed significant differences between friends and nonfriends for the entire sample. None of the interactions of the friend–nonfriend contrast with grade was significant. Thus, the content of the conversations between friends and between other classmates was remarkably similar. Moreover, the content of friends' conversations was like that of other classmates regardless of what the students discussed. In particular, friends did not show more self-disclosure than did classmates when they discussed more intimate issues involving feelings (i.e., things that make children angry and proud).

By contrast, there were significant effects of grade and sex on the topics of the conversations. Seventh graders engaged in more self-disclosure, shared more gossip about peers, and talked more about the research setting than did third graders. (An example of a comment about the research setting would be "How much time do we have to talk about this?") Although these effects could reveal the specific focus of adolescents' conversations (see Gottman & Mettetal, 1986), we note that the grade effect for the most frequent topic of conversation, task-related comments, also approached significance ($p < .07$). It may be, then, that seventh graders simply were more talkative than third graders.

Consistent with past research based on self-report measures, girls showed more self-disclosure than boys did. Girls also talked more about their families than boys did; boys made more comments about the research setting. The sex differences were roughly comparable for friends and for other classmates. That is, the interactions of sex with the friend–nonfriend contrast were nonsignificant.

One of the verbal behaviors showed a significant friend–classmate difference. Disagreements occurred roughly twice as often between friends as between classmates. For two behaviors, the friend–classmate differences varied with grade. Seventh graders agreed less often with friends than with other classmates, but for third graders the friend–classmate difference in agreements was nonsignificant. The friend–classmate differences in these behaviors were equally large when students discussed emotions and when they discussed after-school activities and vacation places.

The findings for disagreements and agreements by seventh graders suggest that friends' conversations may be more frank and, therefore, less polite or positive than other classmates' conversations. The difference in friends' and classmates' whispering for third graders is harder to interpret but may indicate that friends were more willing to speak openly in our setting. In sum, the friends in our study did not have conversations as "friendly" as did nonfriends.

Some researchers might consider the frankness of friends' comments as an indication of the intimacy of their friendships. As mentioned earlier, a scale for frankness is part of one self-report measure of intimacy in friendships (Sharabany et al., 1981). Also, the disagreements that occurred so often between friends could be viewed as signs of the evaluative intimacy of their conversations (K. Rotenberg, personal communication).

We consider such an explanation of our findings as doubtful for two reasons. First, most definitions of intimate relationships assume they are marked by a high level of interpersonal agreement and a low level of disagreement. Of course, some children (and adults) argue frequently and intensely with their friends. These friendships seem paradoxical, however, because positive interactions are prototypical of intimate relationships. If researchers treated frequent disagreements as an indicator of intimacy in friendships, they would have difficulty distinguishing friends from enemies.

Second, in previous descriptions of intimate self-disclosure, the content of disclosures was as important as their affective tone. In previous research (Sharabany et al., 1981), *frankness* referred to a willingness to "talk about almost everything" with a friend, even highly personal topics. Definitions of evaluative intimacy also refer to statements about a person's feelings toward things. Recall the earlier example "I absolutely detest rock music." By contrast, the disagreements in our study often involved little or no self-disclosure and minimal affect. Typically, one child said something like, "Let's choose this one [alternative]," and the friend disagreed by saying, "No, let's pick this one." We conclude that friends were not showing their greater intimacy when they disagreed more frankly with each other. We also conclude that intimate self-disclosure is no greater among friends than among nonfriends in natural and public settings like a schoolroom.

Another explanation of our findings is more plausible. We mentioned that the pairs of other classmates in our study neither strongly liked nor strongly disliked each other. Additional data from a postconversation questionnaire suggested that these pairs had previously had few interactions with each other. Perhaps they behaved so positively during the conversations because they viewed the conversations as a chance to get to know each other and to become friends with each other. This hypothesis would explain why the content of their conversations so closely matched that of friends.

If this alternative explanation is correct, it has important implications for future research on friends' self-disclosure. It implies that researchers will have difficulty devising methods of assessing the differences between friends' and nonfriends' conversations. Although we observed friends and other classmates in the same situation, they may have interpreted the situation differently. To avoid this problem, researchers might focus on the features of friends' conversations rather than the differences between friends' and nonfriends' conversations. Stated differently, pairs of nonfriends may not provide an adequate comparison group for pairs of friends, especially when researchers are studying actual self-disclosure. We will turn to the issue near the end of the chapter when we consider directions for future research on self-disclosure and friendship.

Correlates of reported intimacy and actual self-disclosure

Many researchers have examined the possible effects of intimate self-disclosure on children, adolescents, and adults. Some studies were designed to test Sullivan's (1953) hypotheses about the positive effects of intimate friendships in later childhood or adolescence. Other studies tested more general hypotheses about the effects of supportive social relation-ships (see Sarason & Sarason, 1985; Clark & Reis, 1988). In these studies, intimate disclosure was usually viewed as one means by which friends provided emotional support and advice to each other.

Our heading for this section refers to *correlates* rather than *effects* of intimate self-disclosure because virtually all previous studies had correla-tional designs. Therefore, the results of these studies do not definitely show whether intimate self-disclosure has positive effects on individuals or whether individuals with positive characteristics engage in more intimate self-disclosure. Stated more formally, the studies do not show whether variations in intimate self-disclosure are a cause or an effect of variations in individuals' characteristics.

We also need to distinguish between reports of intimacy in friendships and observations of actual self-disclosure by friends. In previous sections, we have emphasized that the two methods differ greatly and suggest differ-ent conclusions about developmental changes in friendships. We show in this section that the methods also suggest different conclusions about the correlates (and effects) of intimate self-disclosure.

Reports of intimacy in friendships are related to other indicators of closeness between friends. Adolescents who describe their friendships as more intimate also express more satisfaction with their friendships (Reis-man, 1990). In addition, these adolescents rate their friendships as higher in emotional closeness (Camarena et al., 1990). Moreover, adolescents who express concern about a lack of intimacy in their friendships tend, over time, to have less stable friendships (Berndt et al., 1986). Reports of inti-macy are also related to measures of closeness in adults' relationships (Clark & Reis, 1988).

Adolescents who view their friendships as more intimate receive higher scores on measures of self-esteem (Mannarino, 1980; McGuire & Weisz, 1982; Townsend et al., 1988). They also are less likely to suffer from iden-tity diffusion (Papini et al., 1990). These findings are consistent with Sulli-van's hypothesis that intimate friendships contribute to a positive sense of self and to the validation of self-worth. But because the studies are correla-tional, the findings could be interpreted as evidence that adolescents with a better sense of identity and higher self-esteem more often form intimate friendships.

College students who rate themselves as more competent in disclosing intimate information to other people also describe themselves as less anx-ious, shy, lonely, and depressed than do other students (Buhrmester et al., 1988). In addition, the students with high self-ratings are more popular and date more often than do other students. The students' self-reports are also moderately correlated with their roommates' ratings of their competence in intimate self-disclosure. These findings imply that ratings of intimate disclosure are one measure of social competence during the college years and probably earlier.

Buhrmester (1990) recently presented data that suggest reports of intimacy in friendship may be more related to psychological adjustment at 13 to 16 years of age than at 10 to 13 years. He found that the correlations between adolescents' reports on the intimacy of a close friendship and their reports on their psychological adjustment were mostly nonsignificant for the younger group but were mostly significant and fairly strong (.30 to .56) for the older group. Yet these data are difficult to interpret for two reasons.

First, Buhrmester did not find significant differences between the correlations for the younger and older groups when he related adolescents' reports on their adjustment to their friend's ratings of the intimacy of the friendship between them. Moreover, Buhrmester suggested that the discrepancy between the findings for self-ratings and friends' ratings could only be explained by additional research.

Second, many other researchers have found significant correlations between self-reports of intimacy in friendship and measures of psychological adjustment with samples of students the age of Buhrmester's younger group (see Savin-Williams & Berndt, 1990). Research on the relation of intimacy in friendship to self-esteem (e.g., McGuire & Weisz, 1982) is one example. On balance, the evidence suggests that self-reports of intimate disclosure to friends are positively related to adjustment in students as young as 10 years of age. More evidence is needed to judge whether the strength of these relations increases with age.

We noted earlier that researchers have asked people to report the intimacy of their friendships more often than they have observed friends' disclosures during actual conversations. Consequently, more is known about the correlates of reported intimacy than observed disclosure. Our review of the literature revealed only one study in which actual disclosure to friends was related to individuals' characteristics (Costanza, Derlega, & Winstead, 1988). That study had an experimental rather than a correlational design. Moreover, the results of the study suggested that self-disclosure to friends may have negative rather than positive effects.

College students came to a psychology laboratory with a friend. They were told that later in the experiment they would be asked to guide a tarantula through a maze after seeing a model do so. While waiting to perform the task, the students were asked to converse with their friends about one of the following topics: (a) their feelings about the tarantula and the task they would have to do, (b) their ideas about how they might do the task, and (c) other topics unrelated to the task.

Students reported on their anxiety and depression before and after the conversation with the friend. The students who had talked about their feelings with a friend – or engaged in self-disclosure – said they were more anxious and depressed afterward than did the students in the other two groups. These students also kept the tarantula farther away from themselves when they later did the task than did those in the other groups. These results suggest that discussing feelings of anxiety in a stressful situation may increase rather than reduce these feelings. Stated more generally, intimate self-disclosure may be more harmful than helpful in coping with stressful events.

Costanza and his coauthors (1988) mentioned several possible reasons why their experiment did not show beneficial effects of emotional disclosure to friends. First is the possibility that such disclosure is only beneficial when people talk to friends after experiencing a stressful event, not beforehand. That is, self-disclosure may reduce the aftereffects of a stressful event rather than helping people who are about to experience the event. Another possibility is that emotional self-disclosure to friends may be beneficial only when the friends are not going through, and will not go through, the same stressful event. Only when two friends "are in the same boat" and (to continue the metaphor) are *both* about to sink would emotional disclosure to friends be harmful.

Other alternative explanations for the results exist. College students in the three groups were assigned a topic for their conversations before doing the task. Such forced disclosure may be more anxiety provoking and have more negative effects than would spontaneous self-disclosure in natural settings. Perhaps people choose circumstances for self-disclosure that make positive effects more likely.

Second, and more central to the themes of this chapter, is that Costanza et al. may have identified the typical effects of actual disclosures. Their findings may seem contradictory to those of previous research because most previous researchers used a different method, which was to assess people's willingness to disclose intimate information to a friend rather than their actual disclosures. A feeling that a friend is trustworthy, and therefore that the friend can be trusted with intimate information, may have consistently positive effects on adjustment. But participating in an intimate conversation may have more variable effects. To evaluate this possibility, more research will be needed.

Conclusions and research directions

One theme that runs through this chapter is that researchers have often treated children's and adolescents' reports about the intimacy of their friendships as comparable to direct observations of intimate disclosures between friends. Researchers label measures based on verbal reports as measures of self-disclosure (e.g., Buhrmester et al., 1988; Papini et al., 1990). Reviewers take studies of children's and adolescents' reports as evidence about their actual conversations with friends (e.g., Savin-Williams & Berndt, 1990).

We believe that these practices are unwise. Although data are limited, both the developmental changes and the correlates of the reported intimacy of friendship seem to differ from those of observed self-disclosure. One task for future research is to examine the relations between reported intimacy and observed self-disclosure carefully and systematically. This examination must go beyond a simple assessment of the correlation between the two measures in one sample. Researchers must examine the variations in both measures with age and sex and compare the correlations of the two measures with those of other measures. The goal of this research would be to understand the links of reported intimacy and observed self-disclosure to important constructs and to each other.

Research of this kind will not be easy to do. Intimate self-disclosure is difficult to assess in natural settings and difficult to elicit in laboratory settings. Highly intimate self-disclosure is rare in laboratory settings, even when the conditions of observations are as natural as possible (Gottman & Mettetal, 1986). Less intimate self-disclosure may not be distinctive of friendship. It may also occur when children or adolescents are getting acquainted with each other. Consequently, researchers will need to plan their assessments carefully. Previous studies show that obtaining interpretable data is more difficult than placing friends in a room, asking them to talk to each other, and videotaping the conversation.

Despite its difficulty, more research on actual self-discloure is greatly needed. Many psychologists have interpreted the writings of theorists like Sullivan (1953) as extolling the benefits of intimate conversations with friends. If these conversations sometimes have negative effects, as seems to be true with adults (Costanza et al., 1988), then psychologists should be more cautious in advising children or adolescents to "talk it over with your friends." Research is needed to identify when these conversations are beneficial, when they are harmful, and when they have little effect.

Finally, we are not suggesting that researchers should abandon further studies of children's and adolescents' reports on the intimacy of their friendship. These reports have yielded important findings regarding the age changes in friendships and the differences between boys' and girls' friendships. The reports also show how children's and adolescents' perceptions of their friendships are related to their psychological adjustment. Future research could establish more definitely how these reports are influenced by preexisting personality traits and how they influence the development of the children or adolescents who are friends. This research would be a valuable complement to new observations of actual self-disclosure. Continued use of both methods is critical for a complete understanding of friendships in childhood and adolescence.

References

Berndt, T. J. (1981). Relations between social cognition, nonsocial cognition, and social behavior: The case of friendship. In J. H. Flavell and L. D. Ross (Eds.), *Social cognitive development: Frontiers and possible futures* (pp. 176–99). Cambridge University Press.

Berndt, T. J., Hawkins, J. A., & Hoyle, S. G. (1986). Changes in friendship during a school year: Effects on children's and adolescents' impressions of friendship and sharing with friends. *Child Development, 57,* 1284–97.

Berndt, T. J., & Perry, T. B. (1986). Children's perceptions of friendships as supportive relationships. *Developmental Psychology, 22,* 640–8.

Berndt, T. J., Perry, T. B., & Miller, K. E. (1988). Friends' and classmates' interactions on academic tasks. *Journal of Educational Psychology, 80,* 506–13.

Berscheid, E., Snyder, M., & Omoto, A. M. (1989). The Relationship Closeness Inventory: Assessing the closeness of interpersonal relationships. *Journal of Personality and Social Psychology, 57,* 792–807.

Bigelow, B. J. (1977). Children's friendship expectations: A cognitive-developmental study. *Child Development, 48,* 246–53.

Buhrmester, D. (1990). Intimacy of friendship, interpersonal competence, and adjustment during preadolescence and adolescence. *Child Development, 61,* 1101–11.

Buhrmester, D., Furman, W., Wittenberg, M. T., & Reis, H. T. (1988). Five domains of interpersonal competence in peer relationships. *Journal of Personality and Social Psychology, 55,* 991–1008.

Camarena, P. M., Sarigiani, P. A., & Petersen, A. C. (1990). Gender-specific pathways to intimacy in early adolescence. *Journal of Youth and Adolescence, 19,* 19–32.

Clark, M. S., & Reis, H. T. (1988). Interpersonal processes in close relationships. *Annual Review of Psychology, 39,* 609–72.

Costanza, R. S., Derlega, V. J., & Winstead, B. A. (1988). Positive and negative forms of social support: Effects of conversational topics on coping with stress among same-sex friends. *Journal of Experimental Social Psychology, 24,* 182–93.

Douvan, E., & Adelson, J. (1966). *The adolescent experience.* New York: Wiley.

Eckert, P. (1990). Cooperative competition in adolescent "girl talk." Special issue: Gender and conversational interaction. *Discourse Processes, 13,* 91–122.

Furman, W., & Bierman, K. L. (1984). Children's conceptions of friendship: A multidimensional study of developmental changes. *Developmental Psychology, 20,* 925–31.

Furman, W., & Buhrmester, D. (1985). Children's perceptions of the personal relationships in their social networks. *Developmental Psychology, 21,* 1016–24.

Gottman, J. M. (1983). How children become friends. *Monographs of the Society for Research in Child Development, 48*(3, Serial No. 201).

Gottman, J. M., & Mettetal, G. (1986). Speculations about social and affective development: Friendship and acquaintanceship through adolescence. In J. M. Gottman & J. G. Parker (Eds.), *Conversations of friends* (pp. 192–237). Cambridge University Press.

Hornstein, G. A., & Truesdell, S. E. (1988). Development of intimate conversation in close relationships. *Journal of Social and Clinical Psychology, 7,* 49–64.

Jones, G. P., & Dembo, M. H. (1989). Age and sex role differences in intimate friendships during childhood and adolescence. *Merrill-Palmer Quarterly, 35,* 445–62.

Mannarino, A. P. (1980). The development of children's friendships. In H. C. Foot, A. J. Chapman, & J. R. Smith (Eds.), *Friendship and social relations in children* (pp. 45–63). New York: Wiley.

Mazur, E. (1989). Predicting gender differences in same-sex friendships from affiliation motive and value. *Psychology of Women Quarterly, 13,* 277–91.

McGuire, K. D., & Weisz, J. R. (1982). Social cognition and behavior correlates of preadolescent chumships. *Child Development, 53,* 1478–84.

Nelson, J., & Aboud, F. E. (1985). The resolution of social conflict between friends. *Child Development, 56,* 1009–17.

Newcomb, A. F., & Brady, J. E. (1982). Mutuality in boys' friendship relations. *Child Development, 53,* 392–5.

Papini, D. R., Farmer, F. F., Clark, S. M., Micka, J. C., & Barnett, J. K. (1990). Early adolescent age and gender differences in patterns of emotional self-disclosure to parents and friends. *Adolescence, 25,* 959–76.

Reisman, J. M. (1990). Intimacy in same-sex friendships. *Sex Roles, 23,* 65–82.

Rotenberg, K. J., & Sliz, D. (1988). Children's restrictive disclosure to friends. *Merrill-Palmer Quarterly, 34,* 203–15.

Sarason, I. G., & Sarason, B. R. (Eds.). (1985). *Social support: Theory, research and applications.* Dordrecht: Martinus Nijhoff.

Savin-Williams, R. C., & Berndt, T. J. (1990). Friendships and peer relations during adolescence. In S. S. Feldman & G. Elliott (Eds.), *At the threshold: The developing adolescent* (pp. 277–307). Cambridge, MA: Harvard University Press.

Selman, R. L. (1981). The child as a friendship philosopher: A case study in the growth of interpersonal understanding. In S. R. Asher & J. M. Gottman (Eds.), *The development of children's friendships* (pp. 242–72). Cambridge University Press.

Sharabany, R., Gershoni, R., & Hofman, J. E. (1981). Girlfriend, boyfriend: Age and sex differences in intimate friendship. *Developmental Psychology, 17,* 800–808.

Snell, W. E., Miller, R. S., Belk, S. S., Garcia-Falconi, R., & Hernandez-Sanchez, J. E. (1989). Men's and women's emotional disclosures: The impact of disclosure recipient, culture, and the masculine role. *Sex Roles, 21,* 467–86.

Sullivan, H. S. (1953). *The interpersonal theory of psychiatry.* New York: Norton.

Tanner, J. M. (1978). *Foetus into man.* Cambridge, MA: Harvard University Press.

Townsend, A. R., McCracken, H. E., & Wilton, K. M. (1988). Popularity and intimacy as determinants of psychological well-being in adolescent friendships. *Journal of Early Adolescence, 8,* 421–36.

Wright, P. H. (1982). Men's friendships, women's friendships, and the alleged inferiority of the latter. *Sex Roles, 8,* 1–20.

Youniss, J., & Smollar, J. (1985). *Adolescent relations with mothers, fathers, and friends.* Chicago: University of Chicago Press.

4 Self-disclosure and the sibling relationship: What did Romulus tell Remus?

Nina Howe, Jasmin Aquan-Assee, and
William M. Bukowski

Introduction

For many individuals, relationships with siblings form both the "figure" and the "ground" of their lives. Relationships with siblings are the ground in the sense that these relationships often extend across the life span. Almost by definition, relations with siblings are a part of our lives, even though sometimes they may be more in the background than the foreground. However, at specific times, these relationships may acquire a special significance – siblings can become central to our experience as important figures of attachment, as teachers, as companions, or, as we will show in this chapter, as individuals with whom persons engage in intimate self-disclosure. By intimate self-disclosure we mean the reciprocal sharing of confidential, privileged information with one's sibling that is frequently of an affective nature. On the basis of theory derived from empirical research on processes within the sibling relationship and using data from our own studies of children's sibling relationships, we show how the relationship can be an ideal context for self-disclosure. Finally, we discuss how features of the relationship and the broader context are related to the extent of self-disclosure that children experience with their siblings.

Beyond psychological theory and research, the world of literature provides evidence that children, adolescents, and adults frequently engage in self-disclosure with siblings. In fiction, siblings are portrayed as talking in an intimate, confidential, and reciprocal way with each other and sharing private, privileged information, often of an affective nature. For example,

Work on this chapter was made possible by an Internal Research Award from Concordia University to the first author, a grant from Québec's Fond pour la Formation des Chercheurs et l'Aide à Recherche to the second author, and a Faculty Scholar's Award from the W. T. Grant Foundation to the third author. We would like to thank Thalia Feldman, Irving Howe, and Nicholas Howe for their literary advice.

78

in J. D. Salinger's (1951) *Catcher in the Rye,* Holden Caulfield finds himself in search of a confidant during a lonely weekend in New York City after having been kicked out of prep school. After unsuccessful attempts to speak with friends, old girlfriends, and former teachers, he goes to the family apartment to talk to his sister Phoebe. Likewise, in Jane Austen's *Pride and Prejudice,* two sisters, Jane and Elizabeth Bennet, share secrets and act as one another's private confidantes: "The tumult of Elizabeth's mind was allayed by this conversation. She had got rid of two of the secrets which had weighed her for a fortnight, and was certain of a willing listener in Jane, whenever she might wish to talk again of either" (Austen, 1907, p. 194). The sense that siblings communicate in a reciprocal manner is captured by D. H. Lawrence (1971) in *Women in Love,* a story of two adult sisters, Gudrun and Ursula: "She was happy to find Ursula alone. It was a lovely, intimate secluded atmosphere. They talked endlessly and delightedly" (1971, p. 369).

In the classic children's story *The Secret Garden* (Burnett, 1962), two cousins, Mary and Colin, both only children, develop a close relationship, akin to that of siblings. They fight, talk, laugh, and come to share a secret, that of the secret garden long locked away. Mary discovers the key to the garden first and struggles with the question of whether she can trust Colin with this privileged information: "She wanted to discover whether he was the kind of boy you could tell a secret to. . . . he was evidently so pleased with the idea of a garden no one knew anything about that she thought perhaps he could be trusted" (1987, p. 159). Further evidence that siblings know and understand each other's feelings even though circumstances have divided them is seen in Maggie's statement to her brother Tom, in George Eliot's (1985) *The Mill on the Floss:* " 'I can't make you think better of me, Tom, by anything I can say. But I'm not so shut out from all your feelings as you believe me to be. I can see as well as you do' " (1985, p. 450).

Nonfiction also provides examples in which the sibling relationship is a context for self-disclosure. For example, following the demanding and turmoil-filled 1978 baseball season, Reggie Jackson of the champion New York Yankees indicated that he would give a car awarded to him as the World's Series Most Valuable Player to his sister – in gratitude for all the times during the season he called her in search of consolation. Also, for many persons of our generation, the picture of John F. Kennedy seeking advice from his brother Robert in the Oval Office forms an indelible feature of our memories. A further example can be found in the letters between Vincent van Gogh and his brother Theo; their rich correspondence contained frequent references to each other's private thoughts and feelings.

Several premises about the nature of the sibling relationship provide the points of departure for our conceptualization of this particular relationship as an ideal context for self-disclosure. First, the sibling relationship has been identified as having many of the properties of complementary relationships (i.e., hierarchical relationships between children and parents) and reciprocal or equal relationships (i.e., friendships between peers). Reciprocal features may promote trust and mutual understanding, whereas the complementary features may facilitate opportunities for guidance and direction.

A second point of departure is that many sibling pairs possess a shared developmental history. Due to their long period of association, siblings are likely to have had experiences in which they have developed shared meanings. They have the same parents, live in the same home, have the same siblings, relatives, neighbors, perhaps even the same teachers, and they know each other's friends and the events of each other's lives. Indeed, simply because siblings have so much contact with each other and so many opportunities to learn about one other, they are the ones most likely to know each other best. Implicit in this view of how siblings come to develop shared meanings is that it is a process that depends on reciprocity.

Third, particular qualities identified as central to the sibling relationship are likely to be prerequisites for self-disclosure. As we will show, Furman and Buhrmester (1985a) argue that four features central to the sibling relationship are (a) warmth and closeness, (b) conflict, (c) rivalry, and (d) status and power. It is conceivable that at least the first of these features may influence the development of self-disclosure between siblings. As brothers and sisters develop strong emotional ties to one another, they will feel increasingly comfortable telling each other about the thoughts and feelings they would not share with others.

Our discussion of self-disclosure within the sibling relationship begins with the definition of self-disclosure and how the relationship may be an important context within which to nurture disclosure processes. We then present data from three studies indicating (a) that siblings report the relationship is a context for self-disclosure, (b) how aspects of the sibling dyad and features of the family environment are related to self-disclosure between siblings, and (c) how sibling reports of self-disclosure are associated with other aspects of the sibling relationship in a longitudinal sample.

What is self-disclosure?

In the work of Sydney Jourard (1958), one can find a comprehensive and enduring discussion of the phenomenon of self-disclosure. Jourard conceptualized self-disclosure as being no less than the foundation for a healthy personality. He defined self-disclosure as "the act of making yourself manifest, showing yourself so others can perceive you" (Jourard, 1971, p. 19). Central to his conceptualization is the argument that self-disclosure is fundamentally a reciprocal and mutual process. In particular, he believed that one would disclose to individuals who disclosed in return and at a similar level of intimacy. Implicit in this view is the notion that self-disclosure entails a strong sense of privacy on the part of the target, that is, treating the self-disclosed information as both intimate and private and, therefore, not for the gossip mill. This idea of intimacy has also been addressed by Bank and Kahn (1982), who note that we rarely disclose our "innermost self" to others and only to those whom we trust. For Jourard, one of the outcomes of disclosure is that persons learn the extent to which they are similar or different from a specific other in terms of "thoughts, feelings, hopes, reactions to the past, etc." (Jourard, 1971, p. 3). Others have added to the notion that self-disclosure is a form of intentional, intimate, and private verbal communication (Allen, 1974; Chelune, 1979), where presumably the target can be trusted with this special affective information. One norm that has been identified as an important factor facilitating self-disclosure is reciprocity (Cohn & Strassberg, 1983), that is, disclosing to those who disclose to us.

Jourard (1971) was interested in adult relationships and did not specifically address the roots of how one learns to self-disclose. He argued that the source of psychological difficulties, defined as the inability to self-disclose, often emanated from the dynamics of family and married life. Presumably, then, it is within the context of the immediate family that one learns or does not learn to self-disclose. Norrell (1984) proposed that because the family is the primary socializing agent, children first learn to disclose in this context. There is some support, particularly in the adolescent literature (see Norrell, 1984, for a review; also Berg-Cross, Kidd, & Carr, 1990), to suggest that some family dynamics may be conducive to the development of disclosure processes. For example, Papini, Farmer, Clark, Micka, and Barnett (1990) report that self-disclosure to parents was associated with open family communication, family cohesion, and satisfaction with family relationships. One would expect, then, that aspects of the family environment would also be associated with the level of self-disclosure between siblings.

The process of self-disclosure has received less attention from researchers interested in younger children, although there is some work in the areas of disclosure to peers (e.g., Rotenberg & Sliz, 1988) and more general sibling–parental communication (e.g., Bergout Austin, Summers, & Leffler, 1987). In a series of studies, Rotenberg and colleagues have investigated the development of the norm of reciprocity of self-disclosure in peer relationships and associations with loneliness in school-aged children and early adolescents (Rotenberg & Mann, 1986; Rotenberg & Chase, 1992; Rotenberg & Whitney, 1992). Our search of the literature indicated no studies specifically investigating disclosure between young siblings; however, there are studies on mutual confiding or closeness between adult siblings (e.g., Ross & Milgram, 1982; Argyle, Trimboli, & Forgas, 1988; Connidis, 1989) and between adolescent siblings (e.g., Balk, 1983; Bell, Avery, Jenkins, Feld, & Schoenrock, 1985). Although this suggests a gap in the literature, related research on young children's understanding and use of internal-state language (i.e., discussion of feelings and thoughts) may be pertinent, and we shall return to a review of this work shortly.

Recently Derlega and Margulis (1983) identified two types of self-disclosure: (a) descriptive intimacy, or disclosing of otherwise unavailable factual information about the self, and (b) evaluative intimacy, or disclosing personal feelings or judgments. These authors were specifically interested in adult relationships, and this distinction may have a somewhat limited application to disclosures between younger siblings. A number of factors that may or may not facilitate self-disclosures between persons developing friendships or romantic relationships may not be suitable for sibling relationships. Due to the physical proximity of sibling relations (living in the same family), the majority of sibling intimacies presumably would be evaluative. That is, given their common environment, the likelihood of not knowing factual information would probably be lower than in other types of relationships in which there may be a long period of time before the participants meet and interact. Not all siblings engage in reciprocal exchanges of intimate information, and factors underlying individual differences in the propensity to engage in self-disclosure need to be examined. However, now we discuss how the sibling relationship may be a context for self-disclosure.

The sibling relationship as a context for self-disclosure

Relationships consist of both reciprocal interactions, such as returned and similar exchanges, and complementary interactions, such as exchanges where each person's behavior differs from but complements the other's behavior in a hierarchical manner. Hinde (1979) has pointed out that whereas reciprocal interactions are characteristic of peer interactions, complementary interactions are characteristic of parent–child interaction. The sibling relationship is unique in that both types of interactions are prominent (Dunn, 1983); reciprocal interactions are seen in play, positive and negative interactions, whereas complementary interactions are characteristic of caregiving, teaching, and attachment interactions. Dunn (1983) argues that such reciprocity features as "the familiarity and intimacy of the children, the extent to which they recognize and share each other's interests, and the emotional intensity of their relationship" (1983, p. 788) are key in the development of children's social understanding. Nevertheless, the complementary nature of the relationship suggests that siblings, particularly younger ones, may turn to the other for help, instrumental and emotional support or solace, and guidance. Due to the nature of both reciprocal and complementary interactions, siblings are well placed to engage in self-disclosure with one another.

Most of the literature on sibling relations during early childhood emphasizes this as a salient time for sibling influence on development (Lamb & Sutton-Smith, 1982). Siblings have been identified as important members of the child's social network (Hartup, 1979; Furman & Buhrmester, 1985b), and their impact on personality and social development extends into peer and later adult relationships (Lamb & Sutton-Smith, 1982; Hartup, 1989).

The general conclusion from a number of studies examining the child's reaction to the birth of a sibling (e.g., Dunn & Kendrick, 1982a; Gottlieb & Mendelson, 1990; for a review, see Vandell, 1987) is that the stage is set for sibling influence by the child's emotional reaction to the new baby. Within the first 4 years, siblings clearly influenced each other's development (Dunn, 1985). Other studies on early relations have examined associations between family structure (e.g., birth order, sex, and spacing of siblings) and sibling interaction (Berndt & Bulleit, 1985; Abramovitch, Corter, Pepler, & Stanhope, 1986; Dunn & Munn, 1986).

In comparison, sibling relations in middle childhood and early adolescence have been relatively neglected by researchers. Nevertheless, middle childhood is a period of active social and emotional development (Sullivan, 1953; Bryant, 1982); frequently, sibling interactions are intense and children often struggle to manage sibling relations. Moreover, children are attuned to their social status within a variety of contexts (e.g., family, school, home, neighborhood) and siblings play important roles in this process (Bryant, 1982). Although siblings would appear to be the logical recipients of disclosures about critical social and familial experiences, a review of the literature indicates no studies addressing this question.

Interestingly, few studies have examined the sibling relationship from the perspective of the children in the dyad; specifically, relatively little is known about the qualities that children report as characterizing their sibling relationships. Furman and Buhrmester (1985a,b) emphasized that to examine the continuities among different relations in the child's social network, it is important to consider the child's perceptions of those relations. Such information will help us to understand more clearly which conditions facilitate particular experiences and perceptions and thus provide direction for identifying which might foster sibling self-disclosure.

In fact, the different qualities that characterize individual sibling relationships may be an important factor predisposing children to disclose to one another. Several investigators have examined how quality relates to the stuctural features of the sibling relationship. For example, Bowerman and Dobash (1974) examined the level of affect and closeness in adolescent sibling relationships. Females reported high affect toward siblings more frequently than did males, while same-sex siblings indicated a higher level of affect than did opposite-sex pairs. On average, affect was higher toward older than younger siblings. This early study on adolescents' perceptions of their sibling relationships lacked a broad perspective on sibling relationship qualities.

In contrast, Furman and Buhrmester (1985a) used a measure that was designed to assess individual differences in four important sibling dimensions, that is, warmth/closeness, rivalry, relative status and power, and conflict. Birth order and age spacing were differentially associated with the four dimensions; specifically, narrowly spaced dyads reported greater warmth and closeness, whereas eldest children in widely spaced dyads reported engaging in the most caretaking and nurturing behaviors. Children indicated less admiration of their siblings when age spacing was narrow rather than wide. Conflict and agonism occurred more often in narrowly spaced dyads (Minnett, Vandell, & Santrock, 1983; Furman & Buhrmester, 1985a; Summers, 1987). Thus, the child's experiences with siblings is determined partly by his or her standing in the family constellation (see also Buhrmester & Furman, 1990).

The size of the age difference has also been shown to be related to the qualities of the sibling relationship, particularly among school-age children. Stocker and McHale (1988) found that more affection and less hostility by the older sibling were associated with widely spaced dyads, whereas younger children in the widely spaced dyads reported greater sibling rivalry. Recently, Aquan-Assee, Bukowski, Howe, and Gauze (1992) found similar results when examining the relation between the structural properties of the sibling dyad (i.e., age, sex) and the self-reported qualities of the sibling relationship. Relative status and power within the sibling dyad was reported to be highest when the target child was older than the sibling; greater conflict was reported in narrowly spaced dyads and when the target sibling was a boy. Conversely, warmth/closeness was reported to be highest when the target sibling was a girl. In another study, developmental differences in sibling relationship qualities were apparent (Buhrmester & Furman, 1990); relations become more egalitarian and less asymmetrical with age, and adolescents reported less intense relationships than did younger children. Finally, other research demonstrates that being close in age and ability means that siblings inevitably know each other well, have spent a significant portion of their time together playing, teasing, and fighting (Dunn & Munn, 1985, 1987), and certainly have shared the critical affective experiences of family life (e.g., holidays, births, deaths, divorce, family tensions, disputes). For siblings, these affective family matters may be the substance of many sibling disclosures, a point we shall return to shortly.

In summary, the dual features of reciprocity and complementarity characteristic of the relationship suggest possible kinds of interactions that may facilitate self-disclosure in some sibling dyads. Studies that have addressed observed roles or self-reported qualities of sibling relationships have shown that children's relationships with their siblings have a structural and functional dimension. That is, one's sibling experiences and perceptions of the relationship is partly determined by birth order. Presumably, self-disclosure is associated with warmth and closeness in the relationship; these affective dimensions promote an open forum for this type of discussion. As discussed, self-disclosure develops in the family, and although researchers have recently begun to examine family influences on the sibling relationship and the processes by which these influences have their effect, family variables associated with sibling self-disclosures have generally not been investigated. Nevertheless, research on family discourse regarding internal states may provide some direction for our consideration of sibling self-disclosure.

Internal state discourse

The literature investigating the development of young children's ability to employ internal state language in conversation (Bretherton, Fritz, Zahn-Waxler, & Ridgeway, 1986) may be important to our discussion. Internal state language is defined as references to feelings, thoughts, and abilities that occur in ongoing conversations. Although this research has not been framed within the notion of self-disclosure, certainly this process may be occurring during some conversations where children direct references to their siblings about their own or other's feelings, needs, thoughts, and abilities. During such conversations, siblings may be disclosing intimate and sometimes perhaps secret information to one another. Indeed, by definition, the content of self-disclosure is an affective, motivational, and/or cognitive intimate communication (Jourard, 1971; Derlega & Margulis, 1983), which mirrors the content of much internal-state discourse. Nevertheless, not all internal state discourse is meant to reveal private, intimate information. Thus, we do not mean to suggest that all internal state references will necessarily be self-disclosures, although some may be.

Research on internal state discourse has generally examined triadic (mother and two children) family discussions regarding feelings, needs, and abilities (e.g., Dunn, Bretherton, & Munn, 1987); however, preschoolers also direct internal state discourse to their younger siblings (Dunn & Kendrick, 1982a; Howe, 1991). We know that during the second year, toddlers respond to others' feelings and are interested in other's feeling states (Bretherton & Beeghly, 1982). Moreover, four studies have demonstrated individual differences in preschoolers' use of internal state language, as well as examining how such discourse is related to aspects of their sibling relationships.

First, Dunn and Kendrick (1982b) found a positive association between affective communication and positive behavior directed by preschoolers to their 14-month-old siblings. Second, Brown and Dunn (1989) reported a longitudinal correlation between frequent triadic discussions of feelings when the younger sibling was age 3 and the perspective-taking ability of this child at age 6. Third, positive associations were demonstrated between preschoolers' references about the younger sibling's internal states, preschoolers' perspective taking, and friendly sibling interactions (Howe & Ross, 1990). Finally, Howe (1991) reported that preschoolers' references to their younger siblings were more likely to be about the toddlers' internal states than their own and were more likely to be made in mothers' absence than presence. Furthermore, better perspective takers were more likely to engage in internal state discourse, and preschoolers engaging in affective behavior were more likely to direct internal state language to their siblings. In conclusion, these studies suggest that a friendly, warm sibling relationship includes communication regarding internal states, some of which may be considered examples of self-disclosure.

Other evidence suggesting that young children do indeed engage in disclosure was provided by Dunn (1988a) in her recent book on how children come to understand their social worlds. She considers narratives (e.g., telling stories, relating episodes) as a forum for talking about others and reported that an increase in telling narratives was paralleled by an increase in comments about others' mental and feeling states and the causes of their behavior. Dunn argues that one of the outcomes of capturing the attention of another person and sharing an experience is that the child develops a sense of intimacy with others in being able to communicate what particularly interests him or her. Although Dunn did not specifically focus on sibling-directed communication, examples (1988a, p. 146) provided by the

2- to 3-year-olds include some easily defined as self-disclosures. For example, Dunn described one little boy who told the observer that he tramped all over the house with his boots on, a clearly forbidden act in which he took great delight.

Dunn's model of the development of children's social understanding rests on the cornerstone of the family; that is, it is within the context of the child's affective family relationships that knowledge and understanding regarding social and moral matters develops. Implicit in this process is learning how, when, and to whom to disclose intimate, private, and privileged information and when to expect reciprocal kinds of disclosures. As noted earlier, the sibling relationship as an important part of the family experience would appear to be an ideal context to foster this process. The closeness and intimacy that develops between many siblings, along with their vested self-interest in the relationship, may further this process. In addition, the important reciprocal features of the relationship (e.g., play, positive interactions) might facilitate reciprocal self-disclosures by siblings. Certainly, one might expect that siblings who perceive their relationships as close and positive would also engage in more frequent self-disclosures than siblings who did not report friendly relationships. Moreover, in some families a style of discourse that focuses on internal states may be important in the socialization of self-disclosure. To address some of these questions, we now turn to some of our own empirical data.

Empirical studies of siblings and self-disclosure

In this final section, we present data from three studies that focus on different questions regarding self-disclosure and the sibling relationship. First, we addressed a very simple question, namely, whether children report that self-disclosure is a component of their sibling relationships. Second, we looked at the association between the degree of self-disclosure in children's sibling relationships and (a) the structural aspects of the sibling dyad and (b) the family environment. Third, we examined the parameters that underlie young children's use of internal state language in their sibling relationships in a longitudinal sample.

Do siblings engage in self-disclosure?

As part of their participation in a larger study (Aquan-Assee, 1992), 100 children in Grades 4, 5, and 6 were interviewed regarding what they talked about with their siblings. Nearly two-thirds mentioned that they engaged in self-disclosure, that is, sharing private and personal information. In the words of one child, "Well when I need someone to talk to or if I need help with stuff, I don't know, some kind of problem that I have, I just talk to him [brother]." The children often were very specific about what category of information was privileged for which person in their social network. Here are the comments of three children:

Well at home if there's, before my mother or father come home, we just like talk about things, like maybe we wouldn't say to our parents or something, just little things like we didn't steal or anything, just maybe we're too shy to tell our parents. We share together.

Like he has a problem or something he comes and asks what he should do. I go and tell him things, depends if it's personal or not, for like a girl or something I would go to my mum or my sister but if it's something like a big problem or I got in trouble or something I'd go to my brother.

Well sometimes we're both mad at our parents and we try to talk about that, and we talk about everything in school, and stuff like that, we talk about, like if I go to my friend's house and he stays home he asks me what it was like going there and I say I say it was fun and we talk about that kind of stuff. (Aquan-Assee, 1992)

That such a large proportion of these subjects would mention self-disclosure without being specifically prompted to do so is testimony to the place of self-disclosure in the sibling relationship. In the preceding four examples, the variety of themes that may appear in children's disclosure to each other are apparent – their relationship with parents and their friends, whether they are in "trouble" with someone else, and the need for advice about personal matters. Among these comments are themes reflecting reciprocity ("We share together") and complementarity ("[If] he has a problem he comes and asks me what he should do"). One conclusion that can be derived from these comments is that these children see the sibling dyad as a context for self-disclosure.

Self-disclosure, the structure of the sibling dyad, and the family environment

The purpose of our second study was to identify the factors that were related to variations in the extent to which siblings engaged in self-disclosure. Although the previous data indicated that self-disclosure is a characteristic of most children's relations with a sibling, there is much variability in the quality of the sibling relationship (Furman & Buhrmester, 1985a; Buhrmester & Furman, 1990). As discussed earlier, variability in the quality of the sibling relationship has been linked to structural aspects of the sibling relationship. Moreover, a systems approach leads us to expect that the quality of the sibling relationship should be related to the characteristics of the family environment in which it is embedded (Daniels, Dunn, Furstenberg, & Plomin, 1985; Daniels, 1986).

In this second study, associations between early adolescents' perceptions of the degree of self-disclosure in their sibling relationships and three sets of features of the sibling dyad were examined: (a) child characteristics (i.e., age and sex), (b) sibling characteristics (i.e., age and sex of the sibling), and (c) characteristics of the dyad per se (i.e., the age difference between the siblings, whether the dyad was a same-sex or a cross-sex pair, and whether the child was older or younger than the target sibling). Moreover, associations between the degree of self-disclosure and the family environment were also examined.

Our examination of the family was guided by the ideas developed by Olson and his colleagues (Olson et al., 1985; Olson, 1989). Olson's ideas regarding the family emphasized two aspects of the family environment: (a) cohesion (i.e., emotional closeness) and (b) adaptability (i.e., the family's flexibility in their relationships in the face of change). Olson and his colleagues have described families that are very high in cohesion as enmeshed and families that are very low in cohesion as disengaged, while families high in adaptability (i.e., families that are overly responsive to the environment) are seen as chaotic and families that are unresponsive to the environment as rigid.

Olson argued that children's functioning should be related to the family environment in a curvilinear manner, with the most adequate levels of functioning being observed at the center of the distribution for each of the family measures. Relative to these balanced families, families that fall outside the center of the distributions (i.e., either enmeshed or chaotic families) would be likely to show the lowest levels of adjustment. That is, although adaptability and cohesion would be expected to promote adjustment, being too high on either of these dimensions is likely to inhibit healthy adjustment. Consequently, associations between the family environment and sibling self-disclosure were examined according to both linear and curvilinear associations.

The subjects were 138 fourth- through sixth-grade boys and girls and their parents in two schools in Quebec; all the children spoke English fluently. Each child completed Furman and Buhrmester's (1985a) *Sibling Relationship Inventory* (SRI) in reference to their relationship with the sibling who was *most important* to them and also indicated the sibling's age and sex. This measure includes questions concerning the degree of self-disclosure to the sibling (i.e., sharing information, secrets). Parents completed Olson's FACES, a questionnaire that provides indices of the family environment according to the dimensions of adaptability and cohesion.

Two items on the SRI were used to create an index of self-disclosure in the sibling relationship: (a) How much do you and your sibling share secrets and private feelings, and (b) how much do you and your sibling tell each other things you wouldn't tell others? The internal consistency (i.e., reliability) of this score was very high (alpha = .82). This score was used as the dependent variable in a set of multiple regression equations in which four sets of variables were used as the independent variables or predictors. The variables entered into the equation were (a) the subject's age and sex, (b) the sibling's age and sex, (c) whether the siblings were of the same or different gender, the absolute age difference between them, and whether the subject was the older or younger sibling, and (d) the family environment scores (i.e., adaptability and cohesion), which were entered as linear and curvilinear effects.

The results of the first equation, in which the subject's age and sex were the predictor variables, were nonsignificant ($F(1, 125) < 1.0, p > .5$), indicating that self-disclosure was unrelated to the child's age and sex. However, the very small age span in our sample may not have been large enough to provide a very powerful test of whether self-disclosure varied with age. In the second equation, the sibling's age and sex were the predictor variables and the findings were again nonsignificant ($F(2, 125) = 1.89$, $p < .16$), although a marginally significant univariate effect was observed for the sex-of-sibling variable ($F(1, 125) = 3.17, p < .07$). This finding indicated that the self-disclosure score was highest when the sibling was a girl rather than a boy.

The third equation focused on whether self-disclosure was related to (a) whether the siblings were of the same or different gender, (b) the absolute age difference between them, and (c) whether the subject was the older or younger sibling. Again, nonsignificant findings were observed, but as in the second equation, a significant univariate effect was found ($F(1, 124) = 5.02, p < .05$). This significant effect was observed with the variable indicating whether the sibling pair was a same-sex or a cross-sex dyad. Higher self-disclosure scores were observed for same-sex pairs.

In the fourth equation, the family measures were used as predictors. Although no effects were found for the cohesion variable, significant linear ($F(1, 126) = 3.81, p < .05$) and curvilinear ($F(1, 126) = 3.59, p < .06$) effects were found with the adaptation variable. These analyses indicated that self-disclosure increases as adaptability increased, except at the highest levels of adaptability, where there was a decrease in self-disclosure. That is, self-disclosure appeared to increase as families become less rigid, but among families who were overly responsive to external demands, self-disclosure between siblings decreased.

Taken together, our findings show that children were more likely to engage in self-disclosure with their sibling when (a) the sibling was a girl, (b) when they were of the same sex as the sibling, and (c) when their family environment was adaptive to external circumstances, but not overly so. Also, children's perceptions of whether they engaged in self-disclosure with their siblings was observed to be unrelated to their own sex, the age difference between siblings, whether the child was the older or younger sibling, and the amount of cohesion and warmth among family members.

Self-disclosure and the quality of the sibling relationship

The purpose of our third set of data was to examine sibling self-disclosure in a longitudinal study of early sibling relations. As the first step in a longitudinal study, Howe and Ross (1990) examined the associations between the quality of the sibling relationship, maternal socialization techniques, and perspective taking in a sample of 32 3- to 4-year-olds and 14-month-olds. One measure of sibling relationship quality included references that the firstborn directed to the secondborn about internal states (i.e., feelings, needs, and abilities); positive associations were reported between this measure, friendly sibling interactions, and perspective taking (see Howe & Ross, 1990; Howe, 1991, for a more detailed discussion). Families were revisited 2 (Howe, 1992) and then 4 years later when firstborns were a mean age of 8.2 and 5.5 years old. In this chapter, data from time 1 and time 3 will be discussed. Specifically, we were interested in examining (a) whether at time 3 siblings perceived their relationship in a similar manner, including self-disclosure, (b) how siblings viewed different aspects of their relationship, including self-disclosure and closeness at time 3, and (c) if dyads in which internal-state discourse was evident at time 1 were more likely to report engaging in intimate, reciprocal, and close interactions at time 3. Self-disclosure was conceptualized as communicating intimate information and secrets in a reciprocal and affectively close manner with the sibling.

At time 3, 24 of the original 32 sibling dyads were interviewed using a shortened version of the SRI; the 20 items comprising 5 subscales (closeness, positive feelings, conflict, support, companionship) were selected based on a factor analysis of the scale (Mendelson, Aboud, & Lanthier, 1991). Children were asked to rate each question on a 3-point scale ranging from *very like* to *not like* their sibling relationships. In the present sample, Cronbach alphas for the subscales were as follows: older sibling's closeness = .68, younger sibling's closeness = .63, older sibling's positive feelings = .83, younger sibling's positive feelings = .82, older sibling's conflict = .82, younger sibling's conflict = .68, older sibling's support = .76, and younger sibling's support $= .60$. The companionship subscale was not employed because of unacceptable alphas (older sibling's companionship $= .20$, younger sibling's companionship $= .28$). Items selected for the closeness subscale included: (a) How much do you tell your sibling about things that are important to you? (b) How much do you make your sibling feel better when his or her feelings are hurt? (c) How much would you try to help your sibling if he or she needed help? (d) How much do you cheer up your sibling when he or she feels sad? An item concerning telling secrets to siblings was dropped from the closeness subscale to improve the level of alpha.

First, we examined the degree to which children perceived their sibling relationships in a similar manner. Partial correlations (controlling for the age of the older sibling) indicated that first- and secondborn siblings generally did not perceive the relationship in the same way as reflected by the lack of association between sibling ratings on the five subscales ($r = -.21$ to .28, ns). Moreover, the ratings of the two siblings on the 20 individual items ($r = -.22$ to .29, ns) were unrelated except for the following: (a) how much siblings like to do things with one another ($r = .35, p < .05$), (b) how much siblings tell one another things that are important to them ($r = .31$, $p < .07$), (c) how much siblings make the other feel better when his or her feelings are hurt ($r = -.36, p < .05$), and (d) how much the sibling is special ($r = -.33, p < .06$). These associations suggest that in terms of two aspects of intimacy (doing things together, communicating important things), siblings did concur, but they apparently disagreed on how much they helped one another and whether the sibling was special. Interestingly, the 2 items on which siblings did agree are behaviors in which reciprocity is a critical element.

The second question addressed was how siblings viewed different aspects of their relationships, which was assessed by examining partial correlations (controlling for age of the firstborn) between the four subscales of the SRI. For the older siblings, feelings of closeness were positively associated with their own positive feelings ($r = .55, p < .001$) and support ($r = .43$, $p < .05$) and negatively with their own conflict ($r = -.33, p < .06$). Thus, firstborns who reported feeling close to their siblings also felt positive, felt supported, or looked after their siblings and did not perceive the relationship to be conflictual. For the younger siblings, closeness was positively associated with their own positive feelings ($r = .58, p < .001$) and older sibling's support ($r = .43, p < .05$), and negatively with their own conflict ($r = -.35, p < .05$). Similarly, secondborns who perceived their relationships to be close also reported positive feelings about their siblings, less conflict, and being looked after by their firstborn siblings.

The third question investigated longitudinal associations between internal state discourse at time 1 and sibling's perception of their relationships at time 3. Measures of references about internal states that firstborn children directed to their secondborn siblings were collected during naturalistic home observations (Howe & Ross, 1990). Transcriptions of the conversations were coded for preschoolers' references about internal states to toddlers (see Howe, 1991). First, partial correlations (controlling for the age of the firstborn children) were conducted between the measure of internal state references at time 1 and the SRI subscales measured at time 3. Significant positive correlations were apparent between internal-state references and the younger siblings' ratings of the closeness of the relationships $(r = .45, p < .05)$ and the older siblings' ratings of conflict $(r = .34, p < .06)$. Second, cross-time correlations between internal state references and the individual items on the SRI indicated some interesting significant associations; internal state references were positively associated with reports by both children that they would tell their siblings about things important to them $(r = .36$ and $.32$ for older and younger sibling's respectively). For the younger siblings, two other associations were evident with items on the closeness subscale: making sib feel better when his or her feelings were hurt $(r = .51, p < .05)$ and helping sib if he or she needed it $(r = .37, p < .05)$. The notion of reciprocity is implicit in these three items, suggesting that when firstborns discussed internal states with secondborns, over time these dyads engaged in reciprocal, intimate, close types of exchanges.

Discussion

In this chapter we have considered the role of self-disclosure in the sibling relationship during early and middle childhood. We proposed that because the sibling relationship is characterized by both reciprocal and complementary interactions, it is a likely interpersonal context for self-disclosure. Moreover, the notion that siblings have a shared developmental history also provides a common basis of experience that allows for children to engage in self-disclosure. In our data we showed that a majority of children engaged in self-disclosure with their siblings. Moreover, our findings indicated that self-disclosure in the sibling dyad varied according to characteristics of the siblings, the structure of the dyad, and as a function of the family context. Specifically, children reported that they were more likely to self-disclose to a sister than to a brother and to a same-sex sibling rather than an other-sex sibling. With regard to the family, children who were from families that were flexible in their interactions, rather than rigid or chaotic, were most likely to engage in self-disclosure with their siblings. Finally, school-aged siblings did not appear to perceive their relationship in a similar manner, although both children reported positive associations between closeness to their sibling (one aspect of which was self-disclosure) and positive feelings and support. A negative relationship was seen between closeness to sibling and conflict. Moreover, longitudinal associations were evident between internal state discussions and feelings of closeness four years later. In fact, in families where discussions about internal states were encouraged, four years later children reported sharing important intimate information, suggesting that early discussions of feelings, wants, and abilities may facilitate later reciprocal and intimate self-disclosures between siblings.

The questions we have considered regarding the sibling relationship and self-disclosure refer to very broad concerns. Conceivably, self-disclosure between siblings may vary not only according to the properties of the sibling dyad, but also across contexts; self-disclosure may be more frequent at some times than at others. Indeed, knowing about the role of self-disclosure to siblings at times of transition (i.e., going to a new school), distress (e.g., following divorce), or in unique circumstances (e.g., when one sibling is suffering from an acute or chronic illness) would add much to our understanding of how self-disclosure to siblings is related to children's development and adjustment. Finally, little attention has been devoted to the sibling relationship beyond early adolescence, and in our data we were unable to determine how sibling self-disclosure might vary with age. It is conceivable that as children develop stronger relations with peers, self-disclosure to siblings may change in frequency and/or content.

Clearly, a more systematic investigation of self-disclosure between siblings is needed. Our data have suggested that a variety of issues remain to be addressed. For example, a thorough investigation of the content of self-disclosure is warranted. That is, exactly what kinds of evaluative and descriptive intimacies do siblings share with one another, and is this information similar to or different than that exchanged with other family members or friends? Also, there may be developmental differences in children's willingness and ability to engage in intimate and reciprocal self-disclosures with their siblings. Moreover, our findings indicate that family variables may be critical mediating variables; that is, certain family dynamics such as flexibility may facilitate the development of disclosures between family members. Also, our findings suggest that particular kinds of discourse that encourage the discussion of feelings, wants, and abilities between family members may also foster self-disclosure. Thus, family environments that are open, flexible, and sensitive to the feelings and thoughts of the members may create an atmosphere conducive for the development of self-disclosure by siblings. Based on this argument, it seems reasonable that spouses who engage in intimate and reciprocal kinds of disclosures would foster the development of this ability in their children.

Our findings also suggest that the quality of the sibling relationship may be important in fostering self-disclosure between brothers and sisters. Research suggests that the affective quality of the sibling relationship is apparent from the time the secondborn is an infant (e.g., Dunn, 1983) and that it is associated with other behaviors such as perspective taking and positive interactions (Dunn & Kendrick, 1982a; Howe & Ross, 1990; Howe, 1991). Thus, we would predict that siblings who have established friendly relationships that include a fair amount of internal state discourse would turn to one another to disclose intimate information about themselves. Of course, there may be periods or situations, as discussed earlier, in which siblings may be more or less likely to engage in self-disclosure. Thus, an investigation of sibling self-disclosure must take developmental and contextual factors into account. Finally, questions concerning the role and functions of self-disclosure in the sibling relationship remain to be addressed. For example, are the functions of self-disclosure in adult relationships as outlined by Derlega and Margulis (1983) (i.e., expression of feelings, self-clarification, social validation, relationship development, social control) helpful in delineating the functions for young siblings? Or are other functions important? Finally, what is the role of self-disclosure in the sibling relationship, and how does it vary developmentally and in terms of the sex composition of the dyad?

In this chapter, we have adopted the theoretical position that self-disclosure is a reciprocal process involving the exchange of intimate information. In this regard, we have chosen to represent self-disclosure as a property of a relationship rather than as a characteristic of individuals. Nevertheless, it is conceivable that some individuals are more likely to engage in self-disclosure than others. Determining why some persons are more likely to engage in self-disclosure than others is an important and challenging research question. The main difficulty with this question rests in disengaging self-disclosure as a property of an individual from other features of the person's experiences within a relational context.

In this same vein of thought, it should be recognized, of course, that sibling relations are part of a child's broader constellation of relationship experiences. As several persons have proposed (see, e.g., Hinde, 1979; Dunn, 1988b; Sroufe & Fleeson, 1988) an individual's experience within a particular relationship needs to be understood according to experiences within other relationships. In this regard, investigators may wish to assess the association between patterns of self-disclosure in the sibling relationship and the patterns of communication within the broader family context.

On the other hand, it is important also to determine how experience within the sibling relation contributes to or complements experience with peers. Is the sibling relationship a "training camp" for relations with peers, or are these relationships complementary or even independent realms of experience? These issues need to be considered so that a more comprehensive view of sibling interaction can be attained.

In conclusion, psychologists and writers of fiction have both demonstrated that self-disclosure is a feature of the sibling relationship. As we pointed out at the beginning of our chapter, psychologists have not focused on the content of sibling self-disclosure or the role that it plays in this unique relationship. Who knows what Romulus actually said to Remus?

References

Abramovitch, R., Corter, C., Pepler, D., & Stanhope, L. (1986). Sibling and peer interaction: A final follow-up and a comparison. *Child Development, 57*, 217–29.

Allen, J. G. (1974). When does exchanging personal information constitute self-disclosure? *Psychological Reports, 35*, 195–8.

Aquan-Assee, J. (1992). *Family functioning and the sibling relationship: Relationship qualities and interaction during middle childhood.* Unpublished doctoral dissertation, Concordia University, Montreal.

Aquan-Assee, J., Bukowski, W. M., Howe, N., & Gauze, C. (1992, March). *Family environment, structure of the sibling dyad, quality of the sibling relation, and perceived adjustment during early adolescence.* Paper presented at the Society for Research on Adolescence, Washington, DC.

Argyle, M., Trimboli, L., & Forgas, J. (1988). The bank manager/doctor effect: Disclosure profiles in different relationships. *Journal of Social Psychology, 128*, 117–24.

Austen, J. (1907). *Pride and prejudice.* London: Dent.

Balk, D. (1983). Adolescents' grief reactions and self-concept perceptions following sibling death: A study of 33 teenagers. *Journal of Youth and Adolescence, 12*, 137–61.

Bank, S. P., & Kahn, M. D. (1982). *The sibling bond.* New York: Basic.

Bell, N. J., Avery, A. W., Jenkins, D., Feld, J., & Schoenrock, C. J. (1985). Family relationships and social competence during late adolescence. *Journal of Youth and Adolescence, 14*, 109–19.

Berg-Cross, L., Kidd, F., & Carr, P. (1990). Cohesion, affect, and self-disclosure in African-American adolescent families. *Journal of Family Psychology, 4*, 235–50.

Bergout Austin, A. M., Summers, M., & Leffler, A. (1987). Fathers' and mothers' involvement in sibling communication. *Early Childhood Research Quarterly, 2*, 359–65.

Berndt, T. J., & Bulleit, T. N. (1985). Effects of sibling relationships on preschoolers' behavior at home and at school. *Developmental Psychology, 21*, 761–7.

Bowerman, C. E., & Dobash, R. M. (1974). Structural variations in inter-sibling affect. *Journal of Marriage and the Family, 36*, 48–54.

Bretherton, I., & Beeghly, M. (1982). Talking about internal states: The acquisition of an explicit theory of mind. *Developmental Psychology, 18*, 906–21.

Bretherton, I., Fritz, J., Zahn-Waxler, C., & Ridgeway, D. (1986). Learning to talk about emotions: A functionalist perspective. *Child Development, 57,* 529–48.

Brown, J., & Dunn, J. (1989, April). *Patterns of early family talk about feelings and children's later understanding of others' emotions.* Paper presented at the meeting of the Society for Research in Child Development, Kansas City, MO.

Bryant, B. K. (1982). Sibling relations in middle childhood. In M. Lamb and B. Sutton-Smith (Eds.), *Sibling relations* (pp. 87–121). Hillsdale, NJ: Erlbaum.

Buhrmester, W. & Furman, W. (1990). Perceptions of sibling relationships during middle childhood and adolescence. *Child Development, 61,* 1387–98.

Burnet, F. H. (1962). *The secret garden.* New York: Harper Trophy.

Chelune, G. J. (1979). *Self-disclosure: Origins, patterns and implications of openness in interpersonal relationships.* San Francisco: Jossey-Bass.

Cohn, N., & Strassberg, D. (1983). Self-disclosure reciprocity among preadolescents. *Personality and Social Psychology Bulletin, 9,* 97–102.

Connidis, I. A. (1989). Siblings as friends in later life. *American Behavioral Scientist, 33,* 81–93.

Daniels, D. (1986). Differential experiences of siblings in the same family as predictors of adolescent sibling personality differences. *Journal of Personality and Social Psychology, 51,* 339–46.

Daniels, D., Dunn, J., Furstenberg, F. F., & Plomin, R. (1985). Environmental differences within the family and adjustment differences within pairs of adolescent siblings. *Child Development, 56,* 764–74.

Derlega, V. J., & Margulis, S. T. (1983). Loneliness and intimate communication. In D. Perlman & P. C. Cozby (Eds.), *Social psychology* (pp. 208–26). New York: Holt, Rinehart, & Winston.

Dunn, J. (1983). Sibling relationships in early childhood. *Child Development, 54,* 787–811.

Dunn, J. (1985). *Sisters and brothers.* Cambridge, MA: Harvard University Press.

Dunn, J. (1988a). *The beginnings of social understanding.* Oxford: Basil Blackwell.

Dunn, J. (1988b). Connections between relationships: Implications of research on mothers and siblings. In R. A. Hinde & J. Stevenson-Hinde (Eds.), *Relationships within families* (pp. 168–86). Oxford University Press.

Dunn, J., Bretherton, I., & Munn, P. (1987). Conversations about feeling states between mothers and their young children. *Developmental Psychology, 23,* 132–9.

Dunn, J., & Kendrick, C. (1982a). *Siblings.* Cambridge, MA: Harvard University Press.

Dunn, J., & Kendrick, C. (1982b). The speech of two- and three-year olds to infant siblings: "Baby talk" and the context of communication. *Journal of Child Language, 9,* 579–95.

Dunn, J., & Munn, P. (1985). Becoming a family member: Family conflict and the development of social understanding in the second year. *Child Development, 56,* 480–92.

Dunn, J., & Munn, P. (1986). Siblings and the development of prosocial behaviour. *International Journal of Behavioral Development, 9,* 265–84.

Dunn, J., & Munn, P. (1987). Development of justification in disputes with mother and sibling. *Developmental Psychology, 23,* 791–8.

Eliot, G. (1985). *The mill on the floss.* London: Penguin.

Furman, W., & Buhrmester, D. (1985a). Children's perceptions of the qualities of sibling relationships. *Child Development, 56,* 448–61.

Furman, W., & Buhrmester, D. (1985b). Children's perceptions of the personal relationships in their social networks. *Developmental Psychology, 21,* 1016–24.

Gottlieb, L. N., & Mendelson, M. J. (1990). Parental support and first-born girls' adaptation to the birth of a sibling. *Journal of Applied Developmental Psychology, 11,* 29–48.

Hartup, W. W. (1979). The social worlds of childhood. *American Psychologist, 34,* 944–50.

Hartup, W. W. (1989). Social relationships and their developmental significance. *American Psychologist, 44,* 120–6.

Hinde, R. (1979). *Towards understanding relationships.* London: Academic.

Howe, N. (1991). Sibling-directed internal state language, perspective-taking and affective behavior. *Child Development, 62,* 1503–12.

Howe, N. (1992). *Longitudinal stability and consistency in the quality of early sibling relations.* Unpublished manuscript.

Howe, N., & Ross, H. S. (1990). Socialization, perspective-taking and the sibling relationship. *Developmental Psychology, 26,* 160–5.

Jourard, S. M. (1958). *Personal adjustment: An approach through the study of healthy personality.* New York: Macmillan.

Jourard, S. M. (1971). *The transparent self.* New York: Van Nostrand.

Lamb, M. E., & Sutton-Smith, B. (1982). *Sibling relationships.* Hillsdale, NJ: Erlbaum.

Lawrence, D. H. (1971). *Women in love.* New York: Viking.

Mendelson, M. J., Aboud, F. E., & Lanthier, R. P. (1991). Kindergartners' relationships with siblings, peers and friends. Unpublished manuscript.

Minnett, A. M., Vandell, D. L., & Santrock, J. W. (1983). The effects of sibling status on sibling interaction: Influence of birth order, age spacing, sex of child, and sex of sibling. *Child Development, 54,* 1064–72.

Norrell, J. E. (1984). Self-disclosure: Implications for the study of parent–adolescent interaction. *Journal of Youth and Adolescence, 13,* 163–78.

Olson, D. H. (1989). *Circumplex model of family systems: Vol. 8. Family assessment and intervention.* St. Paul, MN: Haworth.

Olson, D. H., McCubbin, H. I., Barnes, H., Larsen, A., Muxen, M., & Wilson, M. (1985). *Family inventories.* St. Paul: Family Social Science, University of Minnesota.

Papini, D. R., Farmer, F. F., Clark, S. M., Micka, J. C., & Barnett, J. K. (1990). Early adolescent age and gender differences in patterns of emotional self-disclosure to parents and friends. *Adolescence, 25,* 959–76.

Ross, H. G., & Milgram, J. I. (1982). Important variables in adult sibling relationships: A qualitative study. In M. E. Lamb & B. Sutton-Smith (Eds.), *Sibling relationships* (pp. 225–50). Hillsdale, NJ: Erlbaum

Rotenberg, K. J., & Chase, N. 1992. Development of the reciprocity of self-disclosure. *Journal of Genetic Psychology, 153,* 75–86.

Rotenberg, K. J., & Mann, L. (1986). The development of the norm of the reciprocity of self-disclosure and its function in children's attraction to peers. *Child Development, 57,* 1349–57.

Rotenberg, K. J., & Sliz, D. (1988). Children's restrictive disclosure to friends. *Merrill-Palmer Quarterly, 34,* 203–15.

Rotenberg, K. J., & Whitney, P. (1992). Loneliness and disclosure processes in preadolescence. *Merrill-Palmer Quarterly, 38,* 401–16.

Salinger, J. D. (1951). *Catcher in the rye.* Boston: Little, Brown.

Sroufe, L. A., & Fleeson, J. (1988). The coherence of family relationships. In R. A. Hinde & J. Stevenson-Hinde (Eds.), *Relationships within families* (pp. 27–47). Oxford University Press.

Stocker, C., & McHale, S. (1988, March). *Sibling relationships in early adolescence.* Paper presented at the Society for Research in Adolescence, Alexandria, VA.

Sullivan, H. S. (1953). *The interpersonal theory of psychiatry.* New York: Norton.

Summers, M. (1987, March). *Imitation, dominance, agonism and prosocial behavior: A meta-analysis of sibling behavior.* Paper presented at the meeting of the Society for Research in Child Development, Baltimore, MD.

Vandell, D. L. (1987). Baby sister/baby brother: Reactions to the birth of a sibling and patterns of early sibling relations. *Journal of Children in Contemporary Society, 19,* 13–37.

5   Lonely preadolescents' disclosure to familiar peers and related social perceptions

Ken J. Rotenberg and Mona Holowatuik

Loneliness is a common and often debilitating problem for individuals in contemporary society (see Peplau & Perlman, 1982). Research has documented the negative psychosocial correlates of loneliness; it has been linked to depression, alcoholism, obesity, and suicide in adults (Peplau & Perlman, 1982; Schumaker, Krejci, Small, & Sargent, 1985; Sadava & Thompson, 1987; Anderson & Harvey, 1988), and to rejection by peers, aggression, shyness, and disruptive behavior in children and adolescents (Asher, Hymel, & Renshaw, 1984; Asher & Wheeler, 1985; Cassidy & Asher, 1992).

Loneliness has been conceptualized in the literature as a state of self-perceived dissatisfaction with social relationships that is accompanied by negative affect (see Solano, Batten, & Parish, 1982). This conceptualization has guided the current measures of loneliness in children, adolescents, and adults (Russell, 1982; Asher et al., 1984) and serves as the basis for discussing loneliness in this chapter.

The focus of this chapter is on loneliness during preadolescence and the potential problems that lonely preadolescents may demonstrate in their disclosure to peers and in related social perceptions. (It should be noted that the term *preadolescence* refers in this chapter to the 10- through 13-year age span, the period of the transition to adolescence.) There are various reasons why this issue should be addressed. First, several authors (Ostrov & Offer, 1978; Jersild, Brook, & Brook 1979; Brennan, 1982) have proposed that the adolescent period, including preadolescence, is marked by widespread loneliness and accompanying psychological problems. Second, according to Sullivan (1953) during preadolescence individuals form chumships that entail intimate disclosures to same-sex peers. Furthermore, it was proposed that forming a chumship plays a significant role in an individual's ability to form intimate relationships later in development. These formulations have received empirical support from a number of

100

studies (see Berndt, 1982; Buhrmester & Furman, 1987; Buhrmester, 1990). It is important to note that Sullivan (1953) explicitly proposed that loneliness first emerges during preadolescence if individuals fail to establish chumships. Based on Sullivan's (1953) formulations, it appears likely that lonely preadolescents have some problems in intimate disclosure to same-sex peers that limits their formation of chumships and, as a consequence, limits their ability to form intimate relationships later in development.

Third, the preadolescent period marks the *beginning* of heterosexual intimate relationships, entailing intimate disclosure to opposite-sex peers (Sharabany, Gershoni, & Hofman, 1981). Problems in intimate disclosure, in this case to opposite-sex peers, would undermine lonely adolescents' early heterosexual relationships and perhaps set the stage for further problems in such relationships later in adulthood.

Research on adults

There has been a lack of research concerning whether lonely preadolescents demonstrate problems in intimate disclosure and related social perceptions. An extensive body of research has revealed that lonely adults show various problems in disclosure and social perceptions, and this provides a perspective on the possible problems that preadolescents may demonstrate.

The research supports the following conclusions about loneliness in *adults*. Lonely adults disclose less intimate information to opposite-sex peer acquaintances and friends than do nonlonely adults (Horowitz & French, 1979; Jones, Hobbs, & Hockenbury, 1982). Nevertheless, during the very early phases of the development of relationships, lonely adults disclose high-intimate information to same-sex peers and low-intimate information to opposite-sex peers, whereas nonlonely adults demonstrate the opposite pattern (Solano et al., 1982). Also during relationship development, lonely adults tend to fail to perceive accurately that they reveal a low level of intimacy to opposite-sex peers (Solano et al., 1982). Finally, lonely adults tend to dislike peers and believe that they themselves are disliked by peers, although peers may not share that perception (Jones, Freemon, & Goswick, 1981).

These findings have led various researchers to propose that the disclosure pattern of lonely adults impairs their development of intimate relationships because it violates norms or limits the intimacy of disclosure in conversations with others (see Chelune, Sultan, & Williams, 1980; Jones et al., 1982; Solano et al., 1982). One controversy concerns whether the disclosure patterns are evidence of social skills (or lack thereof) or a behavioral style. Lack of social skills implies that the lonely person lacks the knowledge or potential for displaying appropriate disclosure (see Vitkus & Horo-witz, 1987), whereas style does not have such implications. Researchers have increasingly recognized that the pattern of disclosure displayed by lonely adults may reflect an interpersonal style rather than a deficit in social skills. This notion underlies recent accounts of lonely adults' social behavior in terms of interpersonal roles (Vitkus & Horowitz, 1987) and social anxiety (Bruch, Kaflowitz, & Lesley, 1988).

Research on children and adolescents

Some attempts have been made to examine the loneliness and disclosure patterns in children and adolescence. Stephen Franzoi and Mark Davis have examined the relation between loneliness and disclosure in a group of high school students in both a cross-sectional study (Franzoi & Davis, 1985) and a longitudinal study (Davis & Franzoi, 1986). Overall, loneliness was associated with self-reported low-intimate disclosure to peers. The path analyses of the cross-sectional data indicated that loneliness caused low-intimate disclosure. However, the path analyses on the longitudinal data indicated that there was some reciprocal causation, with loneliness causing low-intimate disclosure to peers, which in turn caused loneliness. The lonely adolescents showed problems in self-reported disclosure similar to those observed in lonely adults.

Although Franzoi and Davis's findings are revealing, there are various questions that were not addressed. Because self-reports of disclosure were examined, the studies did not reveal whether lonely adolescents demon-strate problems in disclosure *behavior*. Some research may be taken to suggest that the self-disclosure patterns of lonely adults are different from their patterns of actual disclosure (see Solano et al., 1982). Furthermore, Franzoi and Davis did not investigate lonely adolescents' recognition of their tendency to disclose low-intimate information: Do they misperceive the familiarity that they engender in others, as has been found in lonely adults?

The actual disclosure patterns displayed by lonely preadolescents and related social perceptions have been examined by Rotenberg and Whitney (1992). These researchers engaged sixth- and seventh-grade students in conversations with unfamiliar same-age male and female confederates (peer partners). The students were engaged in two exchanges of disclosure in which they could choose to talk about topics varying in intimacy. After the conversations, the students rated how much they were familiar with their partners and how much they thought their partners were familiar with them. Rotenberg and Whitney (1992) found that lonely males provided less intimate disclosure (a) to the female peer than did nonlonely males and (b) to the female peer than to the male peer. In contrast, lonely females provided higher intimate disclosure to the female peer than did nonlonely females. In addition, lonely males demonstrated some problems in recognizing their low-intimate tendencies; they judged that their partners were highly familiar with them. The researchers concluded that lonely male preadolescents showed a shyness toward female peers and were not aware of the low intimacy of their communication to those peers. Also, it was concluded that lonely female preadolescents tend to demonstrate an over-eagerness to their same-sex peers by engaging in the disclosure of high-intimate information to them.

There were three limitations with Rotenberg and Whitney's (1992) study that served as the impetus for our investigation. First, in their study, the preadolescents provided disclosures to unfamiliar (zero history) peers. The question remains whether lonely preadolescents demonstrate the same disclosure patterns toward peers with whom they have had some history of interaction – familiar peers. Second, in Rotenberg and Whitney's (1992) study, the peers were confederates trained to provide sets of disclosures. In normal situations, however, preadolescents interact with peers who vary in interaction along their own personality dimensions, such as loneliness itself. The question of interest is whether lonely and nonlonely preadolescents' disclosure patterns vary as a function of the loneliness of their partners. In particular, are the disclosure patterns of lonely preadolescents different when they are engaged in conversations with lonely peers than with nonlonely peers? Third, Rotenberg and Whitney (1992) assessed the preadolescents' perception of the familiarity they had achieved with their partners only *after* the conversations had been completed. This method is limited because the findings could reflect the preadolescents' perception of how much their partner or even people in general know them rather than the perceived changes in familiarity that occurred as a result of the conversation. For example, it is possible that lonely males simply believe that others in general are very familiar with them. To address this issue appropriately, it is necessary to assess perceived familiarity before and after the conversations. This method was adopted in this study.

Also, this study was designed to assess whether lonely preadolescents demonstrate the perceptions of liking that have been shown by lonely adults. Research has documented that lonely children/preadolescents are more rejected by peers than are nonlonely children/preadolescents (Asher et al., 1984; Asher & Wheeler, 1985; Cassidy & Asher, 1992). If lonely preadolescents hold veridical perceptions of peers, then the preadolescents should believe that they are less liked by familiar peers than are nonlonely preadolescents. The additional question of interest in this context is whether lonely preadolescents' beliefs about how much they are liked by their partners change as a function of conversations with them. Finally, this study addressed whether lonely preadolescents like their peers less than nonlonely peers do, a difference found in adults.

The present study

The subjects in the study were 69 students (27 males and 42 females) from sixth and seventh grades who attended either of two local public schools or a local Catholic school. The students had a mean age of 12 years, 5 months and ranged in age from 11 years, 6 months, to 13 years, 5 months. The preadolescents were administered the Asher et al. (1984) loneliness scale in small groups of between 8 and 15 subjects, although they completed the scale individually and independently. A subsample of 12 preadolescents (6 males and 6 females) who had the highest scores on the Asher et al. (1984) scale within each school served as the lonely group. A subsample of 12 preadolescents (6 males and 6 females) who had the lowest scores on that scale within each school served as the nonlonely group. In practice, a minimum of 12 points on Asher et al.'s (1984) scale (one standard deviation) separated each lonely and nonlonely preadolescent within each school. These selection procedures were successful in establishing two groups of students that were significantly different in loneliness from each other as well as the students who were not selected ($F(2, 66) = 17.70, p < .001$).

For the purposes of this study, the sixth-grade preadolescents were designated as the "subjects," while the seventh-grade preadolescents were designated as the "targets." Each sixth-grade lonely or nonlonely, male or female subject engaged in conversation with each of the seventh-grade lonely male, lonely female, nonlonely male, and nonlonely female targets. The order of conversations with the four different targets was systematically varied. The conversations took place in a room in the subjects'/targets' school. Overall, a "round robin" design was carried out, in which the subjects and targets systematically engaged in conversations with each other. Although the sample sizes of this type of design are often small, they provide extensive information about interpersonal interactions.

The conversations were conducted in the following fashion. The subject and the target were presented the five different topics that have been used by Rotenberg and colleagues (Rotenberg & Sliz, 1988; Rotenberg & Chase, 1992; Rotenberg & Whitney, 1992; Rotenberg, 1993) to elicit disclosures varying in intimacy from children and preadolescents. The topics were, in order of least to most intimate: (a) the description of the environment, (b) the description of people and activities, (c) personal preferences, (d) positive personal, and (e) negative personal. The topics were presented in the form of examples described by Rotenberg and Sliz (1988). The subject and the target took turns choosing a topic and talking about it, with the subject choosing first; in total there were three turns or exchanges. At the beginning, the experimenter promised the subject and target that "what he or she said would be kept a secret." Prior to and after each conversation, the subject and target rated how much he or she (a) liked his or her partner, (b) was liked by his or her partner, and (c) was familiar with his or her partner, as well as (d) how much the partner was familiar with him or her. These judgments were made on 5-point scales, ranging from 1 = *not at all* to 5 = *very, very much,* with the end points varying in direction from one judgment to the next.

The subjects' conversations were transcribed verbatim from the audio-tapes. The accuracy of the transcripts was confirmed by a naive observer who checked 25% of the conversations. The transcribed conversations were scored initially by Gottman's (1983) method of identifying utterances. An *utterance* was defined as a unit of speech that was separated from other speech by either a pause or by a change in the subject or train of thought. The intimacy of each utterance (disclosure) was assessed by Strassberg and Anchor's (1975) Intimacy Rating Scale. This permits the scoring of the intimacy of disclosure across a wide range of topics and yields 3-point ratings: 1 = *low-intimate,* 2 = *moderate-intimate,* and 3 = *high-intimate.* This scale has been used successfully by Cohn and Strassberg (1983) and Rotenberg and Whitney (1992) to score the intimacy of the preadolescents' disclosures. This method was used by two coders, who were naive to the nature of the research, to score the utterances of 25% of the subjects. There was 87% agreement (agreements/agreement + disagreements) be-tween coders. Each coder then used this method to score the utterances of a separate half of the subject sample, and this yielded, in total, complete scoring of the data. For the purpose of analysis, each subject was assigned an intimacy score that was an average of the intimacy of his or her utter-ances. This measure was sensitive to intimacy of disclosure while control-ling for verbosity.

The intimacy of disclosures were subjected to a 2 (sex of subject) × 2 (loneliness of subject) × 2 (sex of target) × 2 (loneliness of target) × 3 (turn) ANOVA with repeated measures on the latter two variables. (A logarithmic transformation + 1 was performed to increase the homogeneity of the variance.) The primary finding was the three-way interaction of loneliness of subject × sex of subject × loneliness of target ($F(1, 8) = 7.13$, $p < .05$), which is shown in Table 5.1 (both the raw and transformed means

Table 5.1 *Raw and transformed means of subjects' disclosure*

		Loneliness of target	
Loneliness of subject	Sex of subject	Lonely	Nonlonely
Lonely	Male	.094	.143
		(1.28)	(1.42)
	Female	.174	.194
		(1.55)	(1.61)
Nonlonely	Male	.114	.116
		(1.32)	(1.32)
	Female	.131	.161
		(1.38)	(1.49)

Note: The raw means are shown in parentheses. Higher numbers denote the greater intimacy of disclosure.

are presented). Simple effects analyses yielded (a) a sex of subject × loneliness of target interaction for lonely subjects ($F(2, 8) = 12.38, p < .05$), (b) a loneliness of subject × loneliness of target interaction for male subjects ($F(2, 8) = 10.66, p < .05$), and (c) a loneliness of subject × loneliness of target interaction for females ($F(2, 8) = 5.78, p < .05$). The following patterns accounted for the effects. First, the lonely male subjects provided less intimate disclosures to lonely than to nonlonely targets. Second, lonely male subjects provided less intimate disclosures to lonely targets than did lonely females either to the same target or to the nonlonely target. Third and finally, lonely females provided more intimate disclosures to both lonely and nonlonely targets than did nonlonely females; both groups provided less intimate disclosures to the former than the latter target (all differences were at $p < .05$ by Tukey a posteriori comparisons).

Several other findings are worthy of note. As expected, the subjects and targets were moderately familiar with each other, as shown by assigning familiarity ratings of 3.5 and 3.6 to each other on the 5-point scale. Also, as expected, lonely subjects believed that they were less liked by their partners than did the nonlonely subjects ($t(8) = 2.56, p < .05; M = 2.13$ and 2.77, respectively). Rather interestingly, that judgment was not matched by partners' liking of lonely preadolescents. In this same context, there was a main effect of time (before and after conversation) on the subjects' perception of how much they were liked by their partners ($F(1, 8) = 6.04$, $p < .05$); subjects believed that their partners liked them more after the conversations than before. That shift was shown equally by lonely subjects ($M = 2.00$ and 2.25, respectively) and nonlonely subjects ($M = 2.63$ and

Table 5.2 *Means of subjects' perceived familiarity by partner*

Loneliness of subject	Sex of subject	Loneliness of target			
		Lonely		Nonlonely	
		Pre-conversation	Post-conversation	Pre-conversation	Post-conversation
Lonely	Male	2.17	2.50	2.00	3.17
	Female	2.33	2.83	2.67	2.83
Nonlonely	Male	2.83	4.17	4.33	3.33
	Female	2.67	3.00	2.33	3.00

Note: Higher numbers correspond to greater perceived familiarity.

2.92, respectively). Also, contrary to expectation, lonely subjects did not report liking their partners less than did nonlonely subjects.

Finally, the 2 (sex of subject) × 2 (loneliness of subject) × 2 (sex of target) × 2 (loneliness of target) × 2 (time – pre/post) ANOVA with repeated measures on the subjects' perceived familiarity by their partners yielded a four-way interaction, loneliness of subject × sex of subject × loneliness of target × time interaction ($F(1, 8) = 7.84, p < .05$), as shown in Table 5.2. Simple effects were not helpful in interpreting this interaction. The interaction appeared to be due to the pattern for male subjects. Lonely male subjects believed that nonlonely partners were more familiar with them after than before the conversations. Nonlonely male subjects believed that lonely partners were more familiar with them after than before conversations. However, nonlonely male subjects believed that nonlonely partners were less familiar with them before than after the conversations (all differences were at $p < .05$ by Tukey a posteriori comparisons). It is not clear why nonlonely males displayed that pattern. One potential cause of the findings, though, lies in potential ceiling effects of nonlonely males' familiarity and some regression toward the mean; they reported a 4.33 familiarity on a 5-point scale, and it may have simply declined with the repeated testing. It is important to note, though, that, contrary to expectation, lonely male subjects' attributions of familiarity to the targets (their partners) indicated that the lonely males were aware that they had provided low-intimate disclosures.

This research did not replicate Rotenberg and Whitney's (1992) finding that lonely preadolescents' disclosure to peers varied as a function of the sex of their peers. However, the research did reveal similar patterns in preadolescents' disclosure to peers as a function of the loneliness of their peers. Specifically, lonely males demonstrated a "shy" pattern toward lonely peers in the form of providing relatively low-intimate disclosures to them, and lonely females demonstrated an overeagerness toward peers in the form of providing high-intimate disclosures to them. The present findings support the conclusion that lonely preadolescents show problems in their disclosure to *familiar* peers.

There are two probable reasons why lonely preadolescents did not demonstrate problems in disclosure to peers as a function of sex in this study. It is possible that the disclosure patterns of lonely preadolescents that were observed by Rotenberg and Whitney (1992) may be evident only in interactions with zero-history peers. Also, the loneliness of the partner was systematically varied in the present study, and that may have overshadowed the potential effects of sex of partner on lonely preadolescents' disclosure.

Unlike the lonely preadolescents in Rotenberg and Whitney's (1992) study, lonely male preadolescents demonstrated an awareness of the low level of intimacy of their disclosure; they were accurate in their perception of the familiarity they had achieved. The tendency for lonely preadolescents not to display misperceptions of their disclosure and the familiarity that they incurred may be due to their familiarity with their partners. It may well be that lonely male preadolescents have attained accurate perceptions of their disclosure and resulting familiarity because they *have had* conversations with the peers. Such conversations may have provided lonely male preadolescents with the basis for adopting a realistic perception of disclosure and familiarity for future interactions. This hypothesis warrants further investigation.

There are some interesting theoretical implications of the observed patterns of disclosure by lonely male preadolescents. The tendency for them to provide higher-intimate disclosures to nonlonely than lonely partners highlights the difference between style and social skills accounts of disclosure patterns. Certainly, lonely preadolescent males were capable of providing intimate disclosures; it depended on the characteristics of their partners. In addition, style is a better means of describing lonely preadolescent females' tendency to provide more intimate disclosures to peers than do nonlonely preadolescent females. The question that remains to be answered is, What is (are) the mechanism(s) responsible for the disclosure patterns of lonely male and female preadolescents? At present the findings are not easily accounted for by the notion that lonely people adopt passive interpersonal roles (Vitkus & Horowitz, 1987), nor by the notion that lonely people experience high social anxiety (Bruch, Kaflowitz, & Lesley, 1988).

As with adults, lonely preadolescents perceived that they were less liked by peers than did nonlonely preadolescents. This was not matched by peers' liking of lonely preadolescents. Whether founded or not, such a perception could serve to handicap lonely preadolescents by increasing their anxiety over social relationships and undermining their success in peer relationships. Also in contrast to the research on lonely adults (e.g., Jones et al., 1981), lonely preadolescents did not like their peers less than did nonlonely preadolescents. Potentially, lonely adults' dislike of their peers is the accumulation of negative social experiences over the course of development.

There are some interesting clinical implications of the observed patterns of disclosure by lonely male preadolescents. In particular, establishing groups or dyads of lonely preadolescent males as a form of clinical treatment would *not* appear to be a viable form of clinical therapy. Under those conditions, the lonely males would not provide intimate disclosures or "open up," and therefore the situation would not serve a therapeutic function. It appears though that establishing a mixed group or dyads of lonely and nonlonely preadolescent males would have therapeutic effects because of lonely males' tendency to "open up" to nonlonely males. Clinical psychologists may wish to examine the utility of these recommendations in the future.

References

Anderson, C. A., & Harvey, R. J. (1988). Discriminating between problems in living: An examination of measures of depression, loneliness, shyness, and social anxiety. *Journal of Social and Clinical Psychology, 6,* 482–91.

Asher, S., Hymel, S., & Renshaw, P. (1984). Loneliness in children. *Child Development, 55,* 1456–64.

Asher, S. R., & Wheeler, V. A. (1985). Children's loneliness: A comparison of rejected and neglected peer status. *Journal of Consulting and Clinical Psychology, 53,* 500–505.

Berndt, T. J. (1982). The features and effects of friendships in early adolescence. *Child Development, 53,* 1447–60.

Brennan, T. (1982). Loneliness at adolescence. In L. Peplau & D. Perlman (Eds.), *Loneliness: A sourcebook of current theory, research and therapy* (pp. 269–90). New York: Wiley-Interscience.

Bruch, M. A., Kaflowitz, N. G., & Lesley, P. (1988). Mediated and nonmediated relationships of personality components to loneliness. *Journal of Social and Clinical Psychology, 6,* 346–55.

Buhrmester, D. (1990). Intimacy of friendship, interpersonal competence, and adjustment during preadolescence and adolescence. *Child Development, 61,* 1101–11.

Buhrmester, D., & Furman, W. (1987). The development of companionship and intimacy. *Child Development, 58,* 1101–13.

Cassidy, J., & Asher, S. R. (1992). Loneliness and peer relations in young children. *Child Development, 63,* 350–65.

Chelune, G., Sultan, F., & Williams, C. (1980). Loneliness, self-disclosure, and interpersonal effectiveness. *Journal of Counseling Psychology, 27,* 462–86.

Cohn, N., & Strassberg, D. (1983). Self-disclosure reciprocity among preadolescents. *Personality and Social Psychology Bulletin, 9,* 97–102.

Davis, M. H., & Franzoi, S. L. (1986). Adolescent loneliness, self-disclosure and private self-consciousness: A longitudinal investigation. *Journal of Personality and Social Psychology, 51,* 595–608.

Franzoi, S. L., & Davis, M. H. (1985). Adolescent self-disclosure and loneliness: Private self-consciousness and parental influences. *Journal of Personality and Social Psychology, 48,* 768–80.

Gottman, J. M. (1983). How children become friends. *Monographs of the Society for Research in Child Development, 48* (3, Serial No. 201).

Horowitz, L., & French, R. (1979). Interpersonal problems of people who describe themselves as lonely. *Journal of Consulting and Clinical Psychology, 47,* 762–4.

Jersild, A. T., Brook, J. S., & Brook, D. W. (1979). *The psychology of adolescence* (3rd ed.). New York: Macmillan.

Jones, W. H., Freemon, J. E., & Goswick, A. A. (1981). The persistence of loneliness and other determinants. *Journal of Personality, 49,* 25–48.

Jones, W. H., Hobbs, S., & Hockenbury, D. (1982). Loneliness and social skill deficits. *Journal of Personality and Social Psychology, 42,* 682–9.

Ostrov, E., & Offer, D. (1978). Loneliness and the adolescent. *Adolescent Psychiatry, 16,* 34–50.

Peplau, L., & Perlman, D. (1982). Perspectives on loneliness. In L. Peplau & D. Perlman (Eds.), *Loneliness: A sourcebook of current theory and therapy* (pp. 1–18). New York: Wiley-Interscience.

Rotenberg, K. J. (1993, March). Development of restrictive disclosure to friends. Paper presented at the meeting of the Society for Research in Child Development, New Orleans.

Rotenberg, K. J., & Chase, N. (1992). Development of the reciprocity of self-disclosure. *Journal of Genetic Psychology, 159,* 39–46.

Rotenberg, K. J., & Sliz, D. (1988). Children's restrictive disclosure to friends. *Merrill-Palmer Quarterly, 34,* 203–15.

Rotenberg, K. J., & Whitney, P. (1992). Loneliness and disclosure processes in preadolescence. *Merrill-Palmer Quarterly, 38,* 401–16.

Russell, D. (1982). The measurement of loneliness. In L. Peplau & D. Perlman (Eds.), *Loneliness: A sourcebook of current theory, research and therapy* (pp. 81–104). New York: Wiley-Interscience.

Sadava, S. W., & Thompson, M. M. (1987). Loneliness, social drinking and vulnerability to alcohol problems. *Canadian Journal of Behavioral Science, 18,* 133–9.

Schumaker, J. F., Krejci, R. C., Small, L., & Sargent, R. G. (1985). Experience of loneliness by obese individuals. *Psychological Reports, 57,* 1147–54.

Sharabany, R., Gershoni, R., & Hofman, J. (1981). Girlfriend, boyfriend: Age and sex differences in intimate friendship. *Developmental Psychology, 17,* 809–15.

Solano, C. H., Batten, P. G., & Parish, E. A. (1982). Loneliness and patterns of self-disclosure. *Journal of Personality and Social Psychology, 43,* 524–31.

Strassberg, D. S., & Anchor, K. N. (1975). Rating intimacy of self-disclosure. *Psychological Reports, 37,* 562.

Sullivan, H.S. (1953). *The interpersonal theory of psychiatry.* New York: Norton.

Vitkus, J., & Horowitz, L. M. (1987). Poor social performance of lonely people: Lacking a skill or adopting a role? *Journal of Personality and Social Psychology, 52,* 1266–73.

6   Children's disclosure of vicariously induced emotions

Nancy Eisenberg and Richard A. Fabes

In recent years, social and developmental psychologists have increasingly studied vicariously induced emotional states. This attention to how individuals respond to other's emotional states and conditions reflects the recognition that emotions are frequently embedded in social interactions (see Eisenberg & Fabes, 1992). Individuals must learn to deal not only with their own directly induced emotions, but also with their reactivity to the emotions of others.

Several types of vicarious emotional responses have been differentiated. For example, *empathy* is defined as an emotional response that is based on the apprehension of another's emotional state or condition and is similar to the emotion of the other person. *Sympathy* is defined as feelings of sorrow or sadness for another, whereas *personal distress* is a vicariously induced aversive emotional reaction such as anxiety or discomfort. The degree to which individuals are willing or able to display vicariously induced emotional reactions varies considerably from person to person. Moreover, the ways in which individuals display these reactions (e.g., verbal and/or nonverbal reactions) also varies considerably from person to person.

In research on vicarious emotional responding, several types of measures may be obtained. For example, subjects often are asked to report their emotional reactions verbally when exposed to needy or distressed people. In addition, facial reactions sometimes are used to index vicarious emotional reactions, particularly in studies involving children. More recently, investigators have begun to use physiological indexes to study

The writing of this chapter was supported by a grant from the National Science Foundation (BNS8807784) to both authors and a Research Scientist Development Award from the National Institute of Mental Health (K02 MH00903-01) to Nancy Eisenberg.

111

questions related to vicarious emotional responding (see Eisenberg & Fabes, 1990).

In regard to self-report and facial measures, at least three things may be tapped by these indexes: (a) the individual's actual vicarious emotional response (e.g., how sad or distressed he or she feels after exposure to the needy or distressed person), (b) the degree to which the individual feels that it is socially acceptable to display or communicate his or her feelings, and (c) the degree to which individuals desire to appear to themselves or others as if they have experienced certain emotions, even if they did not really experience the emotion (because it often is socially desirable to indicate that one has felt empathy or sympathy). Of course, the fact that measures of vicarious emotional responding may reflect a variety of processes is not unique to the study of empathy; many types of self-report and facial measures may be affected by people's attempts to hide, deny, distort, or miscommunicate true thoughts or feelings.

In situations in which people might be expected to experience emotional reactions, these experienced emotions, if they occur, usually will not be detected unless individuals disclose their reactions by means of some observable cue or index (i.e., by reports of the emotion or a facial display). As such, these vicarious emotional reactions can be considered analogous to evaluative intimacy, a type of self-disclosure in which a respondent acknowledges the affect contained in a disclosure and conveys affect him- or herself (Morton, 1978). Thus, in many studies of emotional reactions, researchers are studying self-disclosure as well as the specific targeted emotional reaction. Therefore, it is likely that we can glean valuable information about self-disclosure processes (particularly about evaluative intimacy) by examining data on emotional responding.

In this chapter, we use the literature related to vicarious emotional responding as a vehicle for examining self-disclosure. Specifically, we discuss age and sex differences in verbal and nonverbal cues of vicarious emotional responses and the socialization of such responses. Moreover, we examine closely the role of social desirability in disclosure of vicarious emotional responding. Given that physiological reactions generally are relatively covert and involuntary, we do not focus on physiological data in this chapter. However, it is important to note that, in our studies, subjects usually thought that they were alone when they were exposed to videotaped, sympathy-inducing stimuli (the exception generally was for preschool children); thus, they may not have been concerned about others seeing their emotional reactions (although people's facial displays of emotion sometimes are influenced by the fact that others are nearby, even if other people are not in the room; Fridlund, 1991).

Conceptualization and operationalization of vicarious emotional responding

In our research on vicarious emotional responding, we usually have differentiated between emotional responses that frequently have not been differentiated: empathy, sympathy, and personal distress. In our view (Eisenberg, Shea, Carlo, & Knight, 1991), people exposed to others' sadness, distress, or need frequently experience empathy (i.e., the same, or nearly the same, emotion as the other person). In turn, this empathetic response generally stimulates either sympathy, personal distress, or some of both. Those who experience sympathy frequently try to assist others in distress even if they can escape from dealing with the distressed person (Batson, 1987; Eisenberg & Fabes, 1990). In contrast, people, particularly children, who are anxious or distressed in reaction to others' negative emotions often avoid dealing with the distressing situation (Eisenberg & Fabes, 1990) or may even respond aggressively (Radke-Yarrow & Zahn-Waxler, 1984). Thus, there appear to be basic differences in the degree to which sympathy and personal distress are associated with altruistic and egoistic motivation (Batson, 1991; Eisenberg & Fabes, 1990, 1991).

Sex and age differences in the expression of emotion

Because of differences in cultural expectations for males and females, it is reasonable to expect sex differences in the willingness to disclose information about vicariously induced feelings. Specifically, females frequently are believed to be more emotional, empathetic or sympathetic, and other-oriented than are males (e.g., Block, 1973; Martin, 1987); thus, they would be expected to express sympathetic and distressed reactions more freely than would males. In contrast, because the expression of emotion is stereotypically viewed as feminine, males (particularly those socialized in stereotypic ways) would be expected to try to hide their emotional reactions to others' distress. An exception to the general pattern of greater negative emotional responsivity for females may be in regard to anger (which females may inhibit due to conformity with the feminine role).

General findings in the literature on emotion

In general, research on people's expressions of their own feelings supports the aforementioned expectations. For example, elementary school girls appear to be more willing than boys to report that they would experience sadness and fear in emotion-eliciting situations (Brody, 1984, 1985). Similarly, adolescent girls generally appear more willing to discuss their feelings with friends and parents (Papini, Farmer, Clark, Micka, & Barnett, 1990). However, boys seem more willing to report feelings of anger (Brody, 1984, 1985), perhaps because anger in males is less frequently viewed as inappropriate than is anger in females. Similarly, in elementary school, boys seem to be more adept than girls at inhibiting facial expressions indicative of negative emotions; girls tend to exaggerate positive displays, whereas boys' attempt to hide emotions are more believable than are those of girls (Shennum & Bugental, 1982). However, girls seem to be more likely to hide their disappointment when another person's feelings may be hurt by the expression of disappointment (Cole, 1986). This finding is consistent with the stereotype of females being more sensitive to others' feelings than are males.

In situations in which children have viewed emotion-eliciting tapes, girls tend to display more negative affect, especially fear or distress (Strayer, 1983). The expression of negative affect in such a situation tends to decrease with age, particularly for boys (Strayer, 1983; see Eisenberg, 1988). Similarly, when adults are exposed to slides constructed to elicit positive and negative affect, women are more likely than men to exhibit emotional reactions (Buch, Miller, & Caul, 1974; see Buck, 1984).

Gender differences in infants' and young children's expressivity often have not been found, or have been found for only a few expressions (Field, 1982; Yarczower & Daruns, 1982; Buck, 1984). Thus, it seems likely that the sex differences in the expression of emotion noted among children and adults develop with age and are the consequence of socialization. If this is the case, one would expect sex differences in the expression of sympathy and personal distress to become clearer with age.

Sex and age differences in the expression of empathy, sympathy, and personal distress

In much of the research on empathy and related emotional reactions, vicarious emotional responding has been assessed with self-report measures. Often empathy, sympathy, and personal distress are assessed with questionnaires that are purported to measure individual differences in dispositional levels of vicarious emotional responding (e.g., Mehrabian & Epstein, 1972; Bryant, 1982; Davis, 1983). Another frequently used measure is subjects' self-reported emotional responding in an experimental setting after they have been exposed (e.g., by means of written materials or audio- or videotape recordings) to a person (or people) in distress or need. For example, the stimulus person may be having difficulty dealing with an experimental task (e.g., one involving shock or dealing with a topic such as rape; Batson, 1987; Carlo et al., 1991) or may be in need of money or help with school or household tasks due to an accident (e.g., Toi & Batson, 1982; Eisenberg, Fabes, Miller, Fultz, Mathy, Shell, & Reno, 1989). After being exposed to the needy or distressed person, subjects report how they feel either in their own words, by pointing to pictures of facial expressions (for children; e.g., see Eisenberg et al., 1990), or by rating a series of adjectives that may reflect their feelings (e.g., sympathetic, softhearted, anxious, distressed; see Fultz, Schaller, & Cialdini, 1988; Eisenberg, Fabes, Miller, Fultz, Mathy, Shell, & Reno, 1989). In addition, their facial reactions while viewing pictures or videotapes of the empathy-inducing situation may be taped unobtrusively (e.g., Marcus, 1987; Eisenberg et al., 1990; see Eisenberg & Fabes, 1990, 1991).

Findings on age and sex differences in the expression of vicarious emotions differ somewhat for overt self-report and facial indexes; thus, they are considered separately.

Self-report measures. In general, there are clear gender differences in males' and females' self-reported empathy, sympathy, and personal distress, and there is reason to believe that these differences may increase with age. Moreover, this sex difference appears to be stronger for questionnaire measures than for self-reports in experimental settings (Eisenberg & Lennon, 1983; Lennon & Eisenberg, 1987).

In a meta-analysis of sex differences in empathy and related emotional reactions, Eisenberg and Lennon (1983) statistically combined the results of a number of studies. They found a very strong sex difference favoring females for reports of sympathy and empathy on questionnaire measures. Self-reports of vicarious responding in respone to sympathy-evoking stimuli in the laboratory or in stories also favored females, but the findings for these types of measures were not nearly as significant as for questionnaire measures. Interestingly, generally there were no sex differences in facial measures or physiological measures of empathy and related emotional responses.

Eisenberg and Lennon concluded that sex differences were more apparent when it was obvious to subjects what was being assessed (e.g., as on questionnaire items such as "Seeing people cry upsets me"; Mehrabian & Epstein, 1972) and they could more easily control their responding than when the measures were less obvious or less susceptible to voluntary control (e.g., for physiological measures). When subjects were aware of what was being assessed and could easily control their responses, they seemed to report emotional reactions that mirrored stereotypic gender roles. This is probably for two reasons: because they wanted other people to view them in gender-consistent ways and because they viewed themselves in a manner that was consistent with the prevailing gender roles. Thus, females probably were motivated to view and present themselves as emotionally responsive to others, whereas males sought to appear emotionally controlled. In fact, there is some evidence that females in general report more vicarious emotional responding than do males (Eisenberg, Schaller, Miller, Fultz, Fabes, & Shell, 1988; Foushee, Davis, & Archer, 1979).

Recent findings in which sympathy and personal distress were assessed separately are, for the most part, consistent with the aforementioned pattern of findings (see Eisenberg, Fabes, Schaller, & Miller, 1989; Lennon & Eisenberg, 1987), although sex differences in reported vicarious emotional responding seem to increase somewhat with age. In general, we find relatively few sex differences in preschoolers' self-reported sympathy and personal distress in experimental contexts (Eisenberg, McCreath, & Ahn, 1988; Eisenberg et al., 1990). However, in one study, preschool and second-grade girls were more likely than boys to report fear in response to a tape about children who were scared (Eisenberg, Fabes, Bustamante, Mathy, Miller, & Lindholm, 1988).

Gender differences in self-reported vicarious emotional responding are relatively weak, albeit evident, in older elementary school children. In general, we have found that elementary school girls report more sympathy and personal distress than do boys in experimental settings, but such findings frequently have been only marginally significant and appear in some studies and not in others (see Eisenberg, Fabes, Schaller, & Miller, 1989). Nonetheless, sex differences in children's self reports, when obtained, nearly always indicate that girls report more vicarious emotion than do boys.

By adulthood, gender differences in self-reported emotion in experimental contexts (e.g., in response to viewing a film) are more frequent and stronger, albeit still somewhat ephemeral. For example, in a study with second and fifth graders and adults, girls and women reported marginally more ($p < .10$) distress than boys and men. Girls and boys did not differ in report of sympathy, but such reports increased with age only for girls, and by college age, women reported more sympathy than did men (Eisenberg, Fabes, Miller, Fultz, Mathy, Shell, & Reno, 1989). In some other studies (e.g., Carlo et al., 1991), sex differences in reports of sympathy and personal distress in experimental contexts have not been significant.

Consistent with the conclusions of the Eisenberg and Lennon (1983; Lennon & Eisenberg, 1987) reviews, in our recent research girls and women generally have reported more *dispositional* sympathy and empathy on questionnaires than have boys and men (e.g., Carlo et al., 1991; Eisenberg, Fabes, Schaller, Carlo, & Miller, 1991; Eisenberg, Miller, Schaller, Fabes, Fultz, Shell, & Shea, 1989). For example, adolescent girls tend to report more empathy, sympathy, and perspective taking on questionnaire measures than do adolescent boys (Eisenberg, Miller, Shell, McNalley, & Shea, 1991; also see Davis & Franzoi, 1991). Thus, when it is relatively obvious what is being assessed, sex differences in reported dispositional vicarious emotional responding are clear.

In regard to age differences, older children and adults appear to report more situationally appropriate emotional reactions than do young children. For example, preschoolers are more likely than second graders to report inappropriate positive affect in response to a videotape about a sad or handicapped person (Eisenberg, Fabes, Bustamante, Mathy, Miller, & Lindholm, 1988), whereas second or third graders are more likely to report situationally appropriate concern or sadness (Eisenberg, Fabes, Bustamante, Mathy, Miller, & Lindholm, 1988; Eisenberg, Fabes, Carlo, Troyer, Speer, Karbon, & Switzer, 1992). Similarly, in a study in which children were asked to discuss an event from their past in which they felt threatened or upset, when asked how they responded to this event third-graders reported feeling somewhat more sympathy (which was situationally inappropriate) than did sixth graders (Eisenberg, Schaller, Fabes, Bustamante, Mathy, Shell, & Rhodes, 1988). Thus, younger children may have been more motivated to present themselves as being sympathetic when asked by an adult experimenter.

Our knowledge about age-related changes in sympathy and personal distress is limited because investigators generally study subjects of a limited age span or use different self-report instruments to examine vicarious emotional responding in children and in adolescents or adults. In one study in which the investigators examined change over a 2-year period, Davis and Franzoi (1991) found that high school students' reports of dispositional sympathy (and cognitive perspective taking) increased with age over the 2 years, whereas reports of personal distress decreased. The stability of reports of these characteristics was very high. Similarly, in a longitudinal study of adolescents, Eisenberg and her colleagues (Eisenberg et al., 1987; Eisenberg, Miller, Shell, McNalley, & Shea, 1991) found that sympathy, perspective taking, and personal distress were relatively stable over a 2-year period. Thus, by adolescence, individual differences in the tendency to report differences in empathy and related responses seem to be stable, and reports of relatively desirable modes of response increase, whereas reports of the relatively immature response of personal distress decrease.

In summary, females generally report more vicarious emotional responding than do males, and sex differences in self-reports seem to emerge in the early school years. In addition, situationally appropriate self-reports of empathy and related reactions appear to increase with age. Although it is likely that the capacity for experiencing sympathy increases with age, it also is quite likely that the age- and sex-related patterns of self-reports are due, in part, to changes with age in people's understanding of socially desirable behaviors and gender stereotypes. These changes in social understanding probably affect the degree to which males and females of various ages view themselves as emotionally responsive and are willing to disclose their emotions to others.

Facial/gestural measures. The pattern of findings in regard to sex differences in facial measures is somewhat similar to that for self-report measures, albeit somewhat weaker. In general, sex differences in facial indexes of vicarious emotional responding are infrequent among young children (Eisenberg, McCreath, & Ahn, 1988; Eisenberg et al., 1990) but are found somewhat more often for older samples. However, sex differences in facial reactions are not strong or consistent, even among adults (although they almost always favor females). Moreover, facial reactions indicative of vicarious emotional responding generally decrease with age.

For example, Eisenberg, Fabes, Bustamante, Mathy, Miller, and Lindholm (1988) found that preschool and second-grade girls exhibited more facial sadness than boys in response to an empathy-evoking film in which the film's protagonist was very sad, and boys' facial sadness was less for second graders than preschoolers. In another study involving second and fifth graders and adults, males tended to exhibit less facial distress in reaction to a sympathy-inducing film ($p < .08$), and second graders exhibited significantly more facial sadness and concerned attention than did fifth graders or adults (subjects were alone while watching the film). Subjects also read (for adults) or were read (for children) an appeal for assistance for the film's protagonists, during which time their facial reactions were monitored. For males only, facial sadness was negatively related to age. There also was a marginally significant tendency for younger children to exhibit more facial distress than did adults (Eisenberg, Fabes, Schaller, & Miller, 1989).

Similarly, in a study involving elementary school children (third and sixth graders) and adults, females exhibited more concerned attention than did males when recounting a sympathy-inducing real life event to another person. In addition, adults exhibited less distress and more positive affect than did children (Eisenberg, Schaller, Fabes, Bustamante, Mathy, Shell, & Rhodes, 1988). In two other studies with young elementary school children, there were no sex differences in facial sympathy, sadness, or personal distress (Eisenberg, Fabes, Schaller, Carlo, & Miller, 1991; Eisenberg et al., 1992), although older children exhibited less facial concerned attention in one of the two studies (Eisenberg et al., 1992). In a number of the aforementioned studies (see Eisenberg & Fabes, 1990, 1991), facial expressions reflecting vicarious emotional responding have tended to predict prosocial behavior – a finding that supports the validity of facial indexes.

In brief, gender differences in facial displays of empathy and related emotions are very modest and are not evident until after the preschool years. When sex differences occur, females almost always score higher. In addition, facial displays of vicarious emotion appear to occur less frequently with age.

Socialization and the expression of vicariously induced emotion

As just discussed, according to both the self-report and facial data, sex differences in vicarious emotional responding, when they occur, favor females. Moreover, sex differences in such measures do not occur with any consistency until after the preschool years. However, by middle to late elementary school age, girls are either more responsive to other's emotions, more willing to report their emotional responsiveness, or both. In addition, facial displays of negative emotion decrease somewhat with age, particularly for males.

This pattern of findings is not surprising given the cultural stereotypes (a) that females are more emotional, nurturant, and empathic (Block, 1973; Hoffman, 1977; Martin, 1987) and (b) that adolescent and adult males inhibit or neutralize expressions of sadness and fear more than same-aged females (Fabes & Martin, 1991). Consistent with this stereotype, parents seem to socialize their daughters to be more attuned than sons to others' emotions. For example, Dunn, Bretherton, and Munn (1987) found that mothers made more references to feelings in their conversations with their 1- and 2-year-old girls than boys. Such references to feeling states by mothers and siblings when the children were 18 months old were positively related to children's discussion of feelings at 24 months of age, and by 24 months, girls referred to feeling states more than did boys. In a study with slightly older children, Greif, Alvarez, and Ulman (1981) found that fathers, but not mothers, were more likely to label emotions when telling a story to their 2- to 5-year-old daughters than sons. In another study involving 40-month-olds, Kuebil and Krieger (1991) found that both fathers and mothers used a greater number and variety of emotion words and were more likely to discuss sad aspects of events with daughters than sons.

Consistent with the findings of Dunn et al. (1987), college-aged women were more likely than their male peers to report that their mothers (but not their fathers) had discussed feelings with them (Barnett, Howard, King, & Dino, 1980). Such sex differences in emotion-related socialization would be expected to result both in girls and women being more attuned to others' emotions (see Dunn, Brown, & Beardsall, 1991) *and* in them being more willing than boys and men to discuss and exhibit their feelings. However, these sex differences would be expected to develop over time, which might explain the dearth of significant sex differences is preschool children.

It is interesting that even adult actresses and actors appear to differ in their abilities to communicate sadness, fear, and anger. Women actors are superior at communicating sadness and fear, whereas men are more successful at communicating anger. This pattern of findings suggests that sex differences in the facial disclosure of certain sex-typed emotions may result in differences in the abilities of men and women to communicate these emotions, even when they wish to do so (Wallbott, 1988).

Given the difference in stereotypes regarding emotional responsivity, it is likely that females generally are more motivated than males to appear empathic and sympathetic, both to others and to themselves. Girls and women, relative to boys and men, probably not only believe that others generally will react positively to displays of vicarious emotion, but also want to perceive themselves as nurturant, caring, and emotionally responsive people (see Eisenberg, Miller, Schaller, Fabes, Fultz, Shell, & Shea, 1989). As such, indexes of sympathy and empathy often tell us more about how individuals want to be seen than their true responses.

Regardless of the issue of gender, family interactions likely influence the degree to which children overtly express their emotions. For example, children whose parents minimize, ignore, or punish them for expressing their own negative emotions frequently may hide their negative affect and may have fewer opportunities to learn how to deal constructively with negative emotions than do children whose socializers respond more positively (e.g., by providing emotional support and assistance in learning how to cope with the emotion-arousing situation). Such children may learn to associate feelings with negative outcomes (Buck, 1984); thus, they may become overwhelmed by exposure to others' emotions and, consequently, self-focused in their attempts to regulate the aversive overarousal (i.e., they may be prone to personal distress rather than sympathy; Eisenberg & Fabes, 1990). In addition, however, these same children would be expected to learn over time not to express their negative affective states because they are relatively likely to be ignored, criticized, teased, or punished.

In initial studies, we have found some support for the aforementioned ideas. This evidence is of several sorts. First, we repeatedly have found that parents who are sympathetic and/or who take the cognitive perspective of others tend to have same-sex children who report sympathy or sadness, or exhibit empathic sadness or concerned attention (Fabes, Eisenberg, & Miller, 1990; Eisenberg, Fabes, Schaller, Carlo, & Miller, 1991; Eisenberg et al., 1992). In addition, maternal sympathy/perspective taking has been negatively related to daughters' facial or reported personal distress (Eisenberg, Fabes, Schaller, Carlo, & Miller, 1991; Eisenberg et al., 1992). Moreover, we have found that mothers' and children's facial distress were positively related when they watched a sympathy-inducing film (Eisenberg et al., 1992). It is likely that part of the correspondence between parents and children in their reported or facial emotion is due to children modeling the ways that their parents (particularly same-sex parents) deal with emotion or to genetically shared similarities (or some combination of the two). However, it also is possible that the correspondence is in part due to the effects of sympathetic parenting on children's other-orientation, self-regulation skills, feelings about themselves and others, or other aspects of children's functioning related to vicarious emotional responding. In any case, our findings are consistent with other data indicating that children with empathic, warm parents tend to openly express empathy and sympathy (see Zahn-Waxler, Radke-Yarrow, & King, 1979; Barnett, 1987).

We also have obtained data indicating that the degree that families express emotion is associated with females' (but not males') vicarious emotional responding. In a study with adults, we found that women who said they came from homes in which positive emotions (including sympathy) and subordinant negative emotions (e.g., apologizing, missing someone; see Halberstadt, 1986) were frequently expressed reported relatively high levels of vicarious emotions (e.g., sadness, sympathy, and distress) in reaction to viewing sympathy-inducing and distress-inducing films (Eisenberg, Fabes, Schaller, Miller, Carlo, Poulin, Shea, & Shell, 1991). Similarly, among kindergarten girls (but not boys), maternal reports of negative subordinant emotion in the home have been associated with girls' facial concerned attention when viewing a sympathy-inducing person (Eisenberg et al., 1992). These findings are consistent with Papini et al.'s (1990) finding that adolescents' emotional disclosures to friends are correlated with openness of family communication, family cohesion, and satisfaction with family relationships.

Consistent with the findings regarding familial emotion, mothers' discussions of emotion with their children appear to be associated with children's reports or displays of vicarious emotion. For example, mothers' linking of a film protagonist's emotion with their children's own experiences was associated with girls' and boys' heightened facial emotional responding, including distress as well as sadness or sympathy (Eisenberg et al., 1992). Furthermore, mothers' reports of their own sadness and sympathy while viewing the same sympathy-inducing film with their child were associated with boys' self-reports of sympathy/sadness. Thus, mothers' disclosures of emotion were associated with boys' reports of sympathy/sadness, perhaps in part because mothers who disclose their own emotions encourage the expression of emotion in their sons.

Specific parental reactions to children's experiences of negative emotions also appear to be correlated with children's tendencies to report or display vicarious responding. For example, parental (primarily maternal) emphasis on emotional control of children's own sadness and distress has been positively correlated with children's self-monitoring and with nonverbal evidence of boy's personal distress coupled with their denial of such distress (Eisenberg, Fabes, Schaller, Carlo, & Miller, 1991). Thus, children whose parents teach them to control and hide their negative emotions often may try to monitor their expression of negative emotion.

In summary, our initial research suggests that parental socialization practices are associated with the degree to which children report and display vicarious emotional reactions. Children generally are more likely to report or display sympathy or empathic sadness if their parents do so and if gentle negative emotions are expressed in the home. Additionally, parental emphasis on control of the expression of children's own sadness and anxiety appears to be associated with boys' personal distress and boys' and girls' attempts to monitor their own behavior. Thus, it appears that children learn quite a lot about emotions and the desirability of their expression in the home.

Social desirability and children's vicarious emotional responding

As discussed previously, it is likely that self-presentational concerns (learned in part at home) are one reason that females report and occasionally display more vicariously induced emotion than do males. Recently, we examined the relation of social desirability to children's vicarious emotional responding and gender differences in such responding. In this study, we used multiple measures of children's emotional responding (e.g., facial, verbal, and physiological responding) and examined the relation of these to children's tendencies to present themselves in socially desirable ways.

Subjects and methods

Participants were 71 third graders (39 girls and 41 boys; median age = 109.5 months) and 56 sixth graders (28 girls and 28 boys; median age = 144.2 months). Each child was administered a 10-item version of Crandall, Crandall, and Katkovsky's (1965) Children's Social Desirability Scale (SD; alpha = .74).

The child then watched a videotape (used by Feshbach & Feshbach, 1986) about two boys who are home alone and see a strange man lurking outside their house. The boys are clearly upset and do not know what to do. The film was 110 seconds long and contained 15 seconds of colored bars (for transitional purposes), followed by 38 seconds of neutral content (in which the boys were talking about what to play) and approximately 57 seconds of relatively distressing content (in which the stranger is seen and the boys openly express their anxiety and fear). After a brief introduction, two skin conductance electrodes were attached to the child's nondominant hand. Additionally, two prejelled electrocardiograph electrodes were placed on the left side of the child.

The child was seated facing a partially shielded one-way mirror. The experimenter explained how the physiological equipment worked and tried to allay any anxiety (most of the children had previously viewed the equipment in their classrooms).

The child then viewed the film. (Children also watched a sympathy-inducing film, in counterbalanced order. Results from the viewing of this film are presented in Eisenberg, Fabes, Schaller, Carlo, & Miller, 1991. The order of film viewing was controlled for in the analyses.) The experimenter started the film and left the room until film was over. During the film, the child's physiological responses were recorded, and his or her facial expressions were surreptitiously videotaped from behind the one-way mirror. We also manipulated the observational setting via the instructions given to the child – to watch objectively or to watch and think about how the boys in the film were feeling. However, there were no significant differences as a function of this manipulation, and therefore it is not discussed and is controlled for in the analyses.

After viewing the film, the child's emotional reactions were asssessed by having the child rate his or her reactions to the film using adjectives reflecting happiness (feeling good, feeling happy), distress (feeling nervous or afraid, feeling uncomfortable, feeling worried about oneself), and sympathy/sadness (feeling sad, feeling sorry for others, feeling concerned for others, feeling down, and feeling unhappy). Each phrase was rated using a 5-point scale (1 = *don't feel that way at all;* 5 = *feel that way a whole lot*). To help the child understand the scale, it was presented visually in the form of five stacks of checkers that differed in their heights. The child was asked to indicate how much each of the phrases described how he or she felt while watching the film.

Coding of physiological and facial indexes

Physiological data – heart rate (HR) and skin conductance (SC) – were recorded on audiotapes (sampled every 10 milliseconds for HR, every 100 milliseconds for SC). The data were digitalized as they were recorded and then played into a computer.

Heart rate. Thirteen seconds of HR data during the most evocative period of the film were used in this study. These HR samples were used to compute mean HR per ½-second period (using weighted averages). When there was artifact in the HR data due to movement or talking (as determined by visual inspection of the paper record of the raw HR data and a review of the videotapes), the average of the codable HR beats immediately before and after the artifact was used in place of the uncodable data points (movement artifact was brief and infrequent).

For HR analyses, we computed slopes representing linear change in individual's HR during the evocative portion of the film. Slopes were calculated by computing *for each subject* the correlation between mean HR during the consecutive ½-second periods and the time period of the HR (number from 1 to k, with k being the number of ½-second periods). For two variables, this computation is comparable to computing the beta for linear trend using individualized multiple regression equations (see Knight & Dubro, 1984).

Skin conductance. Skin conductance (SC) data were run through a software program that computed phasic responses. Phasic responses included all SC responses that rose 0.10 micromhos or more (although responses of 2.5 micromhos or larger were assumed to be artifacts and were deleted). Moreover, any phasic response that occurred within 5 seconds after a child displayed a large, gross body movement was considered an artifact and was deleted (editing due to movement occurred in only about 15% of the cases).

For the analyses involving SC responses, we used SC data from the entire 57-second evocative portion of the film. The software program converted the number of SC responses into a rate per minute and also computed the mean amplitude across the individual's phasic responses. We then created a composite SC score that consisted of the sum of the standardized number of phasic responses per minute and the standardized mean amplitude of these SC phasic responses (these SC indexes were significantly correlated, $r = .55, p < .0001$).

Facial reactions. Children's distressed and concerned facial responses during the film were coded by two persons who had no familiarity with the content of the film or the hypotheses of the study. Every 5 seconds, the coders scored the child for distress and concerned-attention facial reactions using a 5-point scoring system ($1 = no \ display;$ $5 = strong \ display$). The 5-second periods of facial reaction data were averaged for the neutral and evocative portions of the film. Facial distress was coded if the child displayed a facial reaction similar to Ekman and Friesen's (1978) mild apprehension expression (e.g., eyebrows somewhat raised and pulled together) or exhibited nonfunctional, nervous mouth or chin movements (e.g., tightening or biting of the lips). The criteria for facial concerned attention (a marker of sympathy) were taken from prior work (e.g., Eisenberg, Fabes, Bustamante, Mathy, & Lindholm, 1988; Eisenberg, Fabes, Miller, Fultz, Mathy, Shell, & Reno, 1989) and included the eyebrows pulled down flat and forward toward the bridge of the nose, furrowing in the center of the brow, head and body oriented forward, and relaxed lower face. Additionally, facial responses indicative of empathic sadness (e.g., triangulated eyelids or eyelids not pulled in tight or raised, downturned mouth) were combined with scores for facial concerned attention (facial sadness occurred very infrequently).

For the analyses of facial indexes, difference scores were used (in which ratings for the neutral period were subtracted from ratings for its respective evocative period) to control for individual differences in facial expressions and averting the gaze in relatively neutral contexts. Interrater reliabilities (Pearson correlations for 35 subjects) for facial codings of distress and concerned attention were .77 and .73, respectively.

Self-reported reactions. Composite indexes of self-reported emotional responses were computed by determining the mean ratings for the happy, sympathy, and distress words. The phrase "feeling concerned about yourself" was dropped because several of the younger children did not understand its meaning and it lowered the internal consistency of the distress index. The alphas for the happy, distress, and sympathy composites were .83, .67, and .70, respectively.

Results

According to a 2 (sex) × 2 (grade) analysis of covariance (covarying tape order and instructional set), girls evidenced significantly higher scores on the social desirability (SD) index than did boys ($M = 3.81$ and 3.28, respectively, $p < .05$). Social desirability measures subjects' need to present themselves in a socially desirable fashion when an adult experimenter was present. Moreover, younger children evidenced significantly higher SD scores than did older children ($M = 3.99$ and 2.93, respectively, $p < .001$).

We computed similar analyses for children's responses to the film (covarying neutral SC for the SC index). Although there were no significant age or sex differences for the situational indexes of children's responses to the distress film, closer examination of the data revealed that children who were relatively high in SD tended to evidence different patterns of response to the film than those children who were relatively low in SD. To examine this pattern, we assigned children to either a high- or a low-SD group (based on a median split) and then computed a series of 2 (sex) × 2 (SD group) analyses covariance (using the same covariates noted earlier, and we covaried grade).

In these analyses, there were significant interactions of sex and SD group for children's self-reports of happy and distressed feelings ($p < .05$ and $.01$, respectively). According to simple effects analyses, there were no significant sex differences for the low-SD group (M for happy = 2.77 and 2.60; M for distress = 2.33 and 2.58 for girls and boys, respectively), but there were significant sex differences for children in the high-SD group. In comparison with girls in the high-SD group, boys in the high-SD group reported feeling significantly more happy ($M = 2.87$ and 3.31, respectively, $p < .05$) and significantly less distressed ($M = 2.65$ and 2.10, respectively, $p < .05$). These differences occurred despite the fact that there were no significant sex differences for any nonverbal index. Thus, the pattern of findings consistent with the gender stereotype regarding disclosure of negative emotional reactions appeared to occur primarily for those children who were especially high in their need to present themselves as socially desirable.

We also examined the partial correlations (controlling for age, instructional set, tape order, and neutral SC for the SC index) among the various measures of vicarious emotional responding (separately for each sex and for each SD group). The results of these findings also supported the notion that children's willingness to disclose or mask vicarious emotional responding varies according to children's levels of SD. Correlations between indexes for children low in SD generally were positive. For example, children's high-HR slope (i.e., HR acceleration, an internal marker of self-oriented distress responses; see Eisenberg & Fabes, 1990) was positively related to facial distress for girls and verbal distress for boys ($r = .38$ and $.48, p < .05$ and $.01$, respectively). Moreover, SC (an internal marker of intensity of personal distress, responding; see Eisenberg & Fabes, 1990) was positively related to girls' reports of distress ($r = .34, p < .05$). Thus, for children low in SD, their verbal reports were congruent with their patterns of nonverbal responding.

In contrast, verbal reports and nonverbal measures of a given construct often were inversely correlated for children high in SD. For girls in the high-SD group, facial distress was inversely related to verbal distress ($r = -.38, p < .05$). For boys, HR slope and SC were inversely related to verbal distress ($r = -.57$ and $-.36$, respectively, $p < .001$ and $.05$), and verbal reports of sympathy were inversely related to facial concerned attention (our marker of facial sympathy, $r = -.36, p < .05$). Finally, we found that children's SD scores were significantly, positively correlated with HR slope ($r = .26$ and $.28, p < .05$, for girls and boys, respectively).

In general, then, the reports of children who were low in SD seemed to be more veridical than those of children high in SD. Children high in SD appeared to report reactions consistent with stereotypic gender roles. Although individual differences in SD appear to influence the degree to which children are willing to disclose vicarious emotional states, little is known about the factors that contribute to the development of these individual differences.

The findings of this study may provide some preliminary insight into these differences. Specifically, the finding that SD correlated with HR slope for both boys and girls suggests that individual differences in the regulation of arousal may be related to children's tendencies to present themselves in socially desirable ways. HR slope can be considered a marker of personal distress and self-focused attention (Eisenberg & Fabes, 1990); children who are distressed when dealing with other's emotions may tend be become self-focused and concerned about how they are evaluated by others (e.g., when an adult experimenter is present). Negative emotional arousal has been found to engender a focus on the self (Wood, Saltzberg, & Goldsamt, 1990), and this self-focus may increase concern about how one is perceived by others. Alternatively, children who typically are concerned about how they appear to others may become easily aroused when exposed to others' negative affect. Certainly, more research into associations among arousal, arousal regulation, social desirability, and self-disclosure is needed.

Conclusions

Several issues arise when considering the data presented herein. One important issue is the extent to which the sex and age difference in self-disclosure reflect differences in individual's willingness to disclose felt emotions versus the extent to which these differences reflect differences in the actual experience of the emotion. As noted previously, when sex differences have been found in measures of vicarious emotional responding, they almost always favor females. What is not clear is whether these differences reflect variations in the expression or the experience of vicariously induced emotions (or a combination of the two).

Sex differences in the expression of vicarious emotionality may arise because of variations in the socialization experiences of males and females. Moreover, because of older children's greater exposure to parental practices and expectations, one would expect to see larger sex differences in older than younger children. Consistent with this conclusion, we have found that sex differences in self-disclosure of vicariously induced emotional responses are not consistently found until the middle of elementary school.

However, to reach a better understanding of the source of sex differences in the self-disclosure of vicarious emotionality, it also is important to consider whether these differences may reflect *actual* differences in the degree to which males and females *experience* vicarious emotions. Popular beliefs about emotions support the notion that males and females may differ in their experience of emotions related to empathy. Fabes and Martin (1990) found that adults believed that females experienced greater levels of sadness, sorrow, sympathy, and concern than did males. Moreover, these perceptions of sex differences held regardless of whether the subjects were referring to children, adolescents, or adults. Similar findings have been found for children's beliefs about sex differences in the experience of sympathy-related emotions (Karbon, Fabes, Carlo, & Martin, 1992). Thus, both adults and children consistently believe that females experience more of these emotions to a greater degree than do males.

The degree to which these stereotypes of sex differences in the experience of vicarious emotionality to others in distress is based on real sex differences is still uncertain. Such evidence has been found in self-report studies. In the Fabes and Martin (1990) study, not only were females perceived to experience more emotions related to sympathy, but women reported that they felt more of these emotions than did men. Other researchers have also found this pattern of results (e.g., Allen & Haccoun, 1976). Moreover, researchers who have studied children find that girls are more likely to report themselves to be more emotionally reactive than are boys (see Brody, 1985, for a review). How well these self-reports reflect the underlying experience rather than social desirability is still unclear.

Although relatively few sex differences in physiological reactivity to sympathy-related stimuli have been found, such research may be particularly valuable in clarifying the nature of sex and age differences in self-disclosure of vicariously induced emotional reactions. For example, Gottman and Levenson (1988) have argued that because males become more physiologically aroused when stressed and are slower to return to prestressor levels, negative affect is more physiologically costly and punishing than it is for females. Thus, Gottman and Levenson (1988) believe that men are more inclined to engage in behaviors that minimize the negative affect and keep it from escalating. To do so, men may be relatively unlikely to disclose negative emotional states and relatively likely to withdraw from aversive social interactions.

It is possible that physiological processes may be related to sex differences in both the experience and expression of variously induced emotional reactions. Males may find the physiological arousal associated with exposure to another's negative state or condition more costly and punishing than do females. As such, males may be more likely than females to experience personal distress, whereas females may be more likely to experience sympathy. In our own work, we have found that females evidence greater physiological reactivity (e.g., skin conductance) than males to sympathy-inducing stimuli (Eisenberg, Fabes, Schaller, Carlo, & Miller, 1991; Eisenberg, Fabes, Schaller, Miller, Carlo, Poulin, Shea, & Shell, 1991). However, in another study (Fabes, Eisenberg, Karbon, Troyer, & Switzer, in press), we have found that boys evidenced greater physiological reactivity to a more evocative videotape depicting other children in distress. Thus, it appears that boys have a more difficult time than girls regulating arousal when the stimulus is more intense and evocative. Because personal distress is likely to occur under relatively evocative conditions, boys may be more inclined to experience personal distress under these conditions than are girls.

As alluded to previously, males and females also may cope with such arousal in different ways. Males may be more inclined to inhibit and repress the expression of negative affect because of their concern regarding its escalation (Gottman & Levenson, 1988). In social contexts, males may be more likely than females to attempt to withdraw and disengage in order to minimize contact with the arousing stimulus person. Some support for these suggestions has been found. For example, Gottman and Levenson (1988) reanalyzed Komarovsky's (1962) data and found that husbands did not self-disclose in unhappy marriages but did so in happy ones. This withdrawal may have a physiological basis. Nonexpressivity under stress has been found to be related to heightened autonomic arousal (Notorius & Levenson, 1979); in addition, coping styles based on repression and denial have been associated with heightened physiological responsiveness to stress (Weinberger, Schwartz, & Davidson, 1979). Moreover, we have found that boys, but not girls, are likely to disengage the stimulus attentionally when aroused (Fabes et al., 1993). Thus, intense negative affect appears to be related to emotional withdrawal in males. With age and increased socialization, these sex differences in reactivity and coping may become even more apparent as high levels of physiological arousal may lead to highly overlearned and automatic behavioral and cognitive routines (Bower & Cohen, 1982).

Clearly, however, there have not been enough physiological studies in which male and female subjects have been exposed to empathy-related stimuli to evaluate these suggestions sufficiently. Moreover, physiological responses may be the consequence, rather than the cause, of differences in males' and females' overt expressions of vicariously induced emotional reactions. Our purpose in discussing these issues is to stimulate thinking about the interactions of physiological and socialization processes as factors in determining self-disclosure in contexts in which one is exposed to others in distress or need.

References

Allen, J. G., & Haccoun, D. M. (1976). Sex differences in emotionality: A multidimensional approach. *Human Relations, 29,* 711–20.

Barnett, M. A. (1987). Empathy and related responses in children. In N. Eisenberg & J. Strayer (Eds.), *Empathy and its development* (pp. 46–162). Cambridge University Press.

Barnett, M. A., Howard, J. A., King, L. M., & Dino, G. A. (1980). Antecedents of empathy: Retrospective accounts of early socialization. *Personality and Social Psychology Bulletin, 6,* 361–65.

Batson, C. D. (1987). Prosocial motivation: Is it ever truly altruistic? In L. Berkowitz (Ed.), *Advances in experimental social psychology* (Vol. 20, pp. 65–122). New York: Academic.

Batson, C. D. (1991). *The altruism question: Toward a social-psychological answer.* Hillsdale, NJ: Erlbaum.

Berg, J. H., & Archer, R. L. (1982). Responses to self-disclosure and interaction goals. *Journal of Experimental Social Psychology, 18,* 501–12.

Block, J. H. (1973). Conceptions of sex role: Some cross-cultural and longitudinal perspectives. *American Psychologist, 28,* 512–26.

Bower, G. H., & Cohen, P. R. (1982). Emotional influences in memory and thinking: Data and theory. In M. S. Clark & S. T. Fiske (Eds.), *Affect and cognition* (pp. 291–331). Hillsdale, NJ: Erlbaum.

Brody, L. R. (1984). Sex and age variations in the quality and intensity of children's emotional attributions to hypothetical situations. *Sex Roles, 11,* 51–9.

Brody, L. R. (1985). Gender differences in emotional development: A review of theories and research. *Journal of Personality, 53,* 102–49.

Bryant, B. K. (1982). An index of empathy for children and adolescents. *Child Development, 53,* 413–25.

Buck, R. (1984). *The communication of emotion.* New York: Guilford.

Buck, R., Miller, R. E., & Caul, W. F. (1974). Sex, personality and physiological variables in the communication of emotion via facial expression. *Journal of Personality and Social Psychology, 30,* 587–96.

Carlo, G., Eisenberg, N., Troyer, D., Switzer, G., & Speer, A. L. (1991). The altruistic personality: In what contexts is it apparent? *Journal of Personality and Social Psychology, 61,* 450–8.

Cole, P. M. (1986). Children's spontaneous control of facial expression. *Child Development, 57,* 1309–21.

Crandall, V. C., Crandall, V. J., & Katkovsky, W. (1965). A child's social desirability questionnaire. *Journal of Consulting Psychology, 29,* 27–36.

Davis, M. H. (1983). Measuring individual differences in empathy: Evidence for a multi-dimensional approach. *Journal of Personality and Social Psychology, 14,* 113–26.

Davis, M. H., & Franzoi, S. (1991). Stability and change in adolescent self-consciousness and empathy. *Journal of Research in Personality, 25,* 70–87.

Dunn, J., Bretherton, I., & Munn, P. (1987). Conversations about feeling states between mothers and their young children. *Developmental Psychology, 23,* 132–9.

Dunn, J., Brown, J., & Beardsall, L. (1991). Family talk about feeling states and children's later understanding of others' emotions. *Developmental Psychology, 27,* 448–55.

Eisenberg, N., & Fabes, R. A. (1990). Empathy: Conceptualization, assessment, and relation to prosocial behavior. *Motivation and Emotion, 14,* 131–49.

Eisenberg, N., & Fabes, R. A. (1991). Prosocial behavior and empathy: A multi-method, developmental perspective. In P. Clark (Ed.), *Review of personality and social psychology* (Vol. 12, pp. 34–61). Newbury Park, CA: Sage.

Eisenberg, N., & Fabes, R. A. (1992). Emotion, self-regulation, and social competence. In M. Clark (Ed.), *Review of personality and social psychology* (pp. 119–50), Newbury Park, CA: Sage.

Eisenberg, N., Fabes, R. A., Bustamante, D., Mathy, R. M., Miller, P., & Lindholm, E. (1988). Differentiation of vicariously-induced emotional reactions in children. *Developmental Psychology, 24,* 237–46.

Eisenberg, N., Fabes, R. A., Carlo, G., Troyer, D., Speer, A. L., Karbon, M., & Switzer, G. (1992). The relations of maternal practices and characteristics to children's vicarious emotional responsiveness. *Child Development, 63,* 583–602.

Eisenberg, N., Fabes, R. A., Miller, P. A., Fultz, J., Mathy, R. M., Shell, R., & Reno, R. R. (1989). The relations of sympathy and personal distress to prosocial behavior: A multimethod study. *Journal of Personality and Social Psychology, 57,* 55–66.

Eisenberg, N., Fabes, R. A., Miller, P. A., Shell, C., Shea, R., & May-Plumee, T. (1990). Preschoolers' vicarious emotional responding and their situational and dispositional prosocial behavior. *Merrill-Palmer Quarterly, 36,* 507–29.

Eisenberg, N., Fabes, R. A., Schaller, M., Carlo, G., & Miller, P. A. (1991). The relations of parental characteristics and practices to children's vicarious emotional responding. *Child Development, 62,* 1393–408.

Eisenberg, N., Fabes, R. A., Schaller, M., & Miller, P. A. (1989). Sympathy and personal distress: Development, gender differences, and interrelations of indexes. *New Directions in Child Development, 44,* 107–26.

Eisenberg, N., Fabes, R. A., Schaller, M., Miller, P. A., Carlo, G., Poulin, R., Shea, C., & Shell, R. (1991). Personality and socialization correlates of vicarious emotional responding. *Journal of Personality and Social Psychology, 61,* 459–71.

Eisenberg, N., & Lennon, R. (1983). Gender differences in empathy and related capacities. *Psychological Bulletin, 94,* 100–131.

Einsenberg, N., Miller, P. A., Schaller, M., Fabes, R. A., Fultz, J., Shell, R., & Shea, C. (1989). The role of sympathy and altruistic personality traits in helping: A re-examination. *Journal of Personality, 57,* 41–67.

Eisenberg, N., Miller, P. A., Shell, R., McNalley, S., & Shea, C. (1991). Prosocial development in adolescence: A longitudinal study. *Developmental Psychology, 27,* 849–57.

Eisenberg, N., McCreath, H., & Ahn, R. (1988). Vicarious emotional responsiveness and prosocial behavior: Their interrelations in young children. *Personality and Social Psychology Bulletin, 14,* 298–311.

Eisenberg, N., Schaller, M., Fabes, R. A., Bustamante, D., Mathy, R., Shell, R., & Rhodes, K. (1988). The differentiation of personal distress and sympathy in children and adults. *Developmental Psychology, 24,* 766–75.

Eisenberg, N., Schaller, M., Miller, P. A., Fultz, J., Fabes, R. A., & Shell, R. (1988). Gender-related traits and helping in a nonemergency situation. *Sex Roles, 19,* 605–18.

Eisenberg, N., Shea, C. L., Carlo, G., & Knight, G. (1991). Empathy-related responding and cognition: A "chicken and the egg" dilemma. In W. Kurtines & J. Gewirtz (Eds.), *Handbook of moral behavior and development: Vol. 2. Research* (pp. 63–88). Hillsdale, NJ: Erlbaum.

Eisenberg, N., Shell, R., Pasternack, J., Lennon, R., Beller, R., & Mathy, R. M. (1987). Prosocial development in middle childhood: A longitudinal study. *Developmental Psychology, 24,* 712–18.

Fabes, R. A., Eisenberg, N., & Eisenbud, L. (1993). Behavioral and physiological correlates of children's reactions to others in distress. *Developmental Psychology, 29,* 655–63.

Fabes, R. A., Eisenberg, N., Karbon, M., Troyer, D., & Switzer, G. (in press). The relations of children's coping to their vicarious emotional responses and comforting behaviors. *Child Development.*

Fabes, R. A., Eisenberg, N., & Miller, P. (1990). Maternal correlates of children's vicarious emotional responsiveness. *Developmental Psychology, 26,* 639–48.

Fabes, R. A., & Martin, C. L. (1990, June). Gender differences in emotionality. Paper presented at the annual meeting of the American Psychological Society, Dallas, TX.

Fabes, R. A., & Martin, C. L. (1991). Gender and age stereotypes of emotionality. *Personality and Social Psychology Bulletin, 17,* 532–40.

Feshbach, S., & Feshbach, N. D. (1986). Aggression and altruism: A personality perspective. In C. Zahn-Waxler, E. M. Cummings, & R. Iannotti (Eds.), *Altruism and aggression: Biological and social origins* (pp. 189–217). Cambridge University Press.

Field, T. (1982). Individual differences in the expressivity of neonates and young children. In R. S. Feldman (Ed.), *Development of nonverbal bahavior in children* (pp. 279–98). New York: Springer-Verlag.

Foushee, H. C., Davis, M. H., & Archer, R. L. (1979). Empathy, masculinity, and femininity. *JSAS: Catalogue of Selected Documents in Psychology, 9,* 85 (MS No. 1974).

Fridlund, A. J. (1991). Sociality of solitary smiling: Potentiation by an implicit audience. *Journal of Personality and Social Psychology, 60,* 229–40.

Fultz, J., Schaller, M., & Cialdini, R. B. (1988). Empathy, sadness, and distress: Three related but distinct vicarious affective responses to another's suffering. *Personality and Social Psychology Bulletin, 14,* 312–25.

Gottman, J. M., & Levenson, R. W. (1988). The social psychophysiology of marriage. In P. Noller & M. A. Fitzpatrick (Eds.), *Perspectives on marital interaction* (pp. 182–200). Philadelphia: Multilingual Matters.

Greif, E. B., Alvarez, M., & Ulman, K. (1981, April). Recognizing emotions in other people: sex differences in socialization. Paper presented at the meeting of the Society for Research in Child Development, Boston.

Halberstadt, A. G. (1986). Family socialization of emotional expression and nonverbal communication styles and skills. *Journal of Personality and Social Psychology, 51,* 827–36.

Hoffman, M. L. (1977). Sex differences in empathy and related behaviors. *Psychological Bulletin, 84,* 712–22.

Karbon, M. M., Fabes, R. A., Carlo, G., & Martin, C. L. (1992). Preschoolers' beliefs about sex and age differences in emotionality. *Sex Roles, 27,* 377–90.

Knight, G. P., & Dubro, A. F. (1984). Cooperative, competitive, and individualistic social values: An individualized regression and clustering approach. *Journal of Personality and Social Psychology, 46,* 98–105.

Komarovsky, M. (1962). *Blue collar marriage.* New York: Random House.

Kuebil, J., & Krieger, E. (1991, April). Emotion and gender in parent–child conversations about the past. Paper presented at the biennial meeting of the Society for Research in Child Development, Seattle.

Lennon, R., & Eisenberg, N. (1987). Gender and age differences in empathy and sympathy. In N. Eisenberg & J. Strayer (Eds.), *Empathy and its development* (pp. 195–217). Cambridge University Press.

Marcus, R. F. (1987). Somatic indices of empathy. In N. Eisenberg & J. Strayer (Eds.), *Empathy and its development* (pp. 374–9). Cambridge University Press.

Martin, C. L. (1987). A ratio measure of sex stereotyping. *Journal of Personality and Social Psychology, 52,* 489–99.

Mehrabian, A., & Epstein, N. A. (1972). A measure of emotional empathy. *Journal of Personality, 40,* 523–43.

Morton, T. L. (1978). Intimacy and reciprocity of exchange: A comparison of spouses and strangers. *Journal of Personality and Social Psychology, 36,* 72–81.

Notorius, C. I., & Levenson, R. W. (1979). Expressive tendencies and physiological responses to stress. *Journal of Personality and Social Psychology, 37,* 1204–10.

Papini, D. R., Farmer, F. F., Clark, S. M., Micka, J. C., & Barnett, J. K. (1990). Early adolescent age and gender differences in patterns of emotional self-disclosure to parents and friends. *Adolescence, 25,* 959–76.

Radke-Yarrow, M., & Zahn-Waxler, C. (1984). Roots, motives, and patterns in children's prosocial behavior. In E. Staub, D. Bar-Tal, J. Karylowski, & J. Reykowski, (Eds.), *Development and maintenance of prosocial behavior: International perspectives on positive behavior* (pp. 81–99). New York: Plenum.

Shennum, W. A., & Bugental, D. B. (1982). The development of control over affective expression in nonverbal behavior. In R. S. Feldman (Ed.), *Development of nonverbal behavior in children* (pp. 101–21). New York: Springer Verlag.

Strayer, J. (1983, April). *Developmental changes in nonverbal affect expression.* Paper presented at the meeting of the society for Research in Child Development, Toronto.

Toi, M., & Batson, C. D. (1982). More evidence that empathy is a source of altruistic motivation. *Journal of Personality and Social Psychology, 43,* 281–92.

Wallbott, H. G. (1988). Big girls don't frown, big boys don't cry – Gender differences of professional actors in communicating emotion via facial expression. *Journal of Nonverbal Behavior, 12,* 98–106.

Weinberger, D. A., Schwartz, G. E., & Davidson, R. J. (1979). Low anxious, high anxious and repressive coping styles: Psychometric patterns and behavioral and physiological responses to stress. *Journal of Abnormal Psychology, 88,* 369–80.

Wood, J. V., Saltzberg, J. A., & Goldsamt, L. A. (1990). Does affect induce self-focused attention? *Journal of Personality and Social Psychology, 58,* 899–908.

Yarczower, M., & Daruns, L. (1982). Social inhibition of spontaneous facial affect in children. *Journal of Personality and Social Psychology, 43,* 831–7.

Zahn-Waxler, C., Radke-Yarrow, M., & King, R. A. (1979). Child rearing and children's prosocial initiations toward victims of distress. *Child Development, 50,* 319–30.

7 Moral development and children's differential disclosure to adults versus peers

Ken J. Rotenberg

Imagine the following situations: (1) Your child has failed a test miserably and is too ashamed to admit it. (2) You search around your house for your cigarettes and find a cigarette butt just outside of your child's room. (3) Your child seems really dozy and his eyes glassy after making model airplanes in his room. (4) You are a storekeeper and you notice a gradual but obvious loss of candies handled by one of the children assisting you. Did the child fail a test, smoke, sniff glue, or steal candies? The answers to these questions frequently depend on the child's willingness to disclose his or her negative feelings and behaviors to adults. Moreover, the extent to which the child is willing to and actually does disclose will most likely play a significant role in parents' and other adults' ability to cope with a child's problems and engage in *appropriate* disciplinary actions.

Also imagine the following situations: (1) Your child does really well in a test at school and he or she is very proud but too timid to brag about it. (2) Your child has a "crush" on someone. (3) Your are a teacher and one of your students has a good idea for a class project. (4) You are a storekeeper and one of the children assisting you has been helpful to the customers. Did the child do well in school, did the child have a crush on someone, did the child have a good idea, or was the child helpful? As with negative feelings/behaviors, the answer to these questions frequently depend on the child's willingness to disclose his or her positive feelings and behaviors to adults. Moreover, the extent to which the child is willing to and actually does disclose will most likely play a significant role in parents' and other adults' ability to deal optimally with a child's positive qualities and engage in behavior to promote them.

These issues have been addressed by theories and research on children's moral development. Children's disclosure of their negative and positive feelings/behaviors to adults is, according to various theories (Sears, Rau, & Alpert, 1965; Kohlberg, 1969), an integral part of moral development and a

135

step toward achieving moral maturity. Rephrased within the theme of this book, children's moral development and maturity rest to some extent on their disclosure processes, specifically their disclosure of negative and positive feelings/behaviors to adults. Two theories of moral development are particularly relevant to this issue: the theory of conscience development and Kohlberg's (1969) cognitive-development theory of moral development.

Children's confession of their transgressions to parents and other adults has been regarded as evidence for children's attainment of a state of conscience (Ausubel, 1955; Sears, Maccoby, & Levin, 1957; Grinder, 1962; Sears, Rau, & Alpert, 1965; Hoffman, 1971). The theories converge in suggesting the following development of conscience in children. As part of the process of identifying with their parents, children internalize their parents' moral standards. Once internalization occurs, children (a) establish self-control that increases the likelihood of resisting temptation and (b) experience guilt when they have violated the acquired moral standards. One consequence of the latter is that children often confess their transgression to adults so as to reduce feelings of guilt.

Several findings have emerged from the theory of and corresponding research on the development of conscience. Sears et al. (1965) found that the mothers' display of warmth to their children was associated with the children's development of conscience in nursery school, which was measured as a resistance to temptation and reactions to deviations from standards of moral behavior (e.g., expression of distress and confession). Sears et al. (1965) reported that even very young children (4-year-olds) confessed their transgressions to adults. Other studies have revealed that children's tendencies to confess transgressions to adults increase from preschool through school age (Sears et al., 1957) and is greater in girls than in boys (Rebelsky, Allinsmith, & Grinder, 1964; Porteus & Johnson, 1965). Finally, Grinder (1962) found that children's confessions of transgressions when they were 5 or 6 years of age predicted their resistance to temptation when they were 11 or 12 years of age.

Another perspective on the issue is provided by Kohlberg's (1969, 1976) cognitive-developmental theory of morality. Kohlberg (1969, 1976) hypothesized and found that young children (approximately 7 to 10 years of age) attain a preconventional level (stages 1 and 2) of moral reasoning. When children adopt that level of moral reasoning, they believe that some acts are wrong, and rules are obeyed because the perpetrator is punished by the superior power of authorities – primarily adults. For children with that level of moral reasoning, conscience is predicated on an "irrational fear of punishment" (Kohlberg, 1969, 381). According to Kohlberg's theory and research, older children attain the conventional level (stages 3 and 4) at which they internalize the moral precepts of right and wrong and experience guilt. There is considerable support for aspects of Kohlberg's theory. For example, researchers have found that using Kohlberg's and related scales of moral development, children from a wide variety of countries/cultures progress from the preconventional to conventional levels of morality at the ages and sequence expected on the basis of the theory (see Snarey, 1985).

The conscience and cognitive-developmental theories and research yield different sets of expectations regarding school-age children's (6 to 10 years of age) disclosure of negative behaviors/feelings to adults. According to the theory and research on the development of conscience, school-age children have established a conscience and therefore are inclined to disclose negative moral behaviors to adults more than to peers or anyone else. However, theory on the development of conscience theory and research suggests that disclosure increases with age and is more prevalent in females than in males. In contrast, Kohlberg's (1969) cognitive-development theory and research supports the conclusion that school-age children base their morality on fear of adults. As a consequence, the children should be motivated to *avoid* disclosing negative moral behaviors to adults and will be less likely to disclose that behavior to adults than to peers or anyone else.

The different theories and research also yield distinct expectations for children's disclosure of positive moral behaviors. Extending Kohlberg's theory, school-age children should be more motivated to disclose positive than negative moral behaviors to adults. Quite simply, the latter but not the former is linked to punishment and the former may even garner praise from adults. According to the theory and research on conscience development, the difference in the disclosure of negative and positive moral behaviors should be attenuated, at least, by the heightened tendency for children to disclose negative moral behaviors because of their feelings of guilt. This study examines the competing expectations regarding children's willingness to disclose negative and positive moral behaviors to adults versus other targets.

Additional insight into these issues is provided by the research on children's disclosure to parents versus peer friends. Research by Hunter and colleague has yielded several relevant findings (Hunter, 1984, 1985; Hunter & Youniss, 1982). Hunter and Youniss (1982) found that fourth-grade children report greater intimacy (comprising measures of disclosure, empathy, companionship, and consensus information) with mothers than with fathers or with same-sex peer friends. However, reported intimacy with same-sex peer friends increased across fourth, seventh, and tenth grades and college years such that, by tenth grade and college, individuals reported greater intimacy with same-sex peer friends than with parents. In addition, females reported greater intimacy with same-sex peers than did males. Highly similar patterns of disclosure were found by Hunter (1985) regarding 12- to 13-year olds', 14- to 15-year olds', and 18- to 20-year-olds' disclosures of academic/vocational and social/ethical information to parents versus same-sex peer friends. Based on preadolescents' and adolescents' reports of their conversations, Hunter (1985) reported that conversations with peer friends were characterized by reciprocal exchanges of disclosures; peer friends equally attempted to express their own views and listen to each other's views. By contrast, conversations with parents were characterized by asymmetrical disclosure in which parents largely explained their views rather than listen to adolescents' views and in the process attempted to control them.

Hunter and Youniss (1982) have broadly concluded that consistent with Piaget's (1932) and Youniss's (1980) theories, parents and peer friends serve different socializing functions. Parents adopt the role of imparting to preadolescents and adolescents already existing knowledge and attempt to enforce given standards of behavior. In contrast, relationships with peer friends are based on equality, and their conversations offer preadolescents and adolescents the opportunity of reciprocating ideas through which they co-construct their personal beliefs and ideas. According to Hunter and Youniss, relationships with peer friends take on increasing importance from preadolescence through adolescence.

Additional insights into the present issue are provided by Buhrmester and Furman's (1987) research. In their study, second, fifth, and eighth graders reported frequencies of companionship and intimacy (telling secrets, private feelings) in their social relations in general and in relationships with specific others, such as mothers, fathers, best same-sex friends, best opposite-sex friends, and siblings. Buhrmester and Furman (1987) found that preadolescents (second graders) perceived the greatest frequency of intimacy in relationships with parents, particularly mothers. Age differences were found for girls: Their perceived frequency of intimacy in relationships with same-sex friends increased with age such that, by eighth grade, girls perceived a greater frequency of intimacy in relationships with same-sex friends than with parents. Age differences were not evident in boys. According to Buhrmester and Furman (1987), the findings supported Sullivan's (1953) hypothesized formation of chumships across preadolescence and adolescence for girls, who displayed corresponding increases with age in intimacy with same-sex peer friends. Buhrmester and Furman (1987) argued that boys may form chumships in accordance with Sullivan's formulations but do so through actions and deeds rather than through the exchange of disclosures. These findings and those of Hunter (Hunter, 1984, 1985; Hunter & Youniss, 1982) are comparable to the findings from a number of other studies (Rivenbark, 1971; Furman & Buhrmester, 1992; see Buhrmester & Prager, Chapter 2, this volume).

Another study is relevant to the issues under consideration. Rotenberg and Sliz (1988) examined whether children displayed a form of intimate friendship called "restrictive disclosure to friends," which is based on the notion that when individuals form intimate friendship, they are more willing to disclose high personal, but not necessarily low personal, information to peer friends than to peer nonfriends. In their study, Rotenberg and Sliz (1988) required kindergarten and second- and fourth-grade children to make tape recorded messages to peer friends and peer nonfriends. Children from each of the three grades showed restrictive disclosure to friends; they provided more high personal disclosures to same-sex peer friends than to same-sex peer nonfriends, while not differentially providing low personal disclosure to those two types of peers. This research points to the importance of considering the distinction between peer friends and nonfriends as targets of children's disclosure and the special status of the former for children.

Issues addressed

This study examined the competing expectations derived from the differing theories and research regarding children's disclosure of negative and positive moral behaviors. To test the competing expectations in a comprehensive fashion, it was necessary to include nonmoral domains of disclosure. This permitted me to determine whether the given disclosure patterns were evident in nonmoral domains rather than exclusively in moral domains, as implied by the differing theories/research of moral development. Because research shows that physical ability and appearance are salient aspects of children's self-concepts (Montemayor & Eisen, 1979), disclosures of those domains of information were included in the study. This study also examined children's willingness to disclose to adults in comparison to nonfriend same-sex peers. This was adopted because of both the special status of same-sex peer friends as targets for children's disclosure and the likelihood that same-sex peer nonfriends most closely represent the broader class of the children's peers. Finally, as indicated earlier, the focus of the study was on children's *willingness* to disclose, and that was assessed by asking children to indicate *whether* they would provide specific disclosures to various targets (termed the *likelihood of disclosing*). This construct and measure were adopted in particular because the various expectations derived from the theories and research on moral development most directly bear on the willingness to disclose. For example, guilt arising from the development of conscience likely increases children's feelings that they *should* reveal their negative moral behaviors. There may be a range of factors that affect children's actual disclosure of moral behavior, such as the likelihood of detection and punishment if detected (see Sears et al., 1965).

Also, this study assessed whether children of different ages display part of Rotenberg and Sliz's (1988) restrictive disclosure, that is, whether children were more willing to disclose positive and negative information to peer friends than nonfriends for *each* of the domains of moral behavior, physical appearance, and physical ability.

Finally, this study assessed whether there are appreciable differences between children's willingness to disclose to adults and to same-sex peer friends, particularly in the domain of moral behavior. Previous research (Hunter & Youniss, 1982; Hunter, 1985; Buhrmester & Furman, 1987), indicates that parents (mothers in particular) are the primary recipients of second and fourth graders' disclosure of social/ethical issues, whereas same-sex friends are the secondary recipients of such disclosure. This study determined whether children display that tendency to the general class of adults and how that pattern compares with children's willingness to disclose to same-sex peer friends.

The study

Sixteen children (8 boys and 8 girls) from kindergarten, 16 (8 boys and 8 girls) from the second grade, and 15 (8 boys and 7 girls) from the fourth grade served as subjects. Their mean ages were 5 years, 4 months; 7 years, 6 months; and 9 years, 3 months, respectively. The children from two public schools located in Thunder Bay, Ontario, were solicited by letters to parents.

All the subjects were tested individually. Initially, each subject was asked to identify by first name a peer friend and a peer who was not a friend. The subject was then presented 12 statements that were composed of 2 valences (positive and negative) × 3 domains of disclosure (moral behavior, physical appearance, and physical ability) × 2 statements each. The following are examples of the disclosures: "I think that I am fat" (negative valence, physical appearance); "I am just the right weight" (positive valence, physical appearance); "I broke my mother's lamp" (negative valence, moral behavior); "I turned in money that I had found" (positive valence, moral behavior); "I am very clumsy" (negative valence, physical ability); and "I can run really fast" (positive valence, physical ability). The subject was

Table 7.1. *Disclosure means as a function of target, valence of disclosure, and domain of disclosure*

Target	Valence	Domain		
		Physical appearance	Moral behavior	Physical ability
Friend (peer)	Positive	2.50	2.50	2.76
	Negative	2.00	2.16	2.62
Nonfriend (peer)	Positive	1.93	1.76	2.00
	Negative	1.33	1.55	1.81
Adult	Positive	2.35	2.45	2.61
	Negative	1.97	1.89	2.40
Anyone	Positive	1.81	1.76	2.14
	Negative	1.40	1.57	1.82

asked to indicate the extent to which he or she would say each statement to each of four target persons – friend (by name), nonfriend (by name), adults, and anyone else – by responding on the following scale: 3 = *yes*, 2 = *maybe*, 1 = *no*. The averaged scores across the pairs of disclosure per domain were subjected to 3 (grade) × 2 (sex) × 4 (targets) × 2 (valence of disclosure) × 3 (domain of disclosure) ANOVA with repeated measures on the latter three variables. The ANOVA yielded a target × valence of disclosure × domain of disclosure interaction ($F(6, 246) = 3.53, p < .01$). Although this was qualified by a five-way interaction, this simpler interaction will be considered in some detail because it helps to interpret the very complex higher-order interaction. The means for this interaction are shown in Table 7.1. Children reported a greater likelihood of disclosing positive-than negative-valenced information, and that differentiation was greater for physical appearance than for physical ability. Tukey a posteriori comparisons indicated that the three-way interaction was due in large part to children reporting a greater likelihood of disclosing positive than negative moral behavior to peer friends ($p < .05$) and, most strongly, to adults ($p < .01$) but *not* to the other two targets. Also, children reported a greater likelihood of disclosing both positive and negative information to peer friends and adults than to either peer nonfriends or anyone else for *each* of the three disclosure domains ($p < .01$).

As indicated, the preceding interaction was qualified by a five-way grade × sex by target × valence of disclosure × domain of disclosure interaction ($F(12, 246) = 2.34, p < .01$). The means for this interaction are shown in Table 7.2. Tests of simple effects yielded a significant target × valence of disclosure × domain of disclosure interaction for fourth-grade children

Table 7.2. *Disclosure means as a function of grade, sex, target, valence of disclosure, and domain of disclosure*

		Domain					
		Boys			Girls		
Target	Valence	Physical appearance	Moral behavior	Physical ability	Physical appearance	Moral behavior	Physical ability
Kindergartners							
Friend	Positive	2.76	2.68	2.91	2.50	2.50	2.80
(peer)	Negative	2.32	2.41	2.77	2.22	2.40	2.76
Nonfriend	Positive	2.27	1.91	2.18	1.60	1.30	1.60
(peer)	Negative	1.68	1.77	1.86	1.00	1.50	2.00
Adult	Positive	2.82	2.59	2.68	2.40	2.40	2.30
	Negative	2.05	1.91	2.73	1.60	1.40	2.20
Anyone	Positive	2.36	2.32	2.87	1.80	1.50	1.60
	Negative	1.96	2.00	2.55	1.20	1.40	1.90
Second graders							
Friend	Positive	2.68	2.48	2.91	2.20	2.60	2.50
(peer)	Negative	1.77	2.05	2.46	1.80	1.70	2.40
Nonfriend	Positive	1.96	1.82	2.05	1.50	1.60	1.70
(peer)	Negative	1.32	1.46	1.86	1.10	1.10	1.20
Adult	Positive	2.32	2.32	2.68	1.90	2.60	2.40
	Negative	1.73	2.09	2.32	1.90	1.30	1.90
Anyone	Positive	1.86	1.68	2.23	1.40	1.70	1.70
	Negative	1.23	1.55	1.46	1.20	1.20	1.10
Fourth graders							
Friend	Positive	2.36	2.43	2.86	2.19	2.31	2.19
(peer)	Negative	2.14	2.44	2.88	2.00	2.00	2.63
Nonfriend	Positive	1.93	1.57	2.21	1.88	2.00	1.94
(peer)	Negative	1.14	1.79	1.71	1.38	1.50	2.00
Adult	Positive	2.14	2.57	2.64	2.19	2.25	2.69
	Negative	2.29	1.71	2.50	2.19	2.32	2.44
Anyone	Positive	1.64	1.64	2.21	1.38	1.40	1.56
	Negative	1.43	1.64	1.96	1.25	1.31	1.69

($F(12, 246) = 3.13$, $p < .001$) and a significant grade × sex × target interaction for the moral disclosure domain ($F(12, 246) = 3.34, p < .001$).

The simple effects coupled with Tukey a posteriori comparisons indicated that the interaction was a product of the following differences. Fourth-grade girls reported a greater likelihood of disclosing negative moral behavior to the adult target than they did to all other targets. Fourth-grade girls also reported a greater likelihood than fourth-grade boys to disclose that same behavior to the adult target ($p < .01$, as shown in Table

7.2). Furthermore, fourth-grade girls reported a greater likelihood of disclosing negative moral behavior to the adult target than did kindergarten and second-grade girls ($p < .01$). In contrast to all other grade-sex groups, fourth-grade girls were the only group *not* to report a greater likelihood of disclosing positive than negative moral behaviors to adults; they showed a slight tendency to display the opposite disclosure pattern.

Some additional Tukey a posteriori comparisons offered further insight into the findings. Second-grade boys reported a greater likelihood of disclosing negative moral behaviors to the adult target than to peer nonfriends or anyone else ($p < .05$), a difference not evident in kindergarten and fourth-grade boys. It should be noted that in none of the cases did the children report a lower likelihood of disclosing negative moral behavior to the adult target than to peer nonfriends or anyone else.

Conclusions

The findings yielded mixed support of the competing expectations derived from the differing theories on moral development. Consistent with the expectations derived from Kohlberg's (1969, 1976) theory, school-age children reported a greater willingness to disclose positive than negative behaviors to adults. Contrary to the expectations based on that theory, however, the children were *not* less willing to disclose negative behavior to adults than to nonfriend peers or anyone else. A number of findings from our study are consistent with the expectations derived from the theory of the development of conscience and indicate that school-age children show evidence of conscience development. Second-grade boys and fourth-grade girls reported, in comparison with children of other ages and sex, a greater willingness to disclose negative behaviors to adults than to nonfriend peers or anyone else. Development of conscience was most clearly displayed by fourth-grade girls, who reported a considerable willingness to disclose negative behavior to adults – so much so that they tended to report a slightly greater willingness to disclose negative than positive moral behavior to adults. Consistent with the notion that the disclosure patterns reflect moral development rather than a broader shift in disclosure, the age and sex differences were evident in the domain of moral behavior rather than in the nonmoral disclosure domains of physical appearance and physical ability.

There are some limitations in concluding that the development of conscience theory and Kohlberg's theory and research are more or less adequate accounts of children's disclosure and moral development on the basis of our findings. First, a small but appreciable number of children attain the conventional level of moral reasoning by 10 years of age (Kohlberg, 1969;

Snarey, 1985). In this context, the finding that the 10-year-old children in this study, particularly the fourth-grade girls, displayed conscience is not *too* discrepant from Kohlberg's theory and research. In future, the issue could be clarified by assessing the relation between children's development of moral reasoning on Kohlberg's scale and their willingness to disclose negative and positive moral behaviors to the various targets. Second, one of the most difficult issues addressed by our study is when, in the course of development, children begin to confess their transgressions. Previous researchers, notably Sears et al. (1965), have concluded that this is evident in children as young as 4 years of age. In our study, evidence for children's tendency to confess their transgressions rested explicitly on their greater willingness to disclose negative behavior to adults than to nonfriend peers or anyone else. Using *these* criteria, the youngest children (5- to 6-year-olds) did not show any evidence of confessing their transgressions; that was only shown by second-grade boys and, most clearly, by fourth-grade girls.

The findings are consistent with a portion of the pattern observed by Rotenberg and Sliz (1988) regarding restrictive disclosure to friends. Children at each of the three ages reported a greater willingness to disclose positive and negative personal information to friends than to nonfriends, and did so across all three domains of disclosure. Overall, same-sex peer friends had a status as disclosure recipients equal to that held by adults, and in the case of negative behavior, a greater status. In particular, the age and sex differences found in children's reported willingness to disclose negative behaviors were *not* evident in their reported willingness to disclose such behaviors to same-sex peer friends. Children of all three ages and both sexes were more willing to disclose negative behavior to peer friends than to peer nonfriends or anyone else. These findings are to some extent different from those obtained by Hunter and colleague (Hunter & Youniss, 1982; Hunter, 1984, 1985) and Buhrmester and Furman (1987), who found that *parents* (mothers in particular) dominated same-sex peer friends as recipients of disclosure, particularly in the social/ethical domain during second and fourth grades. As indicated, however, the previous findings bear directly on children's disclosure to parents rather than on disclosure to the class of adults in general, which was the focus of our study. Our findings may be taken to suggest that there are substantial differences between children's willingness to disclose to same-sex peer friends and to the general class of adults.

Nevertheless, Hunter and Youniss's theory provides an important perspective on the present findings. According to that theory, adults adopt the role of attempting to enforce conventional standards of behavior in their conversations with children. In this light, adults must experience particularly strong pressures to adopt that role when they become targets of children's disclosure of positive or negative behavior and will likely attempt to promote conscience development during the ensuing adult–child conversations. According to Hunter and Youniss's theory, children's conversations with peer friends are more equal and therefore less linked to enforcing moral standards, and through those conversations, children co-construct their ideas about various domains. As a result of children's conversations with peer friends regarding negative and positive moral behaviors in particular, it is quite likely that they establish a system of morality that is different from adult standards. Consistent with these arguments, some research indicates that children adopt differing morality systems in peer relationships than in their relationships with adults (see Brofenbrenner, 1967; Bixenstine, DeCorte, & Bixenstine, 1976). At least in Western culture, peers often promote violations of the moral standards set by adults.

There are four particularly interesting directions for future investigation. First, in this study, the children were asked to report their willingness to disclose to adults in general. It remains to be determined whether the same pattern prevails if children report their willingness to disclose to their parents in particular. Second, the present findings yield insights into children's willingness to disclose various types of information to given targets or classes of targets. Whether the children actually disclose information as they report remains to be examined.

Third, researchers should address whether the presently observed age and sex patterns of children's willingness to disclose negative moral behaviors to adults are a product of their "feelings of guilt." Guilt has been the focus of an extensive and diverse array of research (e.g., Hoffman, 1971; Kagan, 1984). Research indicates that 5- to 6-year-old children *verbalize* their guilt feelings in response to transgressions but also that such verbalizations increase across the school-age period (Zahn-Waxler, Kochanska, Krupnick, & McKnew, 1990; Kochanska, 1991). Of some interest in this context is Ferguson, Stegge, and Damhuis's (1991) investigation of second- and fifth-grade children's understanding of shame and guilt. These researchers found that, on a sorting task, the younger children reported greater preference that guilt-related transgressions remain undetected and not confessed than did older children. These findings are consistent with those from this study. What is surprising is that few studies have examined the relation between guilt feelings and confession of a transgression when the variables are measured independently. Sears et al. (1965) found that there was a modest association between children's distress (a measure of guilt) when they committed transgressions and their confession of transgressions. Also, Grinder and McMichael (1963) administered projective tests of guilt to sixth- and seventh-grade children and found that their expressions of remorse were strongly correlated with their confessions on the projective task. More research is needed to clarify the link between children's guilt feelings and their tendency to disclose negative moral behaviors.

Fourth, there is a lack of research on adults' or parents' reactions to children's disclosure of positive and negative moral behaviors. For example, are adults or parents more or less lenient with children when they confess their transgressions? Does the tendency for children to confess their transgressions to their parents facilitate or inhibit the development of positive relations between them? A number of aspects of this issue warrant further investigation.

References

Ausubel, D. P. (1955). Relationships between shame and guilt in the socialization process. *Psychological Review, 62,* 378–90.

Bixenstine, V. E., DeCorte, M. S., & Bixenstine, B. A. (1976). Conformity to peer-sponsored misconduct at four age levels. *Developmental Psychology, 12,* 226–36.

Brofenbrenner, U. (1967). Response to pressure from peers versus adults among Soviet and American school children. *International Journal of Psychology, 2,* 199–207.

Buhrmester, D., & Furman, W. (1987). The development of companionship and intimacy. *Child Development, 58,* 1101–13.

Ferguson, T. J., Stegge, H., & Damhuis, I. (1991). Children's understanding of guilt and shame. *Child Development, 62,* 827–39.

Furman, W., & Buhrmester, D. (1992). Age and sex differences in perceptions of networks of personal relationships. *Child Development, 63,* 103–15.

Grinder, R. E. (1962). Parental childrearing practices, conscience, and resistance to temptation of sixth-grade children. *Child Development, 33,* 803–20.

Grinder, R. E., & McMichael, R. E. (1963). Cultural influence on conscience development: Resistance to temptation and guilt among Samoans and American Caucasians. *Journal of Abnormal and Social Psychology, 66,* 503–7.

Hoffman, M. L. (1971). Identification and conscience development. *Child Development, 42,* 1071–82.

Hunter, F. T. (1984). Socializing procedures in child–parent and friendship relations during adolescence. *Developmental Psychology, 20,* 1092–9.

Hunter, F. T. (1985). Adolescents' perceptions of discussions with parents and friends. *Developmental Psychology, 21,* 433–40.

Hunter, F. T., & Youniss, J. (1982). Changes in functions of three relations during adolescence. *Developmental Psychology, 18,* 306–11.

Kagan, J. (1984). *The nature of the child.* New York: Basic.

Kochanska, G. (1991). Socialization and temperament in the development of guilt and conscience. *Child Development, 62,* 1379–92.

Kohlberg, L. (1969). Stage and sequence: The cognitive-developmental approach to socialization. In D. A. Goslin (Ed.), *Handbook of socialization theory and research* (pp. 347–404). Chicago: Rand McNally.

Kohlberg, L. (1976). Moral stages and moralization: The cognitive-developmental approach. In Thomas Lickona (Ed.), *Moral development and behavior: Theory, research and social issues* (pp. 31–53). New York: Holt, Rinehart, & Winston.

Montemayor, R., & Eisen, M. (1979). The development of self-conceptions from childhood to adolescence. *Developmental Psychology, 13,* 314–19.

Piaget, J. (1932). *The moral judgment of the child.* New York: Harcourt.

Porteus, B. D., & Johnson, R. C. (1965). Children's responses to two measures of conscience development and their relation to sociometric nomination. *Child Development, 36,* 703–11.

Rebelsky, F. G., Allinsmith, W. A., & Grinder, R. (1964). Sex differences in children's use of fantasy confession and their relation to temptation. *Child Development, 34,* 955–62.

Rotenberg, K. J., & Sliz, D. (1988). Children's restrictive disclosure to peers. *Merrill-Palmer Quarterly, 34,* 203–15.

Rivenbark, W. H. (1971). Self-disclosure patterns among adolescents. *Psychological Reports, 28,* 35–42.

Sears, R. R., Maccoby, E. E., & Levin, H. (1957). *Patterns of child rearing.* Evanston, IL: Row Peterson.

Sears, R. R., Rau, L., & Alpert, R. (1965). *Identification and child rearing.* Stanford, CA: Stanford University Press.

Snarey, J. R. (1985). Cross-cultural universality of social-moral development: A critical review of Kohlbergian research. *Psychological Bulletin, 97,* 202–31.

Sullivan, H. S. (1953). *The interpersonal theory of psychiatry.* New York: Horton.

Youniss, J. (1980). *Parents and peers in social development: A Sullivan-Piaget perspective.* Chicago: University of Chicago Press.

Zahn-Waxler, C., Kochanska, G., Krupnick, J., & McKnew, D. (1990). Patterns of guilt in children of depressed and well mothers. *Developmental Psychology, 26,* 51–9.

8 Parental influences on children's willingness to disclose

Beverly I. Fagot, Karen Luks, and Jovonna Poe

Victimization during childhood is unfortunately not an uncommon event. Children become prey both to family members and to strangers, and to some extent the long-term damage resulting from either sexual or physical abuse appears to be mediated by the feelings of betrayal engendered by the abuse. Abuse by a close family member is the ultimate betrayal and places the child most at risk for keeping the acts a secret (Freyd, 1991). Children who feel they have no one to tell or who are not believed show longer-term, more serious reactions. In their review of the impact of child sex abuse, Browne and Finkelhor (1986) report that the more severely disturbed children had parents who reacted negatively to the children's attempts to disclose. A child's ability to disclose intimate information to a parent is embedded in the larger context of the child's willingness to communicate information about his or her life to the parent. In turn, the ability of the parent to keep communication lines open and to gather information is an important family management skill. But there is suprisingly little research on how parental behaviors affect children's communication.

Communication has been studied mostly in the realm of cognitive development, and the study of the development of cognitive capabilities has been concerned with the origins of intellectual functioning. For many theorists, notably Piaget, cognitive processes emerge in response to pressing internal demands to make sense of the world that surrounds us. But research findings have made it increasingly apparent that the content and processes of cognitive development are strongly influenced by social forces as well. How the child's early practical actions integrate with and are affected by these social forces is a central question when trying to understand effective parenting.

Vygotsky's (1978) concern with creating a psychology that includes the social origins and influences on human cognitive functioning has provided a rich template for addressing this question. For Vygotsky, the social world of

148

the child channels development. He emphasized that development occurs in situations where the child's problem solving is guided by an adult who structures and models ways to solve a problem. Adults can arrange the environment so that children can reach a level beyond their present capabilities when working on their own. This is called "the zone of proximal development" or "distance between the actual developmental level as determined by independent problem solving under adult guidance or in collaboration with more capable peers" (Vygotsky, 1978, p. 86). The child's individual mental functioning develops through experience in the zone of proximal development. The structure provided in communication serves as a scaffold for learning, providing contact between old and new knowledge (Wood & Middleton, 1975). Thus, to understand development of the child's ability to communicate, we must attend to formal and informal instruction provided by the parents in the course of the child's daily activities. Considerable work has been done in this area, first by Sigel and Cocking (1977), who examined the effect of what they label "distancing techniques" on the child's competence. Distancing techniques within this model are cognitive strategies parents use to help a child understand and communicate about an issue or problem. They can range from the concrete (such as asking a child to label) to the abstract (such as synthesizing new structures for the child). More recently, Rogoff (1990) has applied Vygotsky's principles to adults' attempts to provide scaffolds for children's problem solving. Again, the techniques studied have been cognitive strategies to increase the child's understanding of the problem and to help the child move to a new level of thinking.

Too often, parenting studies examining the child's socialization and those on cognitive processing are reviewed separately. Most of the studies just reviewed have examined the cognitive skills of children, although all recognize that social skills and performance are equally important for school achievement and in predicting success beyond school. Socialization studies, which have investigated rather broad parenting skills and very molar child outcomes, show one consistent finding: Parenting behavior cannot be judged on one dimension. Studies on socialization usually come up with two broad factors, a warm versus cold dimension and a structure versus lack of structure dimension. These findings are not new: Sears, Maccoby, and Levin (1957) articulated this two-factor structure extremely well. Baumrind (1971) found that parents whom she termed *authoritative* (i.e., they exerted control when necessary but were warm and sensitive to the child's concerns) had children who were well adjusted and achievement oriented. Within these authoritative families, a dialog between parents and children is firmly established so that the child feels safe in bringing his or her needs and concerns to the parent. Certainly, most developmental psychologists are aware of these findings; yet research studies have too often concentrated on only one parenting dimension.

Finally, there has been some work on children's understanding of emotional states in relation to parenting variables. Saarni (1985) found that the emotional climate of the home was related to the child's emotional expression. Fuchs and Thelen (1988) found an age × sex interaction in children's ability to express anger versus sadness. Clearly, there are indications that both the climate of home and the cognitive and experiential experience of children will influence their ability to both process and express emotions. There has been little work on the parent's understanding of the child's emotional state, but it would seem that a parent must be able to understand the child's affect before he or she can begin to help the child understand emotional states.

There is evidence that in families where abuse takes place, the child is discouraged from attempts to communicate. A group of families under court-referred treatment for child abuse and a group of control families were observed in a family play task by Kavanagh, Youngblade, Reid, and Fagot (1988). Abusive parents responded less often to their children's attempts to talk than did nonabusive parents. In the observation code, when a parent failed to respond to a child's initiation, the interaction sequence was terminated; while if a parent responded positively, the interaction sequence continued. Interaction sequences in abusive families were much shorter than in the nonabusive families. Parents who fail to respond to children's attempt to communicate are in effect saying, "Don't bother me; what you have to say is not important." Even though most of the communications during the play task were nonthreatening, abusive parents were unwilling to listen. What must happen to a child in such a family when he or she attempts to convey some emotionally charged information? We would predict that parents in such families would quickly eliminate the possibility of disclosure.

Fagot, Loeber, and Reid (1988) presented evidence that aggressiveness among siblings is a training ground for aggressive behaviors toward others. When examining families whose children were aggressive toward one another, it appeared that parents rarely intervened to deal with the aggression and often rewarded aggression with positive responses. When a younger child was being abused by an older sibling, parents either ignored the behavior or actively took part in the abuse. Again, one would predict that a child in such a family who attempted to disclose problems would quickly be discouraged. Bugental (1985) hypothesized that the unresponsive child resulted from a transactional system in which adults expected themselves to be powerless and where the behavior of the child confirmed that powerlessness. She used child actors trained to react in responsive or unresponsive ways. Mothers who differed in their attributions of their own power did not differ when faced with a responsive child, but when the child was unresponsive, mothers who felt powerless were more negative and inconsistent. They were also more submissive, or as Bugental put it, they "leaked" their sense of helplessness through their voice tone and posture. Clearly, the mother's own attributions influenced her behavior and, in turn, the behavior directed toward the child. The types of behavior that we have seen in abusive and aggressive families suggest that two types of parental deficits can occur. First is the parent who is extremely power assertive or authoritarian (Baumrind, 1971), one who never attempts to establish two-way patterns of communication but commands and controls the child. The second type of parent is more similar to that described by Bugental, one who feels so powerless that he or she makes no attempt to interact with the child in an instructive way.

Attempts to increase parents' ability to read a child's feelings and gain information have been relatively rare. Hughes and Wilson (1988) compared a parent-training procedure in which parents were taught to manage either through contingency training or through better communication skills. Parents in the communication skills program reported higher rates of acceptance of the child's behavior than those in contingency training, but in general both training programs produced only marginal change. In this chapter, we will report on a pilot program designed to help parents increase their skills in interpreting the child's emotion and in gaining information from the child.

Patterson (1982) described dysfunctional families as having difficulty with several family management skills. One of these skills, monitoring, is described as the parent's ability to know about the child's world outside the family. Monitoring has been a difficult construct to study and has most often been defined by asking the parent to describe the child's friends or to say where the child was at specific times. These measures are the *outcome* of monitoring and teach us little about the *process* by which parents perform monitoring skills. Measured in this way, lack of monitoring is a strong predictor of adolescent problem behaviors (Patterson, Reid, & Dishion, 1992) but does not predict behavior problems in younger children.

Clearly, monitoring is a multidimensional skill, one aspect of which is the ability of the parent to obtain information from the child. Anyone who has tried to question young children about their school day knows how difficult this task can be; however, it is important for parents to know how children are doing in school, who their friends are, and how the they spend free time. Also important, and not always mentioned when discussing family management, is the parent's ability to know what the child is feeling about the events in his or her world. It may be that the parent's ability to understand a child's feeling is the first step in establishing good communication patterns.

The communication task

The communication task presented in this study was developed to examine individual differences in parents' ability to gain information and to communicate with their young children. By observing parents in a standardized laboratory setting, we hoped to discover which parental techniques were successful in encouraging a child to share information. The task takes about 10 minutes and requires only minimal equipment. First, the child plays a 5-minute game with a laboratory assistant. The game is one of two standard commercial products in which there are several pieces to describe. The mother or father stays in another room. The parent is instructed by a second experimenter that he or she will have 5 minutes to find out what the child has been doing and then will be asked to describe the game and the child's feelings about the game. The videotaped parent–child interaction was assessed in two ways: (a) The experimenter subjectively rated parent and child behaviors in the task; and (b) the parent and child were each coded from the videotaped session as on- or off-task with positive or negative valence.

The game and the parent–child interaction

First, the child plays a 5-minute game with an experimenter. In these studies we used commercial games, one called Silly Dilly, the other Dizzy Bee.

Silly Dilly. Silly Dilly is a somewhat active game during which the child picks up colored cardboard disks, using a Slinky-like object called a Silly Dilly. Silly Dilly has a green pickle head, with eyes and a yellow nose. Its head is connected to a green plastic bottom by a flexible plastic spring. The green bottom has three yellow suction cups that enable it to grasp the disks when it is thrust downwards. The participants each hold a Silly Dilly by the head and aim the bottom portion at the disks, which are spread out on the floor. The disks, which are red, yellow, and blue, have big pickle people wearing funny hats on one side. This is the side that faces the participants. On the underside of each disk is a number (1, 2, 3, or 5) and the corresponding amount of little pickle people. The object of the game is to acquire the most points by picking up the disks with the Silly Dilly. Both players play at the same time.

Dizzy Bee. Dizzy Bee is a board game involving a plastic beehive and a wind-up bee. The square board has a pathway of individual flowers that lead from the "Start" to "Home" in a circular route around the beehive. Each player has three honey pots that he or she moves in this pattern. Playing cards with pictures and numbers are used to determine how many flowers to move in a turn. The players take turns moving their honey pots. In the middle of the board lies a yellow beehive with a winder on the top. On a wire connected to the winder sits a yellow and black bee with shiny gold wings. The winner is the first one who gets all of his or her honey pots around the board to Home. The winner then has the privilege of winding up Dizzy Bee and letting it fly a victory lap around the hive.

Parent's instructions. The mother/father stays in another room. The parent is told by a second experimenter that he or she will have 5 minutes to find out what the child had been doing and then will be asked to describe the game and the child's feelings about the game. The procedure for both the child and parent is presented in detail in Table 8.1.

The assessment of communication

Parent–child communication was assessed in two ways: (a) ratings by the experimenter as he or she watched the parent–child interaction and (b) codings of the videotaped 5-minute parent–child interaction by coders unfamiliar with the rest of the family's assessment.

Experimenter ratings. The experimenters were involved in assessing the parents and children in several different tasks. They watched the ongoing interaction live on a video monitor. We were interested in the experimenter's impressions of how supportive the parent was, of the parent's skill in gathering information, and of any threats and directions by the parent. In addition, as the behavior of the child can certainly influence the parent's effectiveness, the experimenter rated the child on positive and negative behaviors (see Table 8.2).

The microsocial coding system. The videotaped parent–child interaction was coded using a relatively simple system. Each 5-minute task was divided into ten 30-second segments. Each segment was coded for both the parent and the child.

Table 8.1. *Procedure for communication task: Silly Dilly game*

1. The specific game to be played will be assigned for each lab visit (see Lab Task Assignment Sheet).
2. Be sure that parent does not see the game box or game components. Seat parent in experiment room, child in game room.

GAME 1: "SILLY DILLY"

Materials

Game box with the following contents: two spring-bodied Silly Dillies, disks, timer. (Do not videotape game play.)

Instructor

Say to child:

Here is a game I want to play with you. We'll play this game for five minutes. Then it will be time to go talk to your mom/dad again. I'll be setting the timer so we'll know when 5 minutes are up.

Do not set timer yet. Open game box and begin setting up game. Point out the game components in the following order:
1. The name of this game is Silly Dilly.
2. This is the Silly Dilly. See, it has a green pickle head and an orange spring body like a Slinky.
3. On the bottom there are three suction cups that can pick up these disks.
4. The disks have funny pickles on one side and numbers for points on the other side.

Demonstrate play while explaining the following:

The idea of this game is to see who can pick up the funniest pickle disks with their Silly Dilly.

Give child a Silly Dilly. Set timer for 5 minutes; make the game mildly competitive, continue play, making sure that child wins. When timer rings, say:

You're the winner! Good game! Now it's time to go talk to your mom/dad. Thanks for playing the game with me.

Take child directly *into experiment room with parent. Instructor and experimenter exit. Monitor videotaping.*

Experimenter

While instructor and child are playing game, seat parent in experiment room. Five minutes before game is over, videotape the following instructions to parent:

Now it's time for the next part of the task. As a parent, sometimes you probably want to find out from [child's name] what he or she has been doing while away from you. This session is like one of those times. [Child] has been playing a game with [instructor's name] for the past five minutes. For the next five minutes, I want you to talk with [child] about the game they played. Ask him or her to describe it to you so that you could describe it to me later. Then find out how [child] felt about the game.

Child enters experiment room; experimenter exits. Continue to videotape through end of task.

Table 8.1 (*cont.*)

Experimenter/instructor

Five minutes after experimenter leaves experiment room, both instructor and experimenter reenter. Instructor says to child:

You and I will wait in the other room while [experimenter's name] and your dad/mom talk for a few minutes.

Instructor and child exit. Experimenter says to parent:

Tell me as much as you can about the game that [child] and [instructor] played together.

Let parent explain; do not prompt until parent is finished. Then ask:

Is there anything else that you can tell me about it?

Instructor times 5 minutes; knocks on experiment room door; turns off camera. Experimenter fills out impressions sheet.

The parent was coded according to the content and affect displayed in the segment. He or she achieved a rating of either on-topic (positive or nonpositive valence) or off-topic (positive or nonpositive valence). The child was coded on the content and the accuracy of his or her description and was scored either on-topic (accurate or inaccurate) or off-topic.

In addition, coders completed ratings of both the parent and the child task behaviors. A 5-point scale was used to rate how well the parent described the game. The coder also recorded whether the parent reported how the child felt about the game. For the child, a 5-point scale was used to determine how well he or she cooperated with the parent and his or her mood during the discussion.

Students from the University of Oregon were trained as coders. Initially, the students became familiar with the task by observing the parent–child interactions and by carefully examining the games. It was crucial for the coders to know the precise terminology used when describing the games to the children. This enabled them to judge whether the child was accurate or inaccurate in his or her description.

Decision rules and guidelines were implemented to minimize discrepancies. For example, if at any time during a 30-second segment the parent was nonpositive, then he or she was coded nonpositive for that entire segment. Similarly, if a child was inaccurate at any time during the segment, then he or she was coded inaccurate. A 3-second rule was employed to determine whether the parent was on-topic or off-topic during a segment. To code a parent off-topic, he or she had to be off-topic for at least 3 seconds during the segment.

For a coder to be reliable, he or she needed to achieve and maintain 70%

Table 8.2. *Experimenter impressions for the communication task*

Game played:	Silly Dilly	Dizzy Bee	Other				
Scale A	Always	Very often	Often	Sometimes	Occasionally	Hardly ever	Never
	1	2	3	4	5	6	7
Scale B	Very (well)			Somewhat		Not at all	
	1	2	3	4	5	6	7

Parent

Was the parent (use scale A for 1–7)
1. Able to keep the child involved in the interaction?
2. Supportive of the child's efforts?
3. Intrusive (interrupting child) in the child's efforts?
4. Asking yes or no questions?
5. Paraphrasing child to check out information?
6. Reframing to check out information?
7. Trying to get a full understanding of the game (probing for his or her own understanding)?
8. Was the child frustrated? 1 = Yes; 0 = No
    a. (If yes) How well did the parent handle the child's frustration (use scale B)?
9. Did the parent ask how the child felt about the game? 1 = Yes; 0 = No
10. How sensitive was the parent (use scale B)?

Child

At the beginning of the session (use scale B for 11–14)
11. Did the child seem to feel well physically?
12. Did the child seem upset about anything?
13. How well did the child describe the toy?
14. How well did the child describe the game?

Was the child (use scale A for 15–21)
15. Involved in the interaction?
16. Directive to the parent? ("Now listen, Mom.")
17. Needing parent's prompting to describe the toy or game?
18. Cooperative with parental questioning?
19. Having fun?
20. Focused on him- or herself (how he or she won as opposed to giving information about the game)?
21. Physically active during the session (use scale B for 22–23)?
22. Likeable?
23. Getting along with the parent?

At the end of the session
24. Did the child seem tired? 1 = Yes; 0 = No

agreement with other reliable coders. During training, reliabilities were checked on at least 50% of the videotapes. Once the coders were reliable, they were randomly checked on 30% of the tapes.

Study 1

Study 1 was a pilot study in which 20 mothers and their 5-year-old children (half boys and half girls) participated. In this study, we were attempting to determine if there were individual differences in parents' ability to gain information from children and if different parental styles were related to how much information was gained.

Subjects

Twenty 5-year-old children, 10 boys and 10 girls, came to the laboratory with their mothers. All were younger siblings of children who had participated in a longitudinal study. In the initial longitudinal study, the majority (83%) of parents were in their first marriages, and 92% of the target children lived with both biological parents. The majority of families had two or more children (e.g., 16% had one child; 49% had two children). Subject families had a median gross income in 1986 of $21,000, placing them below the local median of $28,400 for a family of four (Lane Council of Governments, personal communication, 1987). The parents' mean educational level was some college. Only two of the parents had not completed high school. Approximately half of both the mothers and the fathers were working in unskilled and semiskilled occupations, the other half in skilled and professional occupations. The ethnic background of the children and parents was representative of the area (i.e., 93% of the sample was Caucasian). The families of the children who came in for this task did not differ from the total population in any way.

Results

Experimenter's impressions. The experimenter rated the parent–child interaction on an experimenter's impressions sheet as the task was happening. Three parent composites were created: *parent support* (able to keep child involved, supportive of child's efforts), *parent informational strategy* (asks yes and no questions, paraphrases, reframes, tries to get a full understanding of task, asks how child felt about game), and *parent intrusive insensitive* behavior (interrupts child, unable to handle child's frustration, lack of sensitivity). Three child composites were also created: *child positive, child informative,* and *child inattentive.*

Mothers who were rated as supportive and able to keep the child engaged had children who were cooperative and involved in the interaction ($r(19) = .66, p < .01$). Mothers who were rated as intrusive and insensitive had children who were more physically active and needed more prompting to go on with the interaction ($r(19) = .49, p < .01$). Mothers who used a more informational approach were able to describe the game more accurately after the interaction was complete ($r(19) = .78, p < .001$).

Coding the parent–child interaction. The videotaped parent–child interaction about describing the game was coded using a simple system consisting of ratings of being on-task (positive or negative valence) or off-task (positive or negative valence). The mother and the child were coded separately. In addition, the coder used a 7-point scale to rate how well the parent described the game and also the child's reactions to the game. Mothers' positive on-task behavior correlated with how accurately they described the game ($r(19) = .89, p < .001$) but was unrelated to the accuracy of their description of the child's feelings about the game. The child's negative-valence behaviors during the game were negatively related to the mother's ability to describe the game ($r(19) = -.51, p < .01$). Interestingly, there was no relation between the mother's positive on-task behaviors and the child's negative behaviors. One difficulty with the game was that all children were excited and pleased with their performance, so that there was a ceiling effect on mothers' ratings of the children's reaction to the game.

Discussion

This is a promising approach to the study of communication ability, a facet of parent monitoring that has been difficult to measure in the past. If parents wish to be successful in obtaining information from their children, they must do more than provide a positive situation. Mothers who were consistently positive but allowed the interaction to go off-task were not successful in describing the game the children had just completed. Mothers needed to take an active role in structuring the interaction if they wanted to obtain an adequate description of the game from the children. They needed to probe for information and to help the children by reframing and paraphrasing. It was equally important, however, for the interaction to remain positive; mothers who use negative management skills, such as interrupting, had children who became increasingly negative during the session. Once a child began to whine or complain, the mother was unable to obtain more information about the task.

Study 2

This communication task is now being used as part of a large-scale cross-sectional project to study parental contributions to the development of social competence in young children. In this study, both mothers and fathers participated with boys and girls aged 3, 5, and 7. We were interested in comparing the performance of mothers and fathers in the task as well as assessing different strategies used with boys and girls. We found in Study 1 that children who were more active and needed more prompting had mothers who were more directive and intrusive; therefore, we were interested in examining temperament ratings of the children to see if there was a relation between these ratings and parenting style in the laboratory session.

Method

Subjects. The subjects in this study were 130 children split approximately equally between boys and girls, ages 3, 5, and 7, and their parents.

Assessments. The communication task, ratings, and codes remained the same as in Study 1.

Results

Reliability of the composites from the communication task. The composites from the experimenter ratings for Study 1 were derived rationally; there were not enough children in that study to determine the reliability. Each of the parent composites (support, informational strategy, and intrusive insensitive) and each of the three child composites (positive, informative, and inattentive) consisted of at least three items. Reliability was checked for each scale, and the Cronbach alpha in each case exceeded .80.

Experimenter's impressions. The first analyses were to determine if the correlational analyses from Study 1 were replicated in this larger, more diverse sample and to determine if the pattern of correlations for mothers and fathers were similar. Mothers who were supportive had children who were more positive ($r(130) = .59, p < .001$) and described the game better ($r(130)$ $= .38, p < .001$). Mothers who sought information had children who were more positive ($r(130) = .53, p < .001$) and who described the game better ($r(130) = .41, p < .001$). Mothers who were more directive and intrusive had children who were more active and frustrated ($r(130) = .16, p < .05$). The findings with fathers were very similar. Fathers who were supportive had children who were more positive in their interactions ($r(130) = .64, p < .001$) and described the game better ($r(130) = .46, p < .001$). Fathers who sought information had children who were more positive ($r(130) = .54, p < .001$) and described the game better ($r(130) = .42, p < .001$). Fathers who were more directive and intrusive had children who were more negative and inattentive ($r(130) = .21, p < .05$).

The next set of analyses examined differences in mothers' and fathers' reactions toward boys and girls of three different ages (3, 5, 7) and child differences with their mother and father. Three-way ANOVAs (with parent as a repeated measure, and sex of child and age as between factors) were run on each of the child and parent composites. On the child informative construct, there was a significant age effect, with 3-year-olds being less able than 5-year-olds, who were less able than 7-year-olds. In addition, 3-year-olds were less positive and more negative than either 5- or 7-year olds. There were very few significant findings on the parent measures. Mothers and fathers did not differ in amount of support, information seeking, or intrusiveness. The only significant finding was that parents were more intrusive in interactions with boys than with girls; there were no differences in parent supportiveness or information seeking toward boys and girls. Parents did not appear to modify their styles a great deal for the age of the child, even though there were very great differences in the ways that 3-, 5-, and 7-year-olds responded to the task.

In the next set of analyses, regression equations were run to determine if there were differences in the styles of mothers and fathers toward boys and girls. The child's ability to describe and remain involved with the task (child informative construct) was used as the dependent variable, and the three parent constructs were used as independent variables. Each of the regression equations was significant; however, different parent variables were important for the performance of boys and girls. For girls, the only variable significantly contributing to the ability to describe and stay involved with the task was parent support, and this was true for both mothers and fathers. For boys, parent information seeking contributed significantly to predicting the child's performance with both mothers and fathers. In addition, the mother's lack of negative affect contributed significantly to the boy's information giving.

Coding the parent–child interaction. We used the same interaction code described in Study 1. This is a simple system consisting of being rated as on-task (positive or negative valence) or off-task (positive or negative valence). The parent and the child were coded separately. In addition, coders used a 7-point scale to rate how well the parent described the game and whether the parent could describe the child's reactions to the game. There were no significant differences between the mothers' and fathers' behaviors on this code. In other words, they had an equal number of on- and off-task behaviors and an equal number of positives and negatives. This was also true for boys and girls. There were significant age differences, with 3-year-olds being off-task and negative far more often than 5- and 7-year-olds.

The coded data supported the findings from the experimenter's impressions and replicated the findings from the smaller Study 1. However, due to the increased sample size, many of the findings that did not reach significance in Study 1 were significant in this study. Mothers' and fathers' positive on-task behavior was significantly correlated with how accurately they described both the game and the children's feelings about the game. Negative behaviors on the part of the mother or father, whether on- or off-task, were highly related to negative behaviors on the part of the child, but were also related to the child withdrawing from the interaction and producing no behaviors. The child's negative-valence behaviors during the interaction were negatively related to the mother's and father's ability to describe both the game and how the child felt about the game. Mothers and fathers did not differ in their ability to describe the task or the children's feelings. In general, positive reactions on the part of the parent facilitated the child's performance, while negative reactions either increased negative behaviors on the part of the child or increased the incidence of the child failing to respond. In addition, parents who failed to stay on-task had children who failed to stay on-task; these parents were very poor at describing the game and the child's feeling about the game. Parents, then, have two jobs in this task: They need to stay positive and help the child stay on-task in describing the game.

Study 3

One test of whether the parents' behaviors found in the laboratory studies contribute to their ability to communicate with the child is to determine if teaching the parent these skills improves the level of communication. In Study 3, 19 mothers and their first-grade children took part in an intervention program designed to prevent oppositional problems and academic failure in the classroom.

Method

Mothers and children participated in the communication task both before
and after an intervention designed to enhance parenting skills. Parents
met for approximately 9 hours over a 6-week period and discussed issues
dealing with parenting, promoting school adjustment for children, enhancing child self-esteem, and getting involved with their children's activities
and friends. The children's intervention took place in their classrooms.
Approximately three times a week, children had activities that included
learning to get along with teachers and peers at school, making new
friends, and improving study habits. Mothers and children participated
again in the communication task during the post-assessment, using a second game.

The videotaped interactions were not coded using the communication
code, but raters examined the parent–child interaction using a lab task
impressions sheet. Mothers were coded using the same three composites
that were used in Study 1: parent support, parent informational strategy,
and parent intrusive/insensitive behavior. The child composites were also
identical. In addition, a checklist was used to score the child's description
of the game to the parent and the parent's description of the game to the
experimenter. The raters checked yes or no for the accuracy of reporting
for each element of the game.

Results

Mothers showed significant improvement on support and informational
strategy composites from Time 1 to Time 2 ($t(15) = 3.35, p < .01$). However, most dramatic was the decrease of intrusive/insensitive negative
strategies ($t(15) = 6.21, p < .001$). Mothers also did a better job of describing the game after the parent education program, although this may have
simply been a practice effect. In addition, the child's cooperation with the
parent increased from Time 1 to Time 2. The fact that mothers decreased
their negative questioning and increased both positive support and information seeking is an important confirmation that skills to increase parent–
child communication can be taught.

Discussion

Taken together, the three studies present strong evidence that children's
willingness to communicate information to a parent is dependent on the
parent's behavior. While the communication task deals with information

that is not at all threatening to either the child or the parent, some parents use strategies that very quickly shut down the child's attempts to give information. If such parent behaviors are repeated over and over in everyday situations, one would expect that children will quickly give up. Parents who shut down communication attempts by the child in benign situations certainly will not be seen as a resource by their child in highly emotional situations.

Parents who use negative, intrusive techniques in trying to obtain information from children not only fail to gain information about the situation and their child's behavior; they also fail to read the child's emotional state correctly. We are not surprised that this coercive style (Patterson, 1982) results in a breakdown of communication. However, there is another type of parent who also fails to read correctly his or her child's emotional state as well as to gain information. Recent work in attachment theory has suggested that when such behaviors occur in preschoolers, the parents might best be called *defended,* in that they inhibit communication and affect by the use of avoidance, caregiving, or compliance (Crittenden, Partridge, & Claussen, 1991). Certainly, we see all three of these behaviors in parents who fail to engage their children: Some actively avoid communication by filling out questionnaires or reading the paper, others avoid by picking children up and hugging them or fiddling with their clothes, and others simply agree to switch to children's preferred scripts rather than attempting to keep them on task. We can hypothesize that in such families both parents and children defend against disclosure, resulting in a family system where little emotional interchange takes place and where communication is kept to a minimum.

Disclosure is a product of the level of parent–child involvement and the facilitating behaviors that parents use with children. The results highlight the relation of parent behavior to child information giving. Our studies suggest that there may be different parent behaviors and effective dimensions that facilitate communication for boys versus girls. For boys, information-seeking parental behaviors and the absence of negative affect by mothers were the best predictors of boys' ability to give information. These results make sense in terms of previous findings of the relation between maternal irritability and boys' problem behaviors (Snyder, 1991). Negative affect by mothers is more likely to lead to negative acting-out behavior and create a climate that is not conducive to sharing information. This negative affect can be seen as a barrier to perceiving the mother as a resource. Parents' supportive behaviors were predictive of girls' success in giving information. Again, this follows from preliminary work with older girls showing that positive parent–child interactions are negatively related to reported problem behaviors (Kavanagh & Ray, 1991). The socializing mechanisms for girls compared with boys revolve around supportive and nurturing behaviors. It follows that these same behaviors are intrinsic to the sharing of information.

As suggested in the introduction, it appears that both negative controlling behaviors and lack of input by the parent influence the child's performance. In that sense we have confirmed the findings from the Patterson model, where coercive parents were found to be poor monitors of their children's behavior because their own negative behavior, in effect, shuts the child down. However, we have also confirmed Bugental's findings that parents who make no attempt to influence children will end up powerless, with children who do not give them feedback either about how they are feeling or what they are doing.

The findings from the pilot intervention study strongly suggest that communication can be taught to parents. Mothers improved their skills as a function of participation in a 6-week training program. Listening to children was a specific lesson, and the importance of using positive information-seeking strategies rather than directive and intrusive strategies was emphasized. The communication task itself could be used as a teaching paradigm as well as an assessment procedure. Skills are best practiced with a nonthreatening task, and the paradigm used in this study could be used as a starting point for teaching communication skills.

Parents can offer children practice in information sharing. If time is set aside daily for children and parents to talk together, this will become a habit. If giving information is a daily routine, children will be more likely to use parents as a resource when they are having difficulties or have sensitive information to share. Parent–child communication becomes complex when the information is negative and involves a family member. The ability to disclose difficult information is enhanced if the child has learned in the past that information is respected and not discounted by the parent. A next step in this line of investigation would be to study parent strategies and child behaviors in tasks involving personal information rather than a neutral task.

Parents can be a child's best resource in avoiding problems of victimization. For parents to be effective resources, children need daily opportunities to give information about their lives within and outside the family from their own perspectives. Using strategies that have been found to encourage rather than discourage the children's efforts will increase the likelihood that attempts to communicate will be maximally successful for both parents and children.

References

Baumrind, D. (1971). Current patterns of parental authority. *Developmental Psychology Monographs, 4*(Pt. 2).

Browne, A., & Finkelhor D. (1986). Impact of child sexual abuse: A review of the research. *Psychological Bulletin, 99,* 66–77.

Bugental, D. B. (1985). Unresponsive children and powerless adults. In M. Lewis & C. Saarni (Eds.), *The socialization of emotions* (pp. 239–61). New York: Plenum.

Crittenden, P. M., Partridge, M. F., & Claussen, A. H. (1991). Family patterns of relationship in normative and dysfunctional families. *Development and Psychopathology, 3,* 491–512.

Fagot, B. I., Loeber, R., & Reid, J. B. (1988). Developmental determinants of male-to-female aggression. In G. W. Russsell (Ed.), *Violence in intimate relationships* (pp. 91–105). New York: PMA.

Freyd, J. J. (1991, August). *Memory repression, dissociative states, and other cognitive control processes involved in adult sequelae of childhood trauma.* Paper presented at the Second Annual Conference on a Psychodynamics–Cognitive Science Interface, University of California, San Francisco.

Fuchs, D., & Thelen, M. H. (1988). Children's expected interpersonal consequences of communicating their effective state and reported likelihood of expression. *Child Development, 59,* 1314–22.

Hughes, R.C., & Wilson, P. H. (1988). Behavioral parent training: Contingency management versus communication skills training with or without the participation of the child. *Child and Family Behavior Therapy, 10,* 11–23.

Kavanagh, K. A., & Ray, J. (1991, June). *Differential profiles of pre-adolescents at risk for drug abuse.* Paper presented at the Third Biennial Conference on Community Research and Action, Tempe, AZ.

Kavanagh, K. A., Youngblade, C., Reid, J. B., & Fagot, B. I. (1988). Interactions between abuse versus control parents and children. *Journal of Clinical Child Psychology, 17,* 137–42.

Patterson, G. R. (1982). *Coercive family process.* Eugene, OR: Castalia.

Patterson, G. R., Reid, J. B., & Dishion, T. J. (1992). *Antisocial boys.* Eugene, OR: Castalia.

Rogoff, B. (1990). *Apprenticeship in thinking: Cognitive development in social context.* New York: Oxford University Press.

Saarni, C. (1985). Indirect processes in affect socialization. In M. Lewis & C. Saarni (Eds.), *The socialization of emotions* (pp. 187–209). New York: Plenum.

Sears, R. R., Maccoby, E. E., & Levin, H. (1957). *Patterns of childrearing.* Evanston, IL: Row Peterson.

Sigel, I. E., & Cocking, R. R. (1977). *Cognitive development from childhood to adolescence: A constructivist perspective.* New York: Holt, Rinehart, & Winston.

Snyder, J. (1991). Discipline as a mediator of the impact of maternal stress and mood on child conduct problems. *Development and Psychopathology, 3,* 263–76.

Vygotsky, L. S. (1978). *The mind in society: The development of higher psychological processes.* Cambridge, MA: Harvard University Press.

Wood, D., & Middleton, D. (1975). A study of assessed problem solving. *British Journal of Psychology, 66,* 181–91.

9 Disclosure processes: issues for child sexual abuse victims

Kay Bussey and Elizabeth J. Grimbeek

The definition of child abuse has only recently been extended to include sexual abuse (Burgess, Groth, Holstrom, & Sgroi, 1978; Finkelhor, 1979; Herman, 1981). The pioneering work of Kempe and colleagues (Kempe, Silverman, Steele, Droegemueller, & Silver, 1962) directed the attention of both the public and professionals to severe physical abuse in their description of the battered child syndrome. It is not acknowledged that not only are a substantial number of children victim to physical abuse, but a substantial number are also victim to sexual abuse.

There are many ways in which child sexual abuse differs from physical abuse, but probably the most significant difference lies in the lack of visible external scars to corroborate its occurrence. Consequently, the substantiation of sexual abuse becomes a question of who is believed: the alleged perpetrator, who more often than not denies the abuse, or the child victim, who alleges it. Further, in contrast to physical abuse cases, which are mostly heard in children's courts, sexual abuse cases, at least in North America, England, Australia, and New Zealand, are usually dealt with in criminal courts. The alleged perpetrator of sexual abuse is charged with a criminal offense and the child victim is often required to testify in a criminal court.

Because there is rarely a witness to sexual abuse and very often no physical evidence, the case therefore is a trial of the child victim's word against the adult perpetrator's word. It is thus not surprising that an issue of major concern for child sexual abuse investigators is the reliability and credibility of children's disclosure of sexual abuse, particularly in the legal setting. In this context, one of the most researched issues has been children's memorial skills vis-à-vis their competence to serve as witnesses (Goodman & Reed, 1986; Goodman, Rudy, Bottoms, & Aman, 1990; Rudy & Goodman, 1991). This attention has been correctly placed since

166

children have incurred challenges to their competency to testify in law courts that have not been paralleled by challenges to adult witnesses.

Competence to testify in a court of law, however, does not mean that children will necessarily disclose their experience in that context. The questioning of children's competence to disclose their abusive experiences and credibility of their disclosures when they do so may relate as much to motivational and emotional factors as to children's cognitive abilities. These factors may dramatically reduce children's ability to accurately, completely, and truthfully disclose an incident in which they have been the victim. In this context it is worth noting that adult victims of rape, whose cognitive competence is not at issue, also have great difficulty in disclosing their own sexual victimization and in being believed (Burgess & Holmstrom, 1974). Even the credibility of Freud's theory of personality development, predicated on the widespread sexual abuse of his female patients, was challenged (Masson, 1984; Lerman, 1988). Masson (1984) has advanced an eloquent case to establish that Freud's renunciation of the seduction hypothesis was largely in response to the disbelief and criticisms he received for such views:

In 1895 and 1896 Freud, in listening to his women patients, learned that something dreadful and violent lay in the past. The psychiatrists who had heard these stories before Freud had accused their patients of being hysterical liars and had dismissed their memories as fantasy. Freud was the first psychiatrist who believed his patients were telling the truth. These women were sick, not because they came from "tainted" families, but because something terrible and secret had been done to them as children. (Masson, 1984, p. xviii)

Freud subsequently retracted these ideas (published in *The Aetiology of Hysteria*) in favor of the more "acceptable" view that the memories reported by his female patients were only fantasies. He advanced an explanation of the seductive and abusive scenes as part of the Oedipus complex, in which rather than the parent initiating sexual activity or violence against the child, the child fantasized him- or herself initiating sexual advances toward the parent.

The clinical literature has for some time acknowledged the difficulty that children experience in disclosing sexual abuse, but this has been mainly anecdotal (Sgroi, 1982; MacFarlane & Krebs, 1986). There has been little systematic research into children's disclosure difficulties even though these may contribute to their perceived lack of competence, such as being prone to lying, fantasy, and lack of confidence in recalling details of the abusive episode(s). This chapter aims to redress this neglect by focusing on the disclosure process.

Disclosure processes

Disclosure of information about the self can take different forms (verbal or nonverbal), be of different types (descriptive or evaluative), and serve many different functions [e.g., to express pent-up feelings (expression); to increase personal clarification about an issue (self-clarification); to validate a viewpoint socially (social validation); to facilitate close intimate relationships (relationship development); or to ingratiate oneself with others to gain their approval or make them feel more favorably about oneself (social control); see Perlman & Cozby, 1983]. Whatever the form, type, or function of disclosure, its purpose is to reveal information about the self to others. In context of sexual abuse, the form that disclosure takes would be expected to vary as a function of the age of the child. Younger children who are not aware of the norms regarding sexual activity may inadvertently disclose the abuse nonverbally in the form of sexual behavior learned from the episode (Finkelhor & Williams, 1988). Older children would, however, be expected to rely to a greater extent on verbal disclosure of the abuse and to regulate their disclosure by choosing to whom they disclose and in how much detail.

Disclosure of the abuse could be expected to serve a number of positive functions. Specifically, it could enable the expression of pent-up feelings (expression), clarification of the victim's involvement in the episode, particularly that they were not to blame (self-clarification), and validation that such activity is reprehensible and not normal or acceptable as they may have been informed by the abuser (social validation). This last function is most likely to be served in the court context when there is public apportionment of blame to the abuser and subsequent punishment for the crime. Disclosure of sexual abuse is unlikely to serve the functions of relationship development or social control – as outlined by Perlman and Cozby (1983). It could, however, serve an important additional function: stopping the abuse. While disclosure for the purpose of stopping the abuse would be mainly of a descriptive nature and would be the requirement in the legal context for the substantiation of the abuse, the evaluative aspects of disclosure (e.g., "I feel awful") may be more likely in supportive contexts (e.g., therapeutic and nonformal forensic investigation) and from older rather than younger children.

Despite the number of potentially positive functions that disclosure could serve, such as allowing the expression of pent-up emotions and enabling clarification by the victims that it was not their fault, it appears that children may be reluctant to disclose sexual abuse. Further, even when they do disclose, many regret such disclosure. This reluctance to disclose details about their sexual abuse may result not only from the personal and intimate nature of the abuse, but also because it is often embarrassing, humiliating, and terrifying. Additionally, unlike other information that they disclose, children are frequently threatened with dire consequences should they disclose information about the abuse. Therefore, it is hardly surprising that many children choose not to disclose sexual abuse and only acknowledge it in adulthood or reluctantly if it is suspected by others. Studies of adult survivors of child sexual abuse reveal that many children never reported the abuse when it was happening (Finkelhor, 1979; Herman, 1981).

Before examining the disclosure process in more detail to understand the particular difficulties associated with disclosure of sexual abuse by child victims, we first review the limited data on the children who do report sexual abuse, who they report it to, and the impact of this disclosure. Following this, we briefly examine Summit's (1983) stage model of the disclosure process and then outline the social cognitive theory model (Bandura, 1986). This latter theoretical perspective allows a dynamic interactive analysis of factors that are likely to affect disclosure and provides the explanatory framework in which the disclosure process is conceptualized in this chapter. Finally, this model is illustrated with research relevant to the disclosure of sexual abuse, from the initial report and forensic interview to disclosure within the court context.

Patterns of disclosure and its impact

Although there has been much research on the psychological impact of sexual abuse on children (see Browne & Finkelhor, 1986), there has been comparatively little research into the patterns of children's disclosure of sexual abuse and the psychological impact of such disclosure. Yet it is possible that some of the demonstrated effects of sexual abuse on children may be as much related to factors associated with the disclosure process as to the abuse (Berliner & Conte, 1990; Finkelhor, 1990). It is important to establish the effects of the disclosure process independent of the abusive episode if effective intervention strategies for facilitating disclosure are to be evaluated.

In one of the few studies that has investigated factors associated with the disclosure of sexual abuse, 156 children who had been referred to a program for sexually abused children were evaluated (Sauzier, 1989). The children were aged from infancy through 18 years. For these children, the abuse primarily occurred within the family (usually by a father or father figure), and the majority of the disclosures were either to a parent (usually a mother) or to a parent figure. This study showed that while just over 50% of children disclosed their abuse, almost 50% did not do so; rather, the abuse was suspected by others. Why were so many children unable or reluctant to disclose their abuse?

Three major factors associated with children's disclosure difficulty emerged from this study. The first factor involved the impact of the offender's methods for gaining the child's involvement in the abusive episode. Aggression was equally likely to lead to nondisclosure as to reporting the incident immediately, whereas both threats and coercion had the effect of inhibiting immediate disclosure. Second, characteristics of the abuse influenced disclosure. Although children who never disclosed the abuse themselves were represented in all categories of abuse, they were most concentrated in the extreme categories: the less serious (e.g., attempted sexual activity or nontouching abuse such as exhibitionism and voyeurism) and the most serious categories of abuse (e.g., sexual intercourse). Third, the relationship of the offender to the child also affected disclosure. Children were much less likely to disclose the abuse when the offender was their natural father, whereas they were much more likely to disclose the abuse immediately when the offender was a nonfamily member. The fact that so many children in this and other studies have been found to be abused by somebody that they know implies that disclosure will often be difficult and that many children will not voluntarily disclose their abuse.

Although it might be easier for children to disclose abuse involving a nonfamily than a family member, other studies indicate that young children are also reluctant to disclose abuse involving a nonfamily member. The increased incidence of sexual abuse in day care centers has led to greater attention to sexual abuse and its disclosure in this context (Finkelhor & Williams, 1988). "One of the most perplexing questions about day care sexual abuse has been how could it go undetected for so long. Why don't the children involved tell?" (Burns, Finkelhor, & Williams, 1988, p. 99). In their study of disclosure of sexual abuse involving children under 7 in day care contexts, Burns et al. (1988) showed that while 19% of all cases were disclosed on the same day as the abuse took place, 32% of the children took more than 6 months to disclose the abuse. The majority of the disclosures were made to parents or relatives (86%), and the remaining reports were made to day care staff or other professionals. In this age range, no child disclosed to their peers. For most children (63%), however, disclosure was prompted by an adult's suspicions of sexual abuse such as behavioral changes or physical symptoms shown by the child, or suspicions about the day care personnel. Other disclosures either happened spontaneously or were triggered by other events. For example, some children disclosed when they realized that they were about to return to the day care facility or when they felt safe (e.g., on vacation) and were away from the perpetrator. "Given that approximately 50% of the victims reported that they had been threatened with harm to themselves or their families if they told, it is not surprising that many children were afraid and waited until they felt secure that they [the perpetrator(s)] could not retaliate" (Burns et al., 1988, p. 104). Burns et al. found that whether children disclosed the abuse immediately after it occurred or took longer to disclose, disclosure was not associated with characteristics of the family.

Even when children do disclose the abuse, there is no guarantee that they will be believed. In Burns et al.'s (1988) study, 11% were not believed when they disclosed the abuse. In Sauzier's (1989) study, about one-fifth of the children's disclosures led to no intervention either out of disbelief or through parents simply deciding not to report it to the authorities. When intervention did occur, it often involved disruption to the family unit, which adversely affected all family members. "Most of the 19% of adolescents who regretted their disclosure wanted the abuse to stop but ended up feeling that they had destroyed their families. Their disclosure set into motion forces that they could not control any more than they could their abusers" (Sauzier, 1989, p. 468).

Conte and Berliner (1988) reported that the impact of sexual abuse was likely to be most negative when children feared negative self-consequences for disclosing the abuse and the offenders denied that it occurred. The disbelief and lack of support that children may experience at the time of disclosure have been found to contribute to the emotional disturbance experienced by such children. In comparison, children who received support and were believed by their mothers experienced less emotional disturbance (Adams-Tucker, 1982; Everson, Hunter, Runyan, Edelsohn, & Coulter, 1989). Conte and Schuerman (1987) also reported on the negative impact of the lack of a supportive relationship with either an adult or sibling. Level of maternal support has therefore been implicated as an important attenuator of the effects of disclosure of sexual abuse. Whether or not maternal support is forthcoming, however, has been found to be more closely related to the relationship of the mother to the perpetrator than to child characteristics (Everson et al., 1989). For example, mothers were more supportive of daughters if the disclosure implicated their ex-spouse rather than someone with whom they had a current relationship (Sirles & Franke, 1989).

Because of the difficulty in conducting controlled research on the impact of disclosure on child abuse victims, it is difficult to show conclusively from interview studies of abuse victims whether or not disclosure is beneficial to the victim. Sauzier, however, presents some preliminary findings on the psychological impact of disclosure. She concluded that while not disclosing the abuse may not always be traumatic for one-time abuse or nontouching abuse such as exhibitionism,

on the other hand, children who failed to reveal more serious abuse had the highest fear scores. They described the fear of losing the affection and goodwill of the offender; fear of the consequences of telling (being blamed or punished for the abuse by the non-offending parent); fear of being harmed; and fear of retaliation against someone in their family. (Sauzier, 1989, p. 460)

In contrast, anxiety and hostility scores were lower for children who did not disclose the abuse themselves than for children who did disclose. Sauzier (1989) suggests this indicates that children who did not disclose were not burdened by the added trauma associated with disclosure. More extensive research is required to clarify the impact of disclosure and which aspects of disclosure are troublesome.

Although further research on this topic is required, this does not mean that it is necessary to demonstrate the deleterious effects of abuse and/or its disclosure to justify researching and allocating resources to intervention programs. The view adopted in this chapter is that regardless of the impact of sexual abuse or the effects of disclosure on children, it is necessary to understand and facilitate the disclosure process so that the abuse stops. In most Western countries, sexual abuse is a crime and it is necessary that the crime be exposed. The effect of an armed robbery on a victim and the impact of disclosure on the victim are never debated to justify devoting resources to preventing robbery and facilitating the prosecution of the crime. It is proposed that a similar position be adopted with sexual abuse. In most cases, because of the lack of external signs of the abuse, the only person who can disclose it is the victim. Therefore, it is necessary to understand the disclosure process for two major reasons: first, so that children do not have to remain silent about the abuse and keep it secret, and second, so that disclosure can be facilitated in the least traumatic manner without simultaneously increasing false allegations. We begin a more detailed examination of the disclosure process by considering Summit's (1983) model.

Models of the disclosure process

One of the earliest and most comprehensive attempts to understand the difficulties that many children face in disclosing sexual abuse was advanced by Summit (1983). A child abuse accommodation syndrome, comprising five categories: (a) secrecy, (b) helplessness, (c) entrapment and accommodation, (d) delayed, conflicted, and unconvincing disclosure, and (e) retraction, was proposed. These categories were drawn from clinical accounts of the secondary trauma associated with reporting abuse, where children's allegations were typically disbelieved. Summit wrote:

Most parents are not prepared to believe their child in the face of convincing denials from a responsible adult. Since the majority of adults who molest children occupy a kinship or trusted relationship (Herman, 1981; Russell, 1983) the child is put on the defensive for attacking the credibility of the trusted adult, and for creating a crisis of loyalty which defies comfortable resolution. (Summit, 1983, p. 179)

While the syndrome has not been validated and not all sexually abused children pass through these stages, the reliance on this syndrome by many professionals has led to a greater readiness to take sexual abuse allegations seriously. A brief outline of the model follows.

The first category in this syndrome is *secrecy.* Many children are sworn to secrecy through a variety of means, from threats to bribes, and they often keep the secret to protect the offender or through fear of blame. The second category, *helplessness,* acknowledges children's limited power in relation to the authority exercised over them by adults. Many children do not resist the adult's advances because they do not have the skills and resources to do so. For many victims of abuse by a father, stepfather, or other live-in adult male,

The normal reaction is to "play possum," that is to feign sleep, to shift position and to pull up the covers. Small creatures simply do not call on force to deal with overwhelming threat. When there is no place to run, they have no choice but to try to hide. Children generally learn to cope silently with terrors in the night. Bed covers take on magical powers against monsters, but they are no match for human intruders. (Summit, 1983, p. 183)

Entrapment and accommodation relate particularly to children for whom abuse is an ongoing occurrence. In instances of abuse by parents, children have to deal with the abuse themselves and are told by the abuser that they must protect the other parent from knowing, protect their sibling(s) from being abused, or protect the family from disintegrating. Abusers try to impress upon their victims that "maintaining a lie to keep the secret is the ultimate virtue, while telling the truth would be the greatest sin" (Summit, 1983, p. 185). It is not surprising that many children who attempt to comply with such requests end up by deceiving themselves: The memory of the abuse is repressed. The various ways in which children attempt to cope with such situations is well documented (e.g., Rush, 1980; Blume, 1990). These coping mechanisms obviously have important implications for the long-term adjustment of the child. *Delayed, conflicted, and unconvincing disclosure* refers to the fact that many incidents of sexual abuse are not immediately reported to others within or outside the family (Herman,

1981; Russell, 1983). Children often take a long time to disclose abuse, and as a result their allegations are regarded as less convincing. The final category of the syndrome is *retraction.* Summit argues that unless there is support for the disclosure, and once children realize that they may be institutionalized, they frequently retract their allegation. Retraction clearly reduces the credibility of abused children.

Summit's (1983) model has been valuable in highlighting the many difficulties associated with disclosure of sexual abuse, particularly in instances of intrafamilial sexual abuse. However, although this model provided a sorely needed new perspective on an important issue, it lacks a theoretical base, and no quantitative data are offered in support of the syndrome.

More recently, Sorensen and Snow (1991) have partly redressed the data deficit by establishing a typical disclosure pattern of children who have been sexually abused. They retrospectively analyzed 116 cases, drawn from 630 cases of confirmed sexual abuse, and indeed found support for some of the stages in Summit's model. (The cases had been confirmed either by a confession or guilty plea from the offender, a conviction in a criminal court, or medical evidence consistent with sexual abuse.) Qualitative analysis of the clinical reports associated with these cases yielded a four-stage progressive disclosure process. In the first stage, *denial,* children deny that they have been sexually abused when suspicions of abuse have been raised and they are questioned about it. The second stage, *disclosure,* comprised two phases: tentative and then active disclosure. Tentative disclosure refers to children's partial or vacillating allegations of sexual abuse, while active disclosure refers to children's allegations that they have been sexually abused. *Recantation* was proposed as the third stage in the disclosure process. Here children retract an earlier allegation of sexual abuse. In the final stage of this process, *reaffirmation,* children acknowledge that sexual abuse has occurred despite their previous recantation. In Sorensen and Snow's (1991) sample, 72% of the children initally denied being sexually abused when it was suspected and they were questioned about it. Most of the children (78%) then moved to the middle ground of first tentatively, then actively, disclosing the abuse. Approximately 22% of children then recanted their allegations of sexual abuse. Finally, 92% of these children reaffirmed their allegations.

The study by Sorensen and Snow (1991) is extremely valuable in drawing attention to the difficulty that children experience in disclosing sexual abuse and, consistent with Summit's (1983) accommodation syndrome, highlights the frequent occurrence of retractions. The finding that most children finally confirmed that sexual abuse had occurred underscores the fact that their disclosure of sexual abuse, often tentative, then active, should not be discounted, even if they vacillate about the allegation before the case goes to court. Further, it emphasizes the difficulty in conducting forensic interviews with children about sexual abuse and the need to maintain confidence in the earlier disclosures of children who later recant.

Although these two models of the disclosure process are very helpful, obviously not all children pass through a staged disclosure process, and there is no way to determine which children are likely to recant, then reaffirm their statement, and which children are not. For this reason it would seem necessary to isolate those factors that inhibit children from disclosing abuse and undermine their confidence or willingness to sustain an allegation. Identifying such factors would also facilitate less traumatic, more accurate, and truthful disclosure. Tentative disclosure and retraction make it doubly hard to determine the veracity of children's statements. The next section examines an alternative model of the disclosure process.

A social cognitive model of the disclosure process

Social cognitive theory posits a dynamic interactional model in which disclosure is multidetermined (Bandura, 1986, 1989). A major goal of this model is to provide a basis for intervention after abuse is suspected or after an allegation has been made to facilitate disclosure. It pays attention not only to children's cognitive abilities, but also to social and motivational factors that may affect disclosure (Bandura, 1965).

For children to disclose sexual abuse, they need to have an adequate memory of the events that took place and the necessary skills to communicate details of those events. Simply having these skills does not, however, guarantee that disclosure will occur. Therefore, abuse may not be disclosed because (a) the child is not capable of disclosing it because of either a memory deficit (encoding, storage, or retrieval deficit) or lack of verbal or motor skills for reporting it, or (b) the child elects not to disclose it, actively or by omission. Although the major issue addressed in this chapter, *motivational processes* associated with disclosure, relates to elective nondisclosure, the processes associated with the capacity to disclose the abuse effectively are briefly outlined. These include *attentional, retention,* and *production processes.*

These four component processes were initially proposed by Bandura (1962, 1969, 1986) to explain children's observational learning as bystanders. In sexual abuse cases, however, victims are required to report on a perpetrator's behavior in situations where they typically have been party to the activities. Bandura's observational learning model readily lends itself to the inclusion of participant-observations since there is no reason to believe that processes involved in observational learning would change with observer status. Rather, it is hypothesized that participation would influence the degree to which each of the processes was implicated in observational learning in the same way that the content of the observed event influences the engagement of these processes. For example, the more interesting the observed event, the more the child could be expected to attend to it. Similarly, if participant-observers are more involved in an event than bystander-observers, they may attend more closely to it and spontaneously rehearse it more. However, if bystander-observers need to observe an event to be able to perform it later, they may learn as much about the event as participant-observers. Consequently, degree of involvement and interest in the event may be better predictors of the degree of learning about an event than the status of the observer as bystander or participant (Rudy & Goodman, 1991). It could be that in most situations participant-observers would be more involved in the event than bystander-observers. It is important to note, however, that although increased attention to and rehearsal of the event will facilitate the child's ability to report it, motivational processes will determine whether it is reported or not.

Attentional processes

A number of factors determine what children learn through observation. The modeled activities themselves and the capabilities of the observer are of paramount importance. Abusive episodes could be expected to be salient, affectively charged, relatively simple action sequences that would capture the attention of the child. Many of the events that occur in an abusive encounter would not be expected to overtax the observational capabilities of even young children.

Events are likely to captivate attention the more they engage the observer (Ochsner & Zaragoza, 1988) and the more emotive and personally significant they are to the observer (Keenan & Baillet, 1980; Linton, 1982; Bohannon, 1988). The first requirement is therefore that the abuse is attended to. It would be expected that these events would be emotionally arousing and highly self-relevant. Hence, it is likely that young children's attention would be more focused on this activity than is the case in laboratory studies that are less salient to children. It is possible that less severe forms of abuse such as exhibitionism may harness less of children's attention. Of course, how children interpret the sexual abuse may affect their attentional processes. For example, young children whose knowledge of sexuality is limited may attend to the event differently depending on whether they know that such activity is taboo or not. Even if they are not distressed about sexual activity initially, should they try to stop it later and find they are powerless to do so, their very lack of control may lead to heightened affect and stress. Stress could potentially affect children's attention to the events and hence their ability to accurately report information.

Research has addressed how much children learn during stressful events. While some studies have supported the view that stress has a positive effect on children's memory, other findings have supported the Yerkes–Dodson law (Yerkes & Dodson, 1908) and Easterbrook's extension (1959), which predict adverse effects on memory when there is too much or too little stress; moderate levels of stress are expected to be associated with increased memory performance. Baddeley (1982) has attempted to resolve this by suggesting that high levels of stress may narrow attention, resulting in the more salient elements being better remembered than the less salient elements in the situation.

Goodman and colleagues (Goodman et al., 1990) have also studied children's memory in stressful conditions personally significant to the children. When children aged 3 and 6 years were interviewed after a long delay about routine inoculations received in a medical clinic, the higher their stress level, the more they recalled. Highly stressed children were particularly accurate in their recall of what happened to them (the needle, the bandage, etc.); however, they were less accurate in their identification of the person giving the needle than were the less stressed children. Other studies report the detrimental effects of stress on memory (Peters, 1991), and yet others find little impact of stress on memory (Goodman, Bottoms, Schwartz-Kenney, & Rudy, 1991). Clearly, the relationship between stress and memory is complex.

Certainly, young children's observational capacities would set limits to what they learn about an abusive episode. However, particular details of the abusive experience may facilitate or undermine children's memory for the experience. For example, repeated exposure usually leads to greater memory of the event (Fivush & Hamond, 1989; Price & Goodman, 1990), and unfortunately, many abusive episodes occur repeatedly (Rush, 1980). Hence, children's memory for such experiences may be greater than that demonstrated in one time, less personally relevant memory tasks in the laboratory.

Retention processes

Retention of the event requires that the child transforms the abuse into a symbolic representation such that the information can be more readily remembered. Cognitive representations in the form of images and verbal symbols are stored about the event. Because imaginal representations are abstractions of events, only the most salient details are represented. It has been found that children produce a composite representation of repeated events that contains the essential aspects from specific encounters (Bransford & Franks, 1976). In social cognitive theory, visual memory is accorded an important role in children's representations of abusive events, particularly for younger children with minimal verbal skills. With increasing age it is expected that more of the information about the abusive event would be encoded in a verbal-conceptual form, with both of these systems working jointly with increasing age, so that words evoke corresponding imagery and vice versa.

Observed events are far better remembered if they are rehearsed as close to the time of first observation as possible (Bandura & Jeffery, 1973). Cognitive rehearsal of the event increases retention. Many adult victims of sexual abuse report that they continue to relive the abusive experience in their minds. As much as some may try to wipe the memory from their consciousness, the impossibility of doing so is often reported (Blume, 1990). It is likely that in stressful circumstances this would hold for children too.

Production processes

There are a variety of ways to assess children's memory for an event. For example, children can spontaneously recall witnessed material or retrieve it either through a questioning procedure or a recognition test. Studies have consistently revealed that the younger the child, the less information that is reported during free recall (e.g., Goodman & Reed, 1986; Goodman et al., 1990). Therefore, to establish details about alleged abuse from young victims, the interviewer must ask a greater variety of questions of the child to reconstruct the alleged event than would be required for older children or adults. However, repeated questioning of young children often leads to charges of interviewers being biased and young children's memories becoming contaminated. The implication is that young children easily succumb to an interviewer's belief that sexual abuse has occurred. Consequently, here lies the dilemma. Younger children do not report information to the same extent as older children, so how can this information be drawn from the child for the criminal investigation to proceed without the child's evidence being dismissed on the grounds of contamination? Possible solutions to this dilemma are examined in later sections, particularly the use of props and other aids in the forensic interview. These procedures are used to facilitate retrieval of the memory for the event, and for younger children who may not have the verbal skills to report their knowledge of the event, props and behavioral enactment of the event can serve to increase the amount of information they are able to report.

Most studies of the effects of stress on memory have focused on stress at the time of information acquisition; however, stress may affect children's ability to retrieve information. It could be argued that state-dependent effects would operate and that if the child was stressed during the abuse, stress at the retrieval stage will lead to heightened recall (e.g., Nasby & Yando, 1982). Alternatively, as discussed in the motivational processes section later, the possibility exists that stress will lead to a focus on self-doubting thoughts about difficulties in the disclosure of abuse, and that such self-doubting thoughts will undermine both retrieval and reporting of the abusive episode.

Motivational processes

Social cognitive theory distinguishes between acquisition and performance. This distinction is emphasized because people do not enact everything they learn. They may acquire and retain the capabilities to execute modeled activities adeptly but rarely or never perform them. Discrepancies between learning and performance are most likely to arise when acquired behavior has little functional value or carries high risk of punishment. When positive incentives are provided, observational learning, which has previously remained unexpressed, is promptly translated into action. (Bandura, 1986, p. 68)

In the sexual abuse context, therefore, there are multiple inhibitors to disclosure – for example, threats from perpetrators, or victims' feelings of self-blame or embarrassment. Sociocognitive theory distinguishes three major motivational determinants of nondisclosure: (a) external influences (these can be experienced either as directly affecting oneself or, vicariously, others – for example, fear of punishment from the perpetrator, fear of disbelief); (b) internal influences (e.g., embarrassment or self-blame); and (c) self-efficacy (lack of belief in one's ability to effectively disclose the abuse). The more children anticipate a negative reaction from others to themselves and/or other family members or anticipate self-censure toward themselves for disclosure of the abuse, or the more they feel incapable of disclosing the abuse, the more likely that disclosure will be inhibited.

Concerning the first and second sociocognitive processes of external and internal influences, children's behavior is initially not under any regulatory control. By the end of the second year, children learn to comply with external requests from others, and later they learn to regulate their behavior in accord with the reactions they anticipate from others. Children learn about the diverse reactions of others to different conduct and synthesize this information to formulate their own standards of conduct. Consequently, with increasing cognitive maturity and social experience, children's conduct is regulated not only by their expected reactions of others but by their own self-generated reactions. Children learn to evaluate their own conduct and react with self-praise or self-congratulations when they live up to their standards and with self-criticism when they do not. For children who have developed internal standards, behavior is regulated by an interplay of internal and external factors. The model therefore posits that while younger children's conduct is regulated primarily by external factors, with increasing cognitive competence and appropriate social experience, conduct is increasingly regulated by self-generated influences (Bussey, 1992a; Bussey & Bandura, 1992).

The third sociocognitive process that influences conduct is self-efficacy. Self-efficacy refers to an individual's beliefs in his or her ability to use a skill (Bandura, 1986). With increasing development, individuals self-reflect on their own capabilities. The concept of self-efficacy recognizes a distinction between possessing a particular skill and being able to effectively use that skill. Debilitating thoughts, for example, can undermine the use of a skill to maximum capability. Self-doubts serve to inhibit optimal performance. In this context, self-doubts about being able to disclose alarming and embarrassing material could serve to inhibit disclosure, particularly in the court context.

Before examining these categories of influence on children's reporting of information, it is important to point out that children may sometimes not be motivated to disclose the abuse simply because they are unaware of the taboos associated with such sexual activity involving a person older than themselves.

Inhibition to disclosure: lack of knowledge. One of the reasons for young children not reporting sexual abuse is that they are often not aware that there are societal taboos (translated into laws) about such sexual activity. In the past, it has largely been left to parents to teach children the social conventions associated with sexual behavior.

Rosenfeld, Bailey, Siegel, and Bailey (1986) reported from a sample of 576 children, ranging in age from 2 to 10 years, that younger children were more likely than older children to touch their parents' genitals and mother's breasts, and that this usually occurred out of curiosity in a bathing context. Parents were less likely to bathe with older children and hence less touching of parents' genitals was reported. Overall, some parents used the experience to explain sexual development to their children; however, other parents reacted mildly negatively to such touching. It is hardly surprising that Goldman and Goldman (1984) reported that many children's knowledge of sexuality is limited. Without adequate information from parents about sexual development and sexual mores, many young children will have no basis on which to judge what is acceptable and what is unacceptable sexual conduct. Hence, it is obvious that if children possess little knowledge about sexuality, it is relatively easy for parents and trusted adults to use young children to their own sexual advantage.

If young children with minimal knowledge of sexuality are abused by a trusted adult, particularly a parent, and told that this is normal interaction, the children will have little reason to report the activity. These children may have no idea that such activity is not condoned, and hence it is likely to come to the attention of others only through children's inadvertent sexualized statements and behavior (Finkelhor & Williams, 1988).

Inhibition to disclosure: external influences. Even if children are aware of the taboos against such sexual activity, they may not disclose the abuse because they have been threatened for disclosure. Although there are many strategies that abusers can use to prevent children from disclosing abuse, threat is the most widely reported in the literature (Summit, 1983; Sauzier, 1989). Abusers often swear children to secrecy to prevent disclosure. Thus, abused children can be emotionally stressed both by the sexual abuse itself and by the need to keep the sexual abuse secret (Burgess & Holmstrom, 1978). The overlay of secrecy adds to the difficulty children experience with disclosure.

Finkelhor (1988) found that force and coercion were frequently used by the perpetrators of sexual abuse in day care settings to prevent disclosure:

Getting children to submit to the abuse was the easier part, because it occurred during the time when the children were under the authority of the abusers. To prevent children from telling during times when they were outside that authority and in the care of their parents was a much bigger problem. Thus, much of the threatening that went on in day-care abuse was not to accomplish the molestation but to prevent the children from telling. Children were threatened that if they told, they or their parents or their pets would die or go to jail or that the abusers would do other terrible things to them. (Finkelhor, 1988, p. 95)

Fewer children who were threatened for disclosing their abuse actually disclosed it (47%) than children who had not been threatened for disclosure (61%), although this difference was not statistically significant. Of course, it is not possible to extrapolate from such a field study whether severely threatened children would ever disclose their abuse.

Other studies (Conte & Berliner, 1988; Sauzier, 1989) reveal how prepetrators of sexual abuse use coercion to prevent children from disclosing sexual abuse. However, it may be that the more severe the abuse, the more convincing the abuser is at coercing the young child into not disclosing the abuse. Hence it is necessary to examine the impact of coercive means for silencing children, independent of the severity of the abuse, in more controlled situations.

Children's difficulty in disclosing even a fairly minor misdeed committed by an adult was illustrated in a recent study (Bussey, Lee, & Rickard, 1990). Obviously, it is necessary to examine children's disclosure of information that is either naughty or embarrassing to understand difficulties that children experience in disclosing information about witnessed events. There would be no need for children to withhold neutral information. Because of the ethical difficulties associated with the reporting of sexually embarrassing material as is required in sexual abuse cases, this study examined children's disclosure of an adult male's transgression, the breaking of a prized glass, in which he hid the broken pieces. Fourteen percent of 3-year-olds and 43% of 5-year-olds did not disclose the adult male's transgression after simply being asked not to disclose it. Evidently, the impact of such a direct request by an adult was much greater on older children's than on younger children's disclosure. However, the sterner the request not to disclose the transgression, the more both the 3-year-olds (43%) and the 5-year-olds (71%) inhibited their disclosure by either denying that the transgression occurred (false denial) or refusing to answer any questions about the transgression (disclosure refusal), for example, "I can't tell you what happened." For those children who did disclose the transgression, the majority did not do so spontaneously. While some children disclosed after general nondirective questioning (i.e., after they were asked to tell the interviewer about the game they played in her absence, they were asked, "Did anything else happen while I was gone?"), other children only disclosed after specific questioning about the prized glass ("Have you seen my glass?" or, finally, "Did Mr. X touch my glass?"). Difficulty in disclosing an adult's transgression may induce young children to lie because they are afraid to own up, especially if they anticipate punishment for disclosing the adult's transgression. Even 3-year-olds will lie about their own transgressions (Lewis, Stanger, & Sullivan, 1989), and both 3- and 5-year-olds are more likely to lie if they anticipate punishment for truthfully reporting their transgressions (Bussey, 1992b).

Appeals such as concern for the transgressor, bribery, and trickery had less impact on the disclosure of the 3- than the 5-year-olds. Thus, the more cognitively demanding the reasons used by the transgressor to silence children's disclosure, the more impact they had on the disclosure of the older than the younger children. This is consistent with findings of other studies about the types of requests used by parents and others to gain compliance from children of different ages (Parke, 1969; Kuczynski & Kochanska, 1992).

One of the other striking findings of this study was that when children simply observed the transgression without any reference about nondisclosure by the transgressor, 7% of the 3-year-olds did not disclose compared with 43% of the 5-year-olds. This suggests that with increasing cognitive competence and social experience, children are more selective and have learned to regulate disclosure. They learn to inhibit their disclosure of events, particularly events that they anticipate others might respond to in an unfavorable manner, even when not explicitly asked not to disclose. This is consistent with other research showing that by 5 years of age children have learned to inhibit disclosure; in particular, they show restrictive disclosure to nonfriends in comparison with friends (Rotenberg & Sliz, 1988).

It is also important to note in the Bussey et al. (1990) study, that overall disclosure rates were quite high. Although it could be argued that the task was not sufficiently serious or important to warrant withholding information, comments made by the children confirmed that they regarded the transgression as serious. Further, even though children did disclose the transgression, for many this was a difficult task, often accompanied by expressed concern for the transgressor. Therefore, for children who are sexually abused, it is possible that the more concern they feel for the transgressor and the greater the threat for reporting the abuse, the more likely they would be to comply with the abuser's request not to disclose it. Hence, children need to learn that they can disclose negative information, that they can tell on adults who commit transgressions. If they do not, they will continue to withhold information for fear of negative consequences to themselves or even the transgressor.

Apart from the threatened adverse reactions from the perpetrator, it is likely that victims of child abuse are often reluctant to disclose their abuse because of the reactions they anticipate from the person to whom they disclose it. Such anticipated reactions would often prove to be very real since abuse is not something that adults want to believe has happened to their children, worse still, that someone close to them was the perpetrator. Children themselves often do not think that others will believe their account of a sexually abusive incident (Hursch, 1977).

Some children are, however, believed initially. While this would doubtless be very comforting and reassuring, they still have to convince welfare workers, the police, and finally the judge and jury of the veracity of their allegations. Hence, it is not surprising that the reactions of others involved will be a major factor determining whether or not the allegation will be maintained. Studies that investigate the effect of significant others in facilitating and maintaining disclosure are sorely needed.

Inhibition to disclosure: self-reactions. Apart from negative reactions from others, children's own negative self-reactions may inhibit disclosure. Both types of reactions could work to prevent disclosure. Children who are the victims of incest are often reported as feeling responsible or to blame for the sexual abuse (Finkelhor, 1979; Herman, 1981; German, Habenicht, & Futcher, 1990). Incest often affects adolescent girls' sense of self-worth and they feel guilty about the abuse (Lamb, 1986). Even in hypothetical situations, children are likely to believe that victims of sexual abuse felt "bad" or "guilty" about what happened, even though they in no way instigated the sexual activity (Wurtele & Miller, 1987).

Embarrassment about reporting sexual abuse increases with age, as is demonstrated by older children's inhibition to disclose any events of a sexual nature. This is shown in a study of 5- and 7-year-old children's reports of a routine medical examination (Saywitz, Goodman, Nicholas, & Moan, 1991). For half of the children, the medical examinations involved touching the genitals; the other half underwent an examination for scoliosis in which no genital touching was involved. When children were asked to recall what they experienced during their medical examinations, the 7-year-olds who had the scoliosis examination recalled significantly more accurate information than the 5-year-old children who had either type of examination or the 7-year-olds who had the genital examination. When the children were asked specific questions about the examinations, the 7-year-olds accurately reported as much information in both conditions. Difficulty in disclosing embarrassing sexual material may have contributed to the 7-year-olds' less than complete spontaneous recall about the genital examination. It was obviously not memory failure that led to the lower recall rate, as they answered specific questions to the same degree of accuracy as those children who underwent the scoliosis examination. The younger children, while reporting less information in free recall than the older children, reported equal amounts of information about both the scoliosis and genital examinations. Presumably, younger children did not experience the same degree of embarrassment as the older children in reporting such material because of their more limited understanding of societal taboos regarding sexuality.

Saywitz et al.'s study is important because it not only replicates the finding that older children usually report significantly more information than younger children (results deriving in the main from studies in which children report on emotionally neutral, albeit sometimes stressful events), but also demonstrates that when children are required to report on an embarrassing event (which more closely approximates the sexually abusive episode), the results change. This illustrates that children's reporting of witnessed events is not only dependent on their *competence* to report that information, but also on their *willingness*. Anticipated negative self-reactions as well as anticipated negative reactions from others can also reduce children's propensity to disclose sexual abuse.

Inhibition to disclosure: lack of perceived self-efficacy. Even if children are capable of and want to disclose their abuse, they may not do so because they judge themselves as lacking the skills to communicate the abuse effectively. Particularly when children are fearful and anxious about disclosure, it could be expected that they would judge themselves as lacking in self-efficacy, that is, the perceived skills for reporting the abuse. The more individuals perceive themselves as inefficacious at performing a particular task, the more distressed they become and the less likely they are to perform the task or to perform it adequately (Bandura, 1986). There is a good deal of research to support the relationship between perceived inefficacy and stress reactions (Bandura, Reese, & Adams, 1982). Hence, the more children judge themselves as incapable of disclosing the abuse, the more stress they would be expected to experience and hence the less likely they would be to disclose the abuse. The more confident individuals are that they can disclose an episode, the more likely they would be to disclose it and to do so effectively, even if it is a scary or embarrassing event. Hence, the more children have been forewarned about the difficulties in disclosure and taught disclosure skills, the less stressful children would find the experience and the more capable of disclosure they would judge themselves.

Children need to be taught how to disclose effectively the sometimes fearsome and embarrassing material associated with abuse and to feel a sense of confidence in their ability to do so. Otherwise, judgments of inefficacy will mean that children are overcome with anxiety about disclosing, and the abuse may be recanted or inadequately disclosed. Hence, teaching children how to disclose such information and to judge themselves as being capable of such disclosure would seem to be crucial tasks of prevention programs. Otherwise, sexual abuse will continue to be underreported, with children having little option but to maintain their silence with the consequent self-debilitating thoughts and sense of futility that often characterize long-term victims of sexual abuse (Browne & Finkelhor, 1986).

Age and disclosure

The social cognitive model of disclosure differs from Summit's (1983) and Sorensen and Snow's (1991) models of the disclosure process in that it assumes that the course of disclosure will vary according to children's cognitive capabilities, social experience, and the particular situation in which they find themselves. How long children take to disclose their abuse and whether they maintain their allegation would be dependent on their subjective appraisal of the many situational features associated with disclosure as well as their own self-reactions and perceived capability for disclosure. Hence, in this model, children would not necessarily be expected to pass through a series of stages in the disclosure process, but rather, their disclosure would be better predicted by their evaluative judgments of others' and their own reactions to disclosure as well as their self-perceived efficacy for disclosure. To the extent that children's evaluative judgments are related to their cognitive capacities and social experiences, disclosure would be related to age as well. It should be noted, however, that age is used only as a proxy measure of cognitive capacity and social experience, which should be independently assessed.

Young children who are unaware that abusive sexual activity is not condoned and who have minimal verbal skills are likely to disclose the abuse unintentionally through acting out the sexual activity in which they have engaged. As cognitive abilities and social experience expand, children's disclosure is expected to be more self-regulated. Although they may have a far greater capability for reporting their abuse because of increased attentional, retentional, and production skills, motivational factors may increasingly work to prevent disclosure. Tentative disclosure might be expected as children test the waters to see how "significant others" react to the abuse. Also, the circumstances of the abuse, whether they are threatened or not, will influence their propensity to disclose information. Initially, children may be so paralyzed by the threats from the perpetrator that they feel unable to disclose. Depending on how the initial disclosure is handled, children may volunteer more or less information. Even in laboratory studies in which children were required to report about a genital examination, they were likely to withhold that information unless explicitly asked about it (Saywitz et al., 1991). Hence, it could be expected that even older children, who usually provide more information than younger children under free recall, would leave out embarrassing details. If children are in supportive environments in which they do not anticipate punishment for disclosure, it would be expected that they would be more likely to disclose the abuse than if they expected negative outcomes to themselves or to their family for disclosure.

Because of increasing self-regulatory skills, disclosure would not be expected to increase linearly with age. Rather it is proposed that with increasing age or cognitive capabilities, because of the greater attentional, retention, and production skills, older children will be more capable of disclosure than younger children with less developed cognitive capabilities. However, whether or not disclosure eventuates will be most dependent on motivational processes. Increasingly, disclosure is expected to be determined by an interplay of children's subjective appraisal of others' and their own reactions to disclosure as well as their perceived efficacy for disclosure.

Younger children, who are unaware of the consequences of disclosure, would not be expected to inhibit the disclosure of an event if they are capable of reporting it, unless explicitly threatened for such disclosure. Until children are aware of and anticipate negative reactions for disclosure, it is unlikely that they will intentionally withhold the information. With increasing skills for intentionally withholding information by either lying or omission, it is possible with increasing age to avoid unfavorable outcomes by not disclosing, even though such nondisclosure may be very painful. Self-efficacy for disclosure is likely to increase with age. The ability to reflect on one's capabilities could undermine or enhance reporting ability, depending on children's appraisal of their disclosure skills. In this model of disclosure, what children expect to happen as a result of their disclosure, how they expect to react to their own disclosure, as well as their self-judged capabilities all interact with the specific environment in which they need to disclose the abuse – to a caring counselor and/or in the hostile environs of the courtroom – to determine if and to what extent they will disclose.

Implications from social cognitive theory for facilitating disclosure of sexual abuse in forensic settings

Because the sexual abuse of children is a criminal offense in most countries, the victim, usually the only witness to the crime, is required to testify about the abuse. Consequently, after a child has disclosed the abuse to a nonoffending parent or other person or the abuse has been suspected, the child is interviewed about the abuse by a variety of personnel, including medical officers, welfare workers, and sometimes the police. If the perpetrator is to be prosecuted, the child needs to disclose the abuse to an attorney and then in a court of law. Consequently, in this section we examine how to facilitate disclosure in both precourt forensic interviews and in the courtroom situation. There have been many suggestions of how to facilitate children's disclosure of sexual abuse in the forensic context, but rarely have these suggestions been based on empirical studies, let alone embedded in a firm theoretical basis. In this section we offer some suggestions based on principles of social cognitive theory for facilitating the disclosure of child sexual abuse.

Forensic interviewing

The manner in which a child is interviewed about a witnessed event is a crucial determinant of the quantity and content of information disclosed. In this section we focus on three major aspects expected to facilitate the disclosure of information during the interview process. First, we focus on props that are used to aid children's disclosure. Second, we focus on questioning style, in particular, the types of questions that are asked and the manner in which they are asked. Finally, we examine the effects of multiple interviews.

Props. Props are usually used to aid retention, production, and, to a lesser extent, motivational processes. There are many reasons for having young children use props to reenact the witnessed event during an interview session. First, the limited verbal ability of young children is a major hindrance in communicating an abusive experience. Second, even older children may not know the correct names for the various anatomical parts of the body. They can point to the body parts of an anatomically detailed doll, which may also be less embarrassing than having to state the names out loud. Third, a number of studies have shown that props enhance children's memory of events because they provide retrieval cues for accessing the memory (Fisher & Bullock, 1984; Perlmutter, 1984; Price & Goodman, 1990). However, there has been concern about the use of props, particularly anatomically detailed dolls, in forensic interviews, because it is claimed that such props are suggestive and may lead children to produce false allegations about sexual abuse. This claim has not, however, been supported by the research. For example, Goodman and Aman (1990), did not find that children who had not been abused made false reports of sexual abuse when anatomical dolls were used. The children did play with the dolls' genitals, presumably because of their novelty, but when asked, they did not falsely accuse an adult of sexually abusing them.

Goodman and Aman (1990) did, however, establish that 5-year-olds were better aided by the use of toys and dolls than were 3-year-olds, who were more distracted by the props. Although props may further facilitate memorial processes by providing retrieval strategies, by reducing reliance on language ability, and by being less embarrassing, there are still concerns that children will interact with props in a manner more appropriate to the props than to the events they are reporting on (King & Yuille, 1987). Because of the possible disadvantages of using such props, a promising new computer-assisted method for interviewing children whereby visual elements such as anatomically detailed drawings are depicted on the screen, may provide the facilitatory effects of props without the adverse distractions provided by actual items (Steward, 1989). The benefit of this procedure is that the interviewer can control the presentation of the graphically depicted props when required for clarification of aspects of the child's disclosure.

Questioning style. Concerns about the suggestibility of young witnesses means that leading questions are of considerable concern in forensic interviews. Consequently, less directive and specific questioning procedures are usually preferred in such contexts. However, because of the difficulty in obtaining sufficient information from young children when using vague questioning procedures, interviewers often need to use leading or direct questions with their young interviewees. While children of 4 to 5 years appear to be particularly resistant to leading questions of abuse (Rudy & Goodman, 1991), 3-year-olds may succumb more readily to such questions (Goodman & Aman, 1990). Some children may be more suggestible than others because they do not remember the event but feel pressed to report something and hence look to the adult interviewer for cues as to how to answer the questions "correctly." However, it must be remembered that this is not only the province of the young, as in some situations adults are suggestible too, particularly when they are interviewed by adults of high status (Loftus, 1979). Yet other research has shown that social support – for example, a friend being present during the interview (Moston, 1987) or such social support from the interviewer as being pleasant and comforting and praising them (independent of and unrelated to the content of the children's responses) – reduces rather than increases suggestibility. If young children in particular are scared about and anticipate punishment for disclosure, it is unlikely that they will disclose the abuse unless they feel safe to do so in a supportive environment. We have shown earlier that once children have learned that disclosure can lead to punishment, they are unlikely to disclose information where such outcome expectancies are anticipated.

If children are too stressed in an interview situation, it is likely that their retrieval skills will be compromised, and they will have difficulty recalling the required information (Motson & Engelberg, 1992). In Goodman et al.'s (1991) study, children from two age groups, 4 and 5 years, regardless of social support, recalled equal amounts of accurate information; however, those children provided with social support made fewer inaccurate responses during free recall. Particularly important was the finding that children were less suggestible to misleading information on their second rather than their first interview, and most important, the supportive interviewing style led to all children, irrespective of age, being better able to counter an adult's false suggestions about abuse (e.g., "How many times did she hit you?" and "The nurse kissed you on the mouth, didn't she?"). Goodman et al. (1991) posit that by providing a supportive environment in which to interview the children, intimidation by the interviewer is reduced, and children feel less pressure to comply with adults' suggestions. This interpretation is consistent with the findings of Ceci, Ross, and Toglia (1987), who showed that preschoolers were more resistant to suggestive, misleading questions posed by a child than an adult interviewer. These findings counter claims that provision of a supportive and relaxed atmosphere rather than a more authoritarian and formal atmosphere leads to heightened suggestion (e.g., Underwager & Wakefield, 1990). The provision of social support is thus likely to increase children's ability and willingness to disclose information, particularly negatively valanced information.

Milgram's (1974) classic research drew attention to adult compliance to requests made by those in authority. It would thus hardly be surprising to find that young children are susceptible to such influences, particularly in view of the fact that one of the major goals of socialization is to teach children to comply with adults' requests. Compliance with adults' requests during the first 2 years of life is usually considered a major developmental hallmark, and it has been held that lack of such compliance places children at risk for developing later behavior problems (Patterson, De Baryshe, & Ramsey, 1989). However, other developmental psychologists have argued that children need to learn to assert their own autonomy and that some resistance to parental control (in a socially acceptable manner) may lead to healthy developmental outcomes rather than signifying maladaptive behavior (Kuczynski & Kochanska, 1990). Children's use of negotiation skills with their mothers at age 5 was predicted by the mothers' infrequent use of commands during toddlerhood. Thus, it would not be surprising to find that children comply with an adult's expectations when interviewers use a direct style of questioning with few positive statements.

All children, regardless of whether or not they have been abused, may have had limited experience in negotiating the advances of an adult. "Parents have insisted that children accept all forms of affection from relatives and friends – being picked up, fondled, hugged, kissed, pinched, tickled and squeezed – leaving the child little experience in saying 'no' " (Gager & Schurr, 1976). Children need to be taught that it is acceptable to say no to adults, not only at the abuse stage but later during the forensic interview, and more importantly, how to do it. It would seem especially important, in view of the nature of the information to be disclosed, that the interview be conducted in as relaxed and supportive an environment as possible. Although questioning style does affect retention processes, it probably exerts its major influence through motivational processes in which children are not intimidated about disclosure.

Multiple interviews. From a forensic viewpoint, there are two major concerns about repeated interviews of child abuse victims. One concern is that repeated interviewing may lead to the contamination of memory through the introduction of new information and/or suggestive interviewing practices. The other concern is that it is extremely stressful for children to repeat traumatic material. Some writers even suggest that repeated interviews are a secondary form of abuse. These claims have led to a strong push for legislation to introduce videotaping of children's evidence so that children need only disclose their abuse once. However, neither of these concerns have strong support from the literature (Brainerd & Ornstein, 1991), although multiple interviewing remains a controversial issue (Flin, 1991).

Contrary to the contamination concern, memory research has revealed that repeated interviews serve to maintain children's memory when children are retested either on a free recall measure or in their responses to specific questions (Brainerd, Reyna, Howe, & Kingma, 1990; Tucker, Mertin, & Luszcz, 1990). Even when some of the questions used have been misleading, Goodman et al. (1991) found that children's recall was not affected by multiple interviewing. In fact, in Goodman et al.'s (1991) research, repeated interviewing increased the accuracy of children's answers to specific questions about the identity of the nurse who gave the inoculation and the room in which the children received it, although not to the questions relating to the nurse's actions. Further, those children who were interviewed on two separate occasions demonstrated resistance to misleading questions, particularly to questions concerning the nurse's identity and the room. Consequently, increased testing by way of multiple interviews may actually facilitate memory (Brainerd & Ornstein, 1991).

Not only have children been shown to be less suggestible when interviewed under supportive interviewing conditions, but Tucker et al. (1990) further reported that a greater number of the children in their study responded to the free recall task on the second rather than the first interview. One of the regularly reported difficulties with interviewing young children is that they frequently do not respond to the interviewer's questions. The questions are simply ignored, or the child says, "I don't know." The effect of multiple interviews, however, was to increase the number of children who actually responded to the interviewer's question by reporting information about an inoculation experience. In fact, the children provided more correct information during the second interview than during the first. These results highlight the importance of conducting multiple interviews with young children to obtain the maximum amount of information they are able to provide. This needs to be done in a supportive interviewing style, and it would seem necessary to do this with the same interviewer, although none of the studies involving multiple interviews have investigated the effects of using different interviewers. It could be expected that the rapport building that increases across sessions facilitates children's propensity to disclose information related to their experiences. The more children have been threatened for disclosure and expect to get into trouble, the more important it is to establish an environment in which the child anticipates warmth and support for disclosure. This again highlights the importance of motivational factors as major determinants of disclosure. A supportive atmosphere in which children do not anticipate censure for disclosure is necessary for children to disclose traumatic and embarrassing information. It would appear that concerns about contamination should not solely dictate the interviewing process.

While the data from the inoculation studies (Tucker et al., 1990; Goodman et al., 1991) highlight the facilitatory effect on memory of multiple interviews, these studies shed no light on the degree of trauma associated with multiple interviews. Tedesco and Schnell (1987) have argued that multiple interviews are traumatic for children who have been sexually abused. However, in most of these cases the multiple interviews were conducted by a series of different interviewers such as police, medical officers, and legal personnel. Because of overriding concerns of contaminating evidence, most of these interviews were conducted in a manner unlike that used by Tucker et al. (1990) in which children "were questioned in a supportive atmosphere." The facilitatory effects of a less intimidating interviewing style, incorporating a number of components such as smiling, supportive comments (e.g., "You're doing a great job"), and overt rewards (e.g., cookies and juice) have clearly been demonstrated (Goodman et al., 1991).

Admittedly, children from the inoculation studies were not required to report on experiences nearly as traumatic as those of sexually abused children. Although the children who were inoculated experienced some stress from the procedure, it was comparatively mild. Hence, it could be argued that the experience of recounting abusive experiences on a number of occasions could be detrimental to abuse victims. However, to counter this, there is a growing body of literature in the health psychology field that attests to the negative effects, both psychological and physical, on individuals who harbor negative memories and attempt to repress them (Pennebaker & Susman, 1988; Pennebaker, Barger, & Tiebout, 1989). Pennebaker et al. (1989) found that individuals who disclosed extremely traumatic experiences during an interview and did not try to inhibit distressing thoughts and feelings lowered their skin conductance levels during the interview and achieved long-term health benefits from their disclosure. This contrasts with those individuals who disclosed such experiences in a superficial manner and attempted to inhibit their distressing thoughts and feelings. The physiological work required to inhibit such memories meant that these individuals did not reduce their skin conductance level during the interview or gain the long-term health benefits achieved by those who disclosed their traumatic memories more freely. Therefore, children who talk about their abusive experience in a supportive context and who are adequately prepared to discuss it in the more foreign and often hostile environment of the court (which usually occurs a considerable time after the initial disclosure anyway) may reap important psychological benefits rather than accrue damage to their psyche or physical health. Further research in this area is required.

Disclosure in court

Anecdotal reports indicate that even when children have disclosed the abuse, they sometimes recant their allegations in view of an impending court case. Prosecution attorneys can recount numerous cases where children, on the day of their court appearance, either recant the abuse, state that they no longer want to go to court about it, or, once inside the courtroom, refuse to disclose any details about the abuse. Why might children recant a former allegation at the court stage or refuse to supply any information about the abuse? Unfortunately, few studies have examined the factors influencing children's disclosure in the courtroom. Some analogue studies do, however, address this issue (Hill & Hill, 1987; Bussey, Ross, & Lee, 1991).

These studies have focused on the influence of the perpetrator in affecting children's disclosure. If children have been threatened about disclosure by the perpetrator, their fear is likely to be further exacerbated when the case is heard in court, because they are required to give their testimony in the presence of the perpetrator. For some time there has been anecdotal evidence from clinicians and other practitioners working with actual child witnesses about the distress caused by confronting the accused in the courtroom (Libai, 1969; Burgess & Holmstrom, 1978; Parker, 1982; Whitcomb, Shapiro, & Stellwagen, 1985). More recently, children themselves have reported that the worst part about their impending court appearance was facing the perpetrator (Goodman et al., 1989).

To facilitate children's disclosure in the alien environment of the courtroom, many countries have introduced a barrage of legislation to enable children to testify in court without requiring face-to-face confrontation with the defendant. The American Psychological Association's argument that children should be able to give their testimony without visual contact with the defendant in instances where severe psychological distress could result from facing the accused was accepted in a recent ruling by the U.S. Supreme Court (Goodman, Levine, Melton, & Ogden, 1991). Consequently, in such cases children are allowed to present their evidence via closed circuit television or with a shield separating the defendant from the child victim. While these modifications seem to make common sense in terms of reducing the trauma associated with children facing the alleged perpetrator, some have argued that although disclosure may be facilitated by such procedures, so too may false allegations (*Coy v. Ioua,* 108 S. Ct., at 2800–802).

The small body of research that has been conducted in this area reveals that by not facing the perpetrator, children are in fact not more likely to provide false allegations, but that they are more likely to provide information about events that did occur (Hill & Hill, 1987). Seven- and 9-year-old children who observed a simulated father–daughter confrontation on a videotape were first asked to recall the incident and then asked specific questions either in a mock courtroom in which the "father" in the video sat in the defendant's seat, or in a small research room in which the defendant was absent. Although there was a trend for children who were not tested in the courtroom to recall more information and provide more answers to the specific questions than children interviewed in the courtroom, the most significant difference between the two test conditions was in the number of "don't know" answers given. Children were more likely to give such answers in the courtroom context where they had to face the defendant. Of course, from this study it is impossible to know if children were inhibited from disclosing the interaction between the father and daughter because of the mock courtroom in which they were tested or because of the added dimension of facing the defendant. The results do reveal, however, that testifying in a courtroom situation with the defendant present does affect children's ability to disclose information about a witnessed event. Children who were tested in a more friendly atmosphere than the courtroom were more able to disclose information about the observed father–daughter confrontation. Most importantly perhaps, children tested in both conditions did not falsely accuse the father of actions and statements not witnessed by them.

Another team of investigators have examined the effects of the presence or absence of the perpetrator on children's disclosure (Bussey et al., 1991). The testing was carried out in the same interview room and by the same interviewer for both conditions. Three- and 5-year-old children were less likely to disclose the man's transgression, which involved breaking a prized glass and then hiding the broken pieces to conceal his transgression, in his presence (31% and 25% disclosed the transgression, respectively) than in his absence (63% and 69% disclosed the transgression, respectively). However, his presence or absence did not affect the disclosure of the incident by the 9-year-old children (88% disclosed in both conditions). Hence, the younger children were much more likely to withhold information and not to disclose the man's transgression in his presence than were the older children. For younger children to be able to accurately and truthfully report information they have observed, it would therefore indeed seem necessary that they disclose negative information out of visual contact of the perpetrator. Although the 9-year-old children found it difficult to disclose the man's transgression in his presence, they were able to do so. Older children may find it easier not to comply with an adult's request about not disclosing an event than will younger children, who may be more intimidated by adults. It may very well be that as children get older it is more difficult for adults to silence them into not disclosing wrongful acts. While young children, particularly in sexual abuse day care cases, have been silenced by threats – for example, of killing animals (Finkelhor, 1988) – these threats may hold less sway with older children.

It could be construed that the younger children in these studies concerning the broken glass were less honest than their older counterparts. Yet children of both age groups, when asked, denied that they had been touched by the transgressor – indeed, none of them had been touched. Their denial of the glass breaking and hiding incident would seem to reflect the difficulty that young children have with the disclosure process rather than being a reflection of their honesty. These children were much more likely to disclose the event in the transgressor's absence.

Although research to date has concentrated on the presence of the perpetrator, there are other determinants that could be expected to influence children's disclosure in the courtroom. As noted in the previous section, children's feelings may affect their reporting ability. The more self-blame and embarrassment felt about reporting incidents, the more likely children may be to withhold information. The more children find such disclosure to be aversive, the more likely they may be to deny that the incident occurred. The other sociocognitive determinant that would be expected to influence disclosure in the courtroom context would be children's own perceived self-efficacy for disclosure. It would be expected that the more confident children feel about being able to speak about emotive and embarrassing material in front of others in the courtroom, the more likely they would be to disclose. To the extent that children judge that they could not succeed in this task, the more likely they would be overcome by anxiety. Recantation or noncooperation in such circumstances, particularly where hostile questions from defense attorneys are asked under cross-examination, would not be a surprising outcome.

We have focused on motivational processes that can affect disclosure in the courtroom. This does not mean that retention and production processes are not implicated in courtroom disclosure. Indeed, difficulties with language and communication skills are major hindrances to disclosure in this context (Brennan & Brennan, 1988). Even adults have difficulty comprehending and answering the sometimes convoluted questions of attorneys under cross-examination. This task can be perplexing and stressful for young children, whose verbal skills are less proficient than those of adults.

Although there has been little evaluation of the psychological impact on children who testify in court, Runyan, Everson, Edelsohn, Hunter, and Coulter (1988) did establish therapeutic benefits for child victims who disclosed their sexually abusive experiences in juvenile courts. Children who testified reduced their anxiety levels more rapidly than children who did not testify. Other research, however, has revealed the adverse emotional effects of children's participation in the justice system (Elwell & Ephross, 1987). Further research is therefore needed to clarify the effects of testifying. However, conducting methodologically sound research in this area is no easy task since it is impossible to allocate children randomly to a group that testifies in court versus one that does not. Usually prosecutors decide to prosecute only the most serious cases that involve violence or prolonged abuse. Consequently, adequate methods for dealing with these confounding elements need to be developed, so that the effects of testifying in court can be separated from the effects of the severity of the abuse.

Methods for facilitating children's disclosure in the courtroom context need to be implemented not only for the administration of justice, but also to minimize any adverse psychological effect on children. Of course, not all cases will result in conviction of the accused. Some cases will be dismissed on legal technicalities, and children may have difficulty sustaining their disclosure under hostile cross-examination. It is therefore crucial that children be adequately prepared for their disclosure and the possible outcomes in the court context. Procedures similar to those used to reduce children's anxiety in the medical context (e.g., Melamed & Siegal, 1984) could be used to reduce anxiety in the legal context and thereby facilitate disclosure. Children also need to be provided with realistic expectations of likely outcomes so that they do not recant their disclosure at a crucial stage in the proceedings. Unless the system can provide backup resources to children, such as a supportive adult and resources to keep the family together, children may be justified in their decision not to disclose the abuse. Belle and Burr (1991) found that children with high self-esteem were more aware of reasons for not confiding (the fear of embarrassment and the wish to save face) than were children with low self-esteem. Awareness of the benefits and costs of disclosure may lead children to confide wisely and retain a sense of control. Not only do children need to be helped with disclosure, but society needs to provide safeguards so that children can disclose sexual abuse without their world falling apart. If realistic outcomes of disclosure are known from the start, later recantations as the case progresses may be avoided. Most importantly, ways of reducing the negative outcomes of disclosure, such as the breakup of families, need to be addressed by the authorities and welfare agencies before the major inhibitors of children's disclosure and later recantation of the disclosure can be adequately ameliorated.

Conclusion

While children's capacity to disclose information, particularly about sensitive issues such as sexual abuse, may increase with cognitive development and social experience, their motivation to inhibit disclosure of such information may simultaneously increase. Most research on disclosure has focused on the increase in disclosure with age. However, this disclosure usually serves to foster friendships and build intimacy (e.g., Rotenberg & Mann, 1986; Buhrmester & Furman, 1987). This chapter has highlighted the fact that children may purposefully inhibit their disclosure of certain information. A complete model of disclosure needs to take account of factors that facilitate and inhibit disclosure. Why do children disclose more or less information in different situations about certain topics?

This chapter has outlined the four sociocognitive determinants of disclosure: attention, retention, production, and motivation processes. It has been argued that children may inhibit disclosure because they have not paid sufficient attention to the event (attention processes), they are unable to remember it in sufficient detail (retention processes), they are unable to adequately communicate about the event (production processes), or they are unwilling to report it (motivation processes). A detailed examination of how each of these processes may be inhibiting disclosure for the individual child in his or her special circumstances will enable the adoption of specific strategies to facilitate disclosure. While attention processes cannot be facilitated after the event, retention and production processes can be enhanced particularly during the investigatory interview(s). Motivational factors can be facilitated through the subprocesses outlined in the chapter. In summary, first, children need to know that the sexual activity is wrong so that they feel there is a need to report the abuse. This underscores the value of education programs. Second, the children have probably been threatened, so they need to be interviewed in a relaxed and nonintimidating setting and possibly provided with a support person throughout the disclosure process. If children expect to be seriously hurt or have a family member hurt as a result of their disclosure, they are unlikely to disclose the information. Similarly, if children anticipate being institutionalized, they are unlikely to disclose the abuse. From the perspective of social cognitive theory, the outcomes that children anticipate for disclosure are expected to be important determinants of whether they disclose or not, and these outcomes need to be adequately addressed with the child.

In terms of self-reactions, children need to learn that they are not to blame. Children need to be reassured in talking about embarrassing material. There are many programs that could assist in this process – for example, using videos to demonstrate how other children have successfully dealt with similarly aversive experiences. Finally, self-efficacy boosting is essential for children who have to go to court. Although children could possibly be shielded from the defendant, they may still see this person again or have to live with their visual memory of him or her; hence, teaching children to be efficacious in this context would be important and may indeed lead to a sense of empowerment.

References

Adams-Tucker, C. (1982). Proximate effects of sexual abuse in childhood: A report on 28 children. *American Journal of Psychiatry, 139,* 1252–6.
Baddeley, A. D. (1982). *Your memory: A user's guide.* New York: Macmillan.
Bandura, A. (1962). Social learning through imitation. In M. R. Jones (Ed.), *Nebraska Symposium on Motivation* (Vol. 10, pp. 211–74). Lincoln: University of Nebraska Press.
Bandura, A. (1965). Influence of models' reinforcement contingencies on the acquisition of imitative responses. *Journal of Personality and Social Psychology, 1,* 589–95.

Bandura, A. (1969). Social-learning theory of identificatory processes. In D. A. Goslin (Ed.), *Handbook of socialization theory and research* (pp. 213–62). Chicago: Rand McNally.

Bandura, A. (1986). *Social foundations of thought and action: A social cognitive theory*. Englewood Cliffs, NJ: Prentice-Hall.

Bandura, A. (1989). Social cognitive theory. In R. Vasta (Ed.), *Annals of child development: Six theories of child development* (Vol. 6, pp. 1–60). Greenwich, CT: JAI.

Bandura, A., & Jeffery, R. W. (1973). Role of symbolic coding and rehearsal processes in observational learning. *Journal of Personality and Social Psychology, 26,* 122–30.

Bandura, A., Reese, L., & Adams, N. E. (1982). Micro-analysis of action and fear arousal as a function of differential levels of perceived self-efficacy. *Journal of Personality and Social Psychology, 43,* 5–21.

Belle, D., & Burr, R. (1991). Why children do not confide: An exploratory analysis. *Child Study Journal, 21,* 217–34.

Berliner, L., & Conte, J. R. (1990). The process of victimization: The victim's perspective. *Child Abuse & Neglect, 14,* 29–40.

Blume, E. S. (1990). *Secret survivors: Uncovering incest and its aftereffects in women*. New York: Ballantine.

Bohannon, J. N. (1988). Flashbulb memories for the space shuttle disaster. *Cognition, 29,* 179–96.

Brainerd, C., & Ornstein, P. A. (1991). Children's memory for witnessed events: The developmental backdrop. In J. Doris (Ed.), *The suggestibility of children's recollections* (pp. 10–20). Washington, DC: American Psychological Association.

Brainerd, C. J., Reyna, V. F., Howe, M. L., & Kingma, J. (1990). The development of forgetting and reminiscence. *Monographs of the Society for Research in Child Development, 55*(3–4, Serial No. 222).

Bransford, J. D., & Franks, J. J. (1976). Toward a framework for understanding learning. In G. H. Bower (Ed.), *The psychology of learning and motivation* (Vol. 10, pp. 93–127). New York: Academic.

Brennan, M., & Brennan, R. E. (1988). *Strange language: Child victims under cross examination*. Wagga Wagga, New South Wales: Riverina Murray Institute of Higher Education.

Browne, A., & Finkelhor, D. (1986). Impact of child sexual abuse: A review of the research. *Psychological Bulletin, 99,* 66–77.

Buhrmester, D., & Furman, W. (1987). The development of companionship and intimacy. *Child Development, 58,* 1101–13.

Burgess, A. W., Groth, A. N., Holmstrom, L. L., & Sgroi, S. M. (Eds.). (1978). *Sexual assault of children and adolescents*. Lexington, MA: Lexington Books.

Burgess, A., & Holmstrom, L. (1974). Rape trauma syndrome. *American Journal of Psychiatry, 131,* 981–6.

Burgess, A. W., & Holmstrom, L. L. (1978). Accessory-to-sex: Pressure, sex, and secrecy. In A. W. Burgess, A. N. Groth, L. L. Holmstrom, & S. M. Sgroi (Eds.), *Sexual assault of children and adolescents* (pp. 85–98) Lexington, MA: Lexington Books.

Burns, N., Finkelhor, D., & Williams, L. M. (1988). Disclosure and detection. In D. Finkelhor & L. M. Williams (Eds.), *Nursery crimes: Sexual abuse in day care* (pp. 99–113). Newbury Park, CA: Sage.

Bussey, K., (1992a). Lying and truthfulness: Children's definitions, standards and evaluative reactions. *Child Development, 63,* 129–37.

Bussey, K. (1992b). *Developmental patterns in children's lying*. Manuscript submitted for publication.

Bussey, K., & Bandura, A. (1992). Self-regulatory mechanisms governing gender development. *Child Development, 63,* 1236–50.

Bussey, K., Lee, K., & Richard, K. (1990). *Children's reports of an adult's transgression*. Unpublished manuscript.

Bussey, K., Ross, C., Lee, K. (1991, April). *Factors influencing children's lying and truthfulness*. Paper presented at the meeting of the Society for Research in Child Development, Seattle, WA.

Ceci, S. J., Ross, D. F., & Toglia, M. P. (1987). Age differences in suggestibility: Narrowing the uncertainties. In S. J. Ceci, M. P. Toglia, & D. F. Ross (Eds.), *Children's eyewitness memory* (pp. 57–78). New York: Springer-Verlag.

Conte, J. R., & Berliner, L. (1988). The impact of sexual abuse on children: Empirical findings. In L. Walker (Ed.), *Handbook on sexual abuse of children: Assessment and treatment issues* (pp. 72–93). New York: Springer.

Conte, J. R., & Schuerman, J. R. (1987). Factors associated with an increased impact of child sexual abuse. *Child Abuse & Neglect, 11,* 201–11.

Coy v. Iowa, 487 U.S. 1012 (1988).

Easterbrook, J. A. (1959). The effect of emotion on the utilization and organization of behavior. *Psychological Review, 66,* 183–201.

Elwell, M. E., & Ephross, P. H. (1987). Initial reactions of sexually abused children. *Social Casework: The Journal of Contemporary Social Work* (February), 109–16.

Everson, M. D., Hunter, W. M., Runyan, D. K., Edelsohn, G., & Coulter, M. (1989). Maternal support following disclosure of incest. *American Journal of Orthopsychiatry, 59,* 197–207.

Finkelhor, D. (1979). *Sexually victimized children*. New York: Free Press.

Finkelhor, D. (1988). Dynamics of abuse. In D. Finkelhor & L. M. Williams (Eds.), *Nursery crimes: Sexual abuse in day care* (pp. 84–98). Newbury Park, CA: Sage.

Finkelhor, D. (1990). Early and long-term effects of child sexual abuse: An update. *Professional Psychology: Research and Practice, 21,* 325–30.

Finkelhor, D., & Williams, L. M. (Eds.). (1988). *Nursery crimes: Sexual abuse in day care*. Newbury Park, CA: Sage.

Fischer, K. W., & Bullock, D. (1984). Cognitive development in school-age children: Conclusions and new directions. In W. A. Collins (Ed.), *Development during middle childhood: The years from 6 to 12* (pp. 70–146). Washington, DC: National Academy of Sciences Press.

Fivush, R., & Hamond, N. R. (1989). Time and again: Effects of repetition and retention interval on 2 year olds' event recall. *Journal of Experimental Child Psychology, 47,* 259–73.

Flin, R. (1991). Commentary: A grand memory for forgetting. In J. Doris (Ed.), *The suggestibility of children's recollections* (pp. 21–3). Washington, DC: American Psychologiccal Association.

Gager, N., & Schurr, C. (1976). *Sexual assault: Confronting rape in America*. New York: Grosset & Dunlap.

German, D. E., Habenicht, D. J., & Futcher, W. G. (1990). Psychological profile of the female adolescent incest victim. *Child Abuse & Neglect, 14,* 429–38.

Goldman, R., & Goldman, J. (1984). Perception of sexual experience in childhood: Relating normal development to incest. *Australian Journal of Sex, Marriage & Family, 5,* 159–66.

Goodman, G. S., & Aman, C. (1990). Children's use of anatomically detailed dolls to recount an event. *Child Development, 61,* 1859–71.

Goodman, G. S., Bottoms, B. L., Schwartz-Kenney, B. M., & Rudy, L. (1991). Children's testimony about a stressful event: Improving children's reports. *Journal of Narrative and Life History, 1,* 69–99.

Goodman, G. S., Jones, D. P. H., Pyle-Taub, E., England, P., Port, L., Rudy, L., & Prado-Estrada, L. (1989, August). *Children in court: The emotional effects of criminal court involvement.* Paper presented at the American Psychological Association Convention, New Orleans.

Goodman, G. S., Levine, M., Melton, G. B., & Ogden, D. W. (1991). Child witnesses and the confrontation clause: The American Psychological Association brief in *Maryland v. Craig. Law and Human Behavior, 15,* 13–29.

Goodman, G. S., & Reed, R. S. (1986). Age differences in eyewitness testimony. *Law and Human Behavior, 10,* 317–32.

Goodman, G. S., Rudy, L., Bottoms, B. L., & Aman, C. (1990). Children's concerns and memory: Issues of ecological validity in the study of children's eyewitness testimony. In R. Fivush & J. A. Hudson (Eds.), *Knowing and remembering in young children.* Cambridge University Press.

Herman, J. L. (1981). *Father–daughter incest.* Cambridge, MA: Harvard University Press.

Hill, P. E., & Hill, S. M. (1987). Videotaping children's testimony: An empirical view. *Michigan Law Review, 85,* 809–33.

Hursch, C. J. (1977). *The trouble with rape.* Chicago: Nelson-Hall.

Keenan, J. M., & Baillet, S. D. (1980). Memory for personally and socially relevant events. In R. S. Nickerson (Ed.), *Attention and performance* (Vol. 8, pp. 651–69). Hillsdale, NJ: Erlbaum.

Kempe, C. H., Silverman, F. N., Steele, B. F., Droegemueller, W., & Silver, H. (1962). The battered-child syndrome. *Journal of the American Medical Association, 181,* 17–24.

Kling, M. A., & Yuille, J. C. (1987). Suggestibility and the child witness. In S. J. Ceci, M. P. Toglia, & D. Ross (Eds.), *Children's eyewitness memory* (pp. 24–35). New York: Springer-Verlag.

Kuczynski, L., & Kochanska, G. (1990). The development of children's noncompliance strategies from toddlerhood to age 5. *Developmental Psychology, 26,* 398–408.

Kuczynski, L., & Kochanska, G. (1992). *Function and content of maternal control interventions: Developmental significance of early maturity demands.* Manuscript submitted for publication.

Lamb, S. (1986). Treating sexually abused children: Issues of blame and responsibility. *American Journal of Orthopsychiatry, 56,* 303–7.

Lerman, H. (1988). The psychoanalytic legacy: From whence we come. In L. Walker (Ed.), *Handbook on sexual abuse of children* (pp. 37–52). New York: Springer.

Lewis, M., Stanger, C., & Sullivan, M. W. (1989). Deception in 3-year-olds. *Developmental Psychology, 25,* 439–43.

Libai, D. (1969). The protection of the child victim of a sexual offense in the criminal justice system. *Wayne Law Review, 15,* 977–1032.

Linton, M. (1982). Transformations of memory in everyday life. In U. Neisser (Ed.), *Memory observed: Remembering in natural contexts* (pp. 71–91). New York: Freeman.

Loftus, E. F. (1979). *Eyewitness testimony.* Cambridge, MA: Harvard University Press.

MacFarlane, K., & Krebs, S. (1986). Techniques for interviewing and evidence gathering. In K. MacFarlane & J. Waterman (Eds.), *Sexual abuse of young children* (pp. 67–100). New York: Guilford.

Masson, J. M. (1984). *The assault on truth: Freud's suppression of the seduction theory.* New York: Farr, Straus, & Giroux.

Melamed, B. G., & Siegel, L. J. (1984). Children's reactions to medical stressors: An ecological approach to the study of anxiety. Reprinted in E. M. Hetherington and R. D. Parke (Eds.) (1988), *Contemporary readings in child psychology* (3rd ed). New York: McGraw-Hill.

Milgram, S. (1974). *Obedience to authority: An experimental view.* New York: Harper & Row.

Moston, S. (1987, September). *The effects of the provision of social support in child interviews.* Paper presented at the meeting of the British Psychological Association, York, England.

Moston, S., & Engelberg, T. (1992). The effects of social support on children's eyewitness testimony. *Applied Cognitive Psychology, 6,* 61–75.

Nasby, W., & Yando, R. (1982). Selective encoding and retrieval of affectively valent information: Two cognitive consequences of children's mood states. *Journal of Personality and Social Psychology, 43,* 1244–53.

Ochsner, J. E., & Zaragoza, M. S. (1988, March). *The accuracy and suggestibility of children's memory for neutral and criminal eyewitness events.* Paper presented at the American Psychology and Law Association meetings, Miami, FL.

Parke, R. D. (1969). Effectiveness of punishment as an interaction of intensity, timing, agent nurturance, and cognitive structuring. *Child Development, 40,* 213–36.

Parker, J. (1982). The rights of child witnesses: Is the court a protector or perpetrator? *New England Law Review, 17,* 643–717.

Patterson, G. R., De Baryshe, B. D., & Ramsey, E. (1989). A developmental perspective on antisocial behavior. *American Psychologist, 44,* 329–35.

Pennebaker, J. W., Barger, S. D., & Tiebout, J. (1989). Disclosure of traumas and health among Holocaust survivors. *Psychosomatic Medicine, 51,* 577–89.

Pennebaker, J. W., & Susman, J. (1988). Disclosure of traumas and psychosomatic processes. *Social Science & Medicine, 26,* 327–32.

Perlman, D., & Cozby, P. C. (1983). *Social psychology.* New York: Holt, Rinehart, & Winston.

Perlmutter, M. (1984). Continuities and discontinuities in early human memory paradigms, processes, and performance. In R. Kail & N. E. Spear (Eds.), *Comparative perspective on the development of memory* (pp. 253–86). Hillsdale, NJ: Erlbaum.

Peters, D. P. (1991). The influence of stress and arousal on the child witness. In J. Doris (Ed.), *The suggestibility of children's recollections* (pp. 60–76). Washington, DC: American Psychological Association.

Price, D. W. W., & Goodman, G. S. (1990). Visiting the wizard: Children's memory of a recurring event. *Child Development, 61,* 664–80.

Rosenfeld, A., Bailey, R., Siegel, B., & Bailey, G. (1986). Determining incestuous contact between parent and child: Frequency of children touching parents' genitals in a nonclinical population. *Journal of the American Academy of Child Psychiatry, 25,* 481–4.

Rotenberg, K. J., & Mann, L. (1986). The development of the norm of the reciprocity of self-disclosure and its function in children's attraction to peers. *Child Development, 57,* 1349–57.

Rotenberg, K. J., & Sliz, D. (1988). Children's restrictive disclosure to friends. *Merrill-Palmer Quarterly, 34,* 203–15.

Rudy, L., & Goodman, G. S. (1991). Effects of participation on children's reports: Implications for children's testimony. *Developmental Psychology, 27,* 527–38.

Runyan, D. K., Everson, M. D., Edelsohn, G. A., Hunter, W. M., & Coulter, M. L. (1988). Impact of legal intervention on sexually abused children. *Journal of Pediatrics, 113,* 647–57.

Rush, F. (1980). *The best kept secret: Sexual abuse of children.* New York: McGraw-Hill.

Russell, D. E. H. (1983). The incidence and prevalence of intrafamilial and extrafamilial sexual abuse of female children. *Child Abuse and Neglect, 7,* 133–46.

Sauzier, M. (1989). Disclosure of child sexual abuse: For better or for worse. *Pyschiatric Clinics of North America, 12,* 455–69.

Saywitz, K. J., Goodman, G. S., Nicholas, E., & Moan, S. F. (1991). Children's memories of a physical examination involving genital touch: Implications for reports of child sexual abuse. *Journal of Consulting and Clinical Psychology, 59,* 682–91.

Sgroi, S. M. (1982). *Handbook of clinical intervention in child sexual abuse.* Lexington, MA: Lexington Books.

Sirles, E. A., & Franke, P. J. (1989). Factors influencing mothers' reactions to intrafamily sexual abuse. *Child Abuse and Neglect, 13,* 131–9.

Sorensen, T., & Snow, B. (1991). How children tell: The process of disclosure in child sexual abuse. *Child Welfare, 70,* 3–15.

Steward, M. S. (1989). *The development of a model interview for young child victims of sexual abuse: Comparing the effectiveness of anatomical dolls, drawings and video graphics.* (Grant No. 90CA1332). Washington, DC: National Center on Child Abuse and Neglect.

Summit, R. C. (1983). The child sexual abuse accommodation syndrome. *Child Abuse and Neglect, 7,* 177–93.

Tedesco, J. F., & Schnell, S. V. (1987). Children's reactions to sex abuse investigation and litigation. *Child Abuse and Neglect, 11,* 267–72.

Tucker, A., Mertin, P., & Luszcz, M. (1990). The effect of a repeated interview on young children's eyewitness memory. *Australian and New Zealand Journal of Criminology, 23,* 117–24.

Underwager, R., & Wakefield, H. (1990). *The real world of child interrogations.* Springfield, IL: Thomas.

Whitcomb, D., Shapiro, E. R., & Stellwagen, L. D. (1985). *When the victim is a child: Issues for judges and prosecutors,* Washington, DC: National Institute of Justice.

Wurtele, S. K., & Miller, C. L. (1987). Children's conceptions of sexual abuse. *Journal of Clinical Child Psychology, 16,* 184–91.

Yerkes, R. M., & Dobson, J. D. (1908). The relation of strength of stimulus to rapidity of habit formation. *Journal of Comparative Neurology and Psychology, 18,* 459–82.

10 Self-disclosure in adolescents: a family systems perspective

H. Russell Searight, Susan L. Thomas,
Christopher M. Manley, and Timothy U. Ketterson

Contemporary clinical family therapy theory is founded upon an interactional model in which individuals are deemphasized in favor of higher-order social patterns. This paradigm, often labeled "general systems theory," has been adopted from the physical and biological sciences and applied to an understanding of family interaction (Von Bertalanfy, 1969; Bateson, 1972).

Family systems theory and self-disclosure

From the perspective of systems theory, the family is perceived as a holistic organismic unit rather than a set of individuals (Nichols, 1984; Searight & Openlander, 1986). The interdependent elements interact in a circular rather than a linear manner (Nichols, 1984). These patterns of interaction within a system are oriented toward maintaining the homeostasis or stability of the family. Negative feedback loops are the primary mechanism for self-regulation through reduction of the effect of any change-oriented process (Jackson, 1957). This is often an adaptive process but may be maladaptive when the family's homeostasis includes a dysfunctional child or adolescent. Thus, while a symptomatic child represents systems-wide distress, the dysfunctional child simultaneously serves to maintain a particular pattern of family organization – for example, an overinvolved mother and an emotionally distant father. Positive feedback, in contrast, amplifies certain family patterns past the equilibrium point such that the family becomes reorganized (Hoffman, 1981). The goal of family therapy is to enact a positive feedback process that results in the family functioning without a symptomatic member (Hoffman, 1981).

Self-disclosure is traditionally viewed as a process by which persons make themselves known to each other (Norrell, 1984). Historically, the importance of self-disclosure as a construct is usually seen as originating with Jouard (1971), who viewed this process as a form of self-discovery (Norell, 1984). From this perspective, self-disclosure occurred when an individual communicated genuine thoughts and feelings. Jouard's approach, while important for highlighting the role of self-disclosure in healthy development, did not lend itself to the measurement of developmental processes and age-related changes in disclosure.

Social and developmental psychologists have attempted to focus the definition of self-disclosure to emphasize the communication of information, by one person to another, that was previously unknown to the recipient (Cozby, 1973; Chelune, 1979). With respect to families, there has been little direct investigation of self-disclosure between members. While there is a growing literature on verbal interaction patterns within parent–child dyads, there have been relatively few studies of self-disclosure as a specific type of communication. While there is some data suggesting that there is a reduction in disclosure by children to parents with the onset of adolescence (West & Zingle, 1969; Komarovsky, 1974; Norell, 1984) and greater self-disclosure by daughters versus sons (Dalusio, 1972; Norell, 1984), the majority of these studies focus on dyadic, linear communication patterns.

In contrast, systems theory emphasizes higher-order social patterns, such as homeostatic mechanisms, which govern the family as a holistic unit (Nichols, 1984). Systems theory views individual personality variables and psychological states as "context markers" for more pervasive interaction patterns (Bateson, 1972). Seemingly "individual" behavior is no longer attributed to a particular person (Henggeler & Borduin, 1990). Personality itself becomes a questionable construct. A child's communication style, rather than reflecting individual characteristics such as trust, is more accurately perceived as part of an interactional sequence. As Henggeler and Borduin (1990) note, it is not appropriate to label a child as "shy," "withdrawn," or "open" but more accurate to say the child shows these features as part of a circular pattern of family interaction. Behavior cannot be isolated from the social systems within which the child participates (Broffenbrenner, 1986).

In this chapter, family communication processes relevant to self-disclosure will be examined. As noted earlier, there has been relatively little direct empirical investigation of self-disclosure in clinical and nonclinical families in family therapy. However, family therapists such as Levant (1986) have suggested that self-disclosure plays an important role in family health. To link family theory to self-disclosure, important family systems process and concepts will be alternatively interpreted from the perspectives of social and developmental psychology. It is hoped that these linkages will suggest directions for future theoretical development and research.

The extent and types of self-disclosure between parents and children are likely to be influenced by both the developmental stage of the family and the individual development of the children. In line with a systems approach, it is not enough to look at just the family unit, the individual child, or the parent–child dyad in isolation. Moreover, without appreciating the continuing development of the family and its individual members, an understanding of the antecedents of parent–child self-disclosure cannot be realized.

Family life cycle perspective

Similar to individually oriented developmental models, the life cycle is a schema for understanding how normative transitions affect family functioning (Carter & McGoldrick, 1989). These temporal challenges have been termed "horizontal stressors," and they interact with "vertical stressors," which take the form of preexisting dysfunction (Carter & McGoldrick, 1989). For example, while self-disclosure between children and parents may reach its highest levels immediately prior to adolescence (Riskin, 1982), the presence of a vertical stressor such as parental alcoholism is likely to alter this traditional developmental pattern. Research such as Borduin and Henggeler's (1987) finding that there was less warmth and decreased communicative sharing between mothers and adolescent sons in families experiencing divorce in the preceding 5 to 10 years lends indirect support to this model. However, the pattern of interaction between horizontal and vertical stressors is currently open to investigation.

While the child-rearing years are the focus of interest for understanding parent–child self-disclosure, it is important to recognize that preexisiting patterns such as communication style from each parent's family of origin are likely to influence current family functioning (Carter & McGoldrick, 1989). Thus, it is useful to understand the overall process of the family life cycle.

Carter and McGoldrick (1989) describe six basic family life cycle stages. Each stage has certain emotional processes that are connected with the transitions as well as changes that the family must make to advance developmentally. In the first stage, young adults need to accept responsibility for themselves separate from the family of origin, develop close peer relationships, and seek employment and financial sufficiency. When a couple marries, there is a commitment to a new family system. This new system begins to take form, and each spouse learns to accommodate and assimilate the new sets of friends and extended families. With the acceptance of each new child in the system, the marital couple adjusts the current living arrangements by making space for the child(ren), setting out new rules concerning parenting, and determining responsibility for household duties and financial responsibilities. Along with those adjustments, the couple will experience changes in their relationships with the extended families and will need to understand the role of the new grandparents. As the children become adolescents, the parents will need to increase the flexibility in their boundaries due to the adolescent's push for autonomy. Also, the parents' focus will shift in a number of ways during midlife, with attention to career issues, caring for their aging parents, and reevaluating the marriage itself. Before entering the final stage, it will be necessary for the family to accept the inevitable leaving home of the child(ren) as well as realign the family as a marital dyad, realize and interact with their children as adults, adjust their relationships with the extended families, and prepare for the disabilities or death of their parents. Finally, the family will undergo many adaptations to the changing generational roles, such as coping with the interpersonal effects of their own physiological decline and the possible loss of loved ones, whether immediate family members, extended family, or friends. Even though this cycle could be considered limited in scope, it provides a core from which variations that may effect transitions can be discussed, such as divorce and remarriage, as well as economic and cultural differences (Carter & McGoldrick 1989).

Cowan (1991) and Elder (1991) have contributed another dimension to Carter and McGoldrick's (1989) molar stage model by highlighting the molecular processes that take place at each phase. Transitions may occur simultaneously (getting married and changing jobs), be overlapping (adolescence and career choice), or happen sequentially (marriage, childbearing, children leaving home). Similarly, Elder (1991) suggests that transitions are processes that have aspects of duration, timing, and order. That is, the length of the transition, the appropriateness of when it happens, and whether it occurs in its proper developmental sequence all contribute to the effects the change may have on the family and the individual.

As suggested earlier, vertical stressors in the form of preexisting patterns of family interaction often impact these transitions. There are suggestions that communication patterns are an important factor in facilitating or impairing adjustment to family life cycle transitions (Baumrind, 1991; Blechman, 1991). For example, Baumrind's (1991) research suggests that supportive parents who encourage positive, rational, and interactive communication while they use firm and consistent discipline (i.e., authoritative parents) have children that are higher in competence and self-esteem. These children are better equipped to deal with life events and transitions. In particular, the transition into adolescence is one that requires autonomy while avoiding self-destructive behavior during an inherently demanding process of individuation.

Further support for the role of communication in family adjustment comes from Blechman (1991), who describes communication deficits as the central issue in the destructive patterns of multiproblem families. Blechman's review concluded that the common characteristics of a multiproblem family generally include marital distress, maternal depression, and child antisocial behavior. These families lack the single best indicator of successful transitions, which is communication skill. Normative transitions in these families are extremely difficult because of rigidity and resistance to change. Furthermore, the communication deficits in these families incapacitate the members from accepting new and valuable information that can facilitate appropriate change and transitions.

Transactional model

Moving to an examination of individual development is not a departure from, but rather a complement to, the family life cycle perspective. In a transactional model approach to development, any particular outcome is the result of the interaction between the individual and his or her family and social context (Sameroff, 1983, 1987). Moreover, outcomes are the result of the interpretation of the interaction between the child and his or her experiences over time. Thus, a child's behavior cannot be directly linked to any one antecedent. From this perspective, the self-disclosure patterns of adolescents cannot be tied to any one event or target person; it is the adolescents' interpretation of all relevant preceding stimuli that determine the adolescents' responses. To this point in time, the application of the transactional model has been restricted to parent–infant interactions; however, because of its focus on the interpretation of interactions, the model offers many insights into the self-disclosure of adolescents within their families. In particular, new insights may be gained by focusing on the adolescent's perceptions of the family and its environment. Stated briefly, the transactional model postulates that a child's behavior is a result of transactions between the child (the phenotype), external experiences (the environment), and genetics (the genotype). Because genetics are a given for any particular child, it is the transactional role of the "environtype" that is of importance for adolescents' self-disclosure. The environtype is composed of family and cultural socialization patterns that regulate, and it is achieved through a series of codes at the cultural, family, and individual parent level. The cultural code employs both social supports and social controls to organize a society's child-rearing system. The purpose of the cultural code is to direct the fit between a social system and its members. In terms of self-disclosure, the cultural code may play a role in establishing appropriate areas of discussion between family members. For example, discussions about sexual activity were once taboo. The culture dictated that premarital sex be treated as if it did not exist; and thus, few adolescents felt comfortable talking to their parents about it. However, with the advent of, among other things, the "free love" generation, sex education in the schools, and a growing awareness of the dangers of sexually transmitted diseases, the cultural restrictions on families may be changing such that children are more likely to see their parents as legitimate targets for their disclosures and parents may be becoming more willing to listen. Thus, as the cultural code changes, the areas of self-disclosure change.

Like the cultural code, the family code also serves a regulatory function. Its primary purpose is to manage the fit between individuals and their families. The family code is composed of rituals (distinctive behaviors for nonroutine events), stories (family folklore), myths [non-reality-based, usually affectively charged beliefs about family member(s); Kramer, 1985], and paradigms (core rules of family functioning; Reiss, 1981). Although the least well articulated, it is the paradigms that offer the most insight into self-disclosure patterns. It is the rules of the family that determine its structure, and it is the structure of the family that determines its organization and patterning of relationships (Sroufe, 1989). Many family rules pertain to the expression of feelings or other highly personal information. Once established, the family will go to great lengths to assure that the rules are not broken or, if they are broken, that they are reestablished as quickly as possible (Sroufe, 1989). Thus, in a highly self-disclosing family, a recalcitrant adolescent may be goaded and cajoled into stating things he or she would prefer to keep private. On the opposite end of the spectrum, any self-disclosing statements made in a very restricted environment may be met with negative feedback intended to terminate such behavior. Just as the cultural and family codes exert a strong influence on the self-disclosing behavior of adolescents, these codes also exert a strong influence on the parents. These influences are manifested in the individual code of the parent. Parents bring many attributions to their roles, with these attributions affecting their reactions to their children's behaviors. For example, even though a family may express a desire for its individual members to share their feelings, one of the parents may come from an authoritarian family in which "a child should be seen and not heard." Given this individual code about disclosure, when a child attempts to express his or her feelings about a particular subject, this parent will more than likely greet such attempts with a negative response.

By combining the transactional model with the family life cycle perspective, the multiplicity of determinants for adolescent self-disclosure become clear. This combined approach suggests that the complexity of such disclosive behavior may be better understood by taking not only the behavior of the individual child into account, but also the perceptions of this child of his or her cultural rules, family paradigm (which in part may be determined by its stage in the life cycle), and the beliefs held by his or her parents about self-disclosure.

Parent–child interaction and communication: implications for self-disclosure

Because the perceptions of the child are so important in determining self-disclosure behavior, it is not surprising that the importance of parents versus peers as sources of intimacy appear to change as a function of development. As the culture sends messages that certain topics are not to be discussed with parents and the adolescents learn the power that can be associated with self-disclosing, the pattern of disclosing within the family is destined to change.

In general, children appear to experience greater intimacy with their mothers until approximately 11 to 12 years of age (Buhrmester & Furman, 1987). The importance of peers as sources of intimacy begins to increase at around age 9. There are suggestions that the degree of intimacy with same-sex peers is greater for girls than boys (Buhrmester & Furman, 1987). While parents remain the most important confidants for children and adolescents through ages 15 to 16, their importance appears to plateau at around age 11, while that of peers progressively increases (Santrock, 1990). By ages 15 to 16, friends are rated significantly higher than family members as sources of intimacy (Hunter & Youniss, 1982).

Research on self-disclosure within families has focused almost exclusively on adolescent–parent communication. Generally, mothers appear to receive more disclosure than fathers, and daughters appear to disclose more than sons (Norrell, 1984). It has been suggested that adolescents may disclose less to parents because the content may become less acceptable. Additionally, a stronger personal boundary between the adolescent and parent may be initiated by the adolescent as part of the process of developing greater autonomy.

Csikszentmihalyi and Larson (1984) conducted a phenomenological study of adolescents that suggests some of the possible reasons for adolescents' reduced disclosure to parents. The teenagers wore beepers programmed to go off at random times during the day. When beeped, the teenagers recorded what they were doing, who they were with, and what they were thinking and feeling. Comparable to the findings noted earlier, there was a decline in the amount of time spent with family members during the high school years, with 15-year-olds spending 25% and 17- to 18-year-olds only 15% of waking time with family members. With respect to mood and thought content, adolescents often experienced this family time very negatively. Adolescents often experienced parents as intruding upon the boundaries of their own consciousness (Csikszentmihalyi & Larson, 1984). The teenagers became particularly angry when their self-boundary (Derlega & Margulis, 1983) was repeatedly invaded by parental requests to perform tasks representative of parental values. Thus, while the respondents were begrudingly willing to pick up clothes or clean the house, they reacted strongly to the intrusion upon autonomy when parents insisted they perform tasks "exactly this way." These findings suggest that reduced self-disclosure in adolescence is part of the developmental process of separation and individuation from the family of origin; the manner in which the parents approach the adolescent also plays a major role.

Baumrind's (1967, 1978) longitudinal studies of parent–child interaction, which were mentioned earlier, suggest some insight into distinct parenting styles and the effects of these styles on the children. Based on a typology of restrictiveness, Baumrind classified parents into five types: authoritarian, authoritative, permissive, nonconformist, and harmonious. Both authoritarian and authoritative parents are highly restrictive; the difference between the two lies in how they tried to control their children. Authoritarian parents believe in unquestioning acceptance of their rules; communication between parent and child is poor. Authoritative parents, on the other hand, expect their children to follow their rules, but they explain the reasoning behind their rules. Moreover, they respectfully and lovingly listen to their children's points of view, while still maintaining the final word on the subject. On the low end of the restrictiveness continuum are the permissive and nonconformist parents. Both of these types make few attempts to control their children. The difference between the two is that permissive parents show a lack of control due to being uninvolved, while nonconformist parents are very involved and use the lack of control to give their children the freedom to develop. In terms of communication, little communication occurs between the permissive parent and child because the parent readily gives in to the child's demands. Communication is much better between the nonconformist parent and child as the parent actively supports the child in developing his or her own point of view. The final group of parents, the harmonious type, are neither restrictive nor permissive; they have never found a need to control their children's behaviors because the children always lived up to the parents' expectations. Like the authoritative type, these parents willingly listen to their children's opinions.

The implication of this typology for self-disclosure is readily apparent. In families where parents support and encourage their children to express their own points of view, self-disclosure among adolescents should be high. Conversely, low communication between parents and children should effectively diminish any self-disclosure behavior. Although no studies have been found that directly address these implications, a study by Snoek and Rothblum (1979) found that parental affection and responsiveness were associated with high self-disclosure to parents, friends, and strangers.

Researchers (Youniss, 1983; Hauser et al., 1984) relying on cognitive and psychoanalytic formulations have found a similar pattern. These investigators concluded that the level of adolescents' ego development was positively related to family interactions featuring shared perspectives and challenges accompanied by support (Grotevant & Cooper, 1985).

The finding that shared perspective increases self-disclosures adds an interesting addendum to the parenting styles typology. It may be that the parents who are warm and supportive are also those who disclose more information about themselves (Norrell, 1984). By being willing to be self-disclosive, these parents established an equitable information-sharing relationship with their adolescents; the ratio of adolescent input (receiving information) to output (sharing information) is approximately equal to the parental input–output ratio (Adams, 1965; Greenberg & Cohen, 1982). Thus, the adolescent views communication with the parent as a shared endeavor and is more willing to offer information. However, it must be noted that an equitable relationship does not involve the sharing of the same information. Parent–child boundaries can still be maintained in equitable relationships.

The role of parent–child boundaries in self-disclosure becomes clear from descriptions of clinical families. While self-disclosure is generally viewed as an indication of psychological health, Jouard (1971), Minuchin (1974), and other family therapists argue that enmeshed families, characterized by poorly defined individual boundaries, often exhibit inappropriate self-disclosure crossing intergenerational boundaries. For example, a teenager in an enmeshed system may self-disclose to parents about his or her experimentation with alcohol or sex. Similarly, a mother may disclose to her adolescent son that the husband is having an extramarital affair. Conversely, it has been suggested that when boundaries between parent and adolescent are highly permeable, one or both parties may inhibit self-disclosure in order to obtain approval (Grotevant & Cooper, 1985).

While the specific dimension of self-disclosure has not been examined empirically, there is some evidence relating enmeshment and disengagement to adolescent psychopathology. Mann, Borduin, Henggeler, and Blaske (1990) describe "cross-generational coalitions," a characteristic of enmeshed families where the child and one parent develop an implicit coalition against the other parent, as is characteristic of families with a delinquent adolescent.

These coalitions generally take the form of a peerlike relationship between mother and child against the father. When compared with families with nondelinquent adolescents, Mann et al. (1990) found that families of delinquents exhibited greater rates of verbal activity between the mother and adolescent, less verbal activity between the father and adolescent, and higher rates of adolescent–father as well as mother–father hostility.

Disengaged families, however, are likely to demonstrate relatively little self-disclosure since individual boundaries are relatively impermeable (Derlega & Margulis, 1983). While a moderate level of social and emotional autonomy from parents is important for developing self-reliance and responsibility, excessive autonomy from parents leaves the adolescent without the behavioral guidance and emotional support necessary to avoid deviant peer activity (Henggeler & Borduin, 1990). In particular, there are suggestions that adolescent substance abuse appears to be associated with greater familial disengagement.

Family factors associated with substance abuse consistently include emotional detachment (Turner, Irwin, & Millstein, 1991) and an absence of warmth (Barnes, Farrel, & Windle, 1990; Brook, Whiteman, & Gordon, 1983). Barnes et al. (1990) found that the presence of maternal nurturance was far more important than parental control in reducing substance abuse. Brook et al. (1983) concluded that the absence of maternal warmth together with maternal unconventionality was associated with higher levels of adolescent abuse.

While not empirically studied, it is likely that experimentation with drugs or alcohol is a common adolescent experience that is not disclosed to parents but is frequently disclosed to peers. Indirect suppport for this hypothesis comes from several studies indicating a much stronger orientation to peers versus parents among adolescent substance abusers (Brook et al., 1983; Barnes et al., 1990).

Enmeshed and disengaged family structures both appear to be associated with adolescent psychopathology (Minuchin, Rosman, & Baker, 1978; Henggeler & Borduin, 1990). Thus, there are suggestions that both too much as well as too little self-disclosure between adolescents and parents characterizes maladjusted families. This relationship should be the topic of further investigation. It is likely that certain psychiatric conditions such as anorexia nervosa and somatoform disorders, which appear clinically to be more common among overly close families (Minuchin et al., 1978), may be characterized by abnormally high levels of self-disclosure. In contrast, substance abuse and conduct disorders, which appear more prevalent among disengaged families, may be characterized by less self-disclosure to parents and more self-disclosure to peers.

Self-disclosure and clinical family therapy

While the role of self-disclosure has been the subject of considerable study as well as a central theoretical construct in individual therapy (Rogers, 1951; Jouard, 1971), there has been relatively little attention devoted to self-disclosure processes in clinical family therapy. The majority of clinical family therapists focus on larger-scale relational patterns (Selvini Palazzoli, Boscolo, Cecchin, & Prata, 1978), power and control hierarchies (Haley, 1976), or cross-generational detouring of conflict (Minuchin, 1974) rather than examine dyadic and intrapersonal dimensions such as self-disclosure. An exception to this practice is the systematic integration of client-centered therapy and communication skills in structured psychoeducational programs such as Guerney's (1977) relationship enhancement therapy. In relationship enhancement, couples are taught to become aware of feelings relevant to the relationship and to communicate these experiences in a manner that will be sensitively understood. Similarly, couples are also instructed in empathic listening as well as when to switch from a listening to a sharing modality (Levant, 1986). Evaluations of this approach have consistently found that it positively affects marital communication. However, significant improvement in marital adjustment has been more difficult to document (Levant, 1986).

When compared with individual treatment, one of the unique dimensions of family therapy is that clients communicate about personal problems and interpersonal issues in the presence of all members of the social system (Bednar, Burlingame, & Masters, 1988). This process is likely to be associated with "higher levels of immediacy and intensity . . . [because family members] are 'doing it' as compared to 'talking about it' " (Bednar et al., 1988). The impact of this immediacy on self-disclosure is highlighted in a study of family therapy with drug-abusing adolescents and their families conducted by Quinn, Kuehl, Thomas, and Joanning (1988). The authors departed from traditional behavioral coding or self-report measures and utilized a qualitative, ethnographic methodology featuring semistructured interviews as the primary data-gathering technique. Family members were interviewed after completing a treatment course of approximately eight sessions. The early stage of therapy centered around emphasizing the seriousness of the adolescents' problem and its impact on the parents. However, therapists who "bore down" on the adolescent and tried to force disclosures with statements such as "What are you angry about? We cannot help you unless you tell us why you are sad" were usually greeted with minimal response; these questions only served to "seal the shell which the adolescent . . . [had already] . . . constructed." Another common therapist tactic to elicit self-disclosure is silence. This strategy also was doomed to failure. When queried by the researcher after the treatment sessions, adolescents recalled this stage as being one in which they were fearful of extreme therapist confrontation and said "as little as possible to anyone" (Quinn et al., 1988). Parents were encouraged to talk very specifically about the adolescent's drug use. The therapist then focused on developing a coalition while generally deemphasizing the adolescent's input. Family members described the therapist as "digging down" and probing all family members for "weak spots" (Newfield, Kuehl, Joanning, & Quinn, 1987). The therapist would then provide the parents with alternatives and suggestions about limit setting for their teen.

While adolescents' disclosures in the treatment sessions were minimal, they became increasingly active outside of sessions. They appeared to believe that their disclosures were used as part of a larger "confidence game" designed to control their behavior (Brehm, 1976) and refused to "play along." The teenagers would attempt to talk their parents out of following the therapist's suggestions. A number of tactics were employed toward this end, including disparaging the therapist, telling parents that treatment was worthless, attempting to instill doubt in parents about the credibility of therapeutic advice, and violating rules established during treatment to see if parents would really follow through. Those families that had been treated successfully exhibited strong parental dyads that held firm to decisions. In unsuccessful treatment, parents reported feeling stuck and helpless, adolescents indicated that they had continued to "bullshit" the therapist and their parents, and, for some teens, drug use actually increased. The bullshitting process appears to be manifestation of a communicative style in which misleading information is provided to provoke others to change behavior or reveal their intention (Derlega & Margulis, 1983).

Posttherapy accounts revealed that a critical element in successful treatment was whether the therapist was perceived in early stages as both caring and able to help (Quinn et al., 1988). If this trusting foundation had not been established, family members were less likely to share important information and did not communicate freely. In keeping with self-disclosure theory, a nonsympathetic authority is unlikely to be successful in eliciting important personal information (Derlega & Marqulis, 1983).

When the therapist did not have the family's confidence and an adequate understanding of them, the suggestions and directives were less likely to be followed. Families who completed all phases of treatment described their therapist as caring and able to cooperate with the parents in formulating useful, practical, suggestions.

While Quinn and colleagues (1988) were not directly investigating self-disclosure, these descriptions highlight the distinction between communication and disclosure. The process of bullshitting is an act of communication but not a form of self-disclosure. The teenagers later reported that they found this process useful so that they could learn how much both the therapist and their parents knew about the behavior. From a social psychological perspective, one could argue that the teenagers were being appropriately self-protective since they did not know how their disclosures would be used in subsequent therapy sessions (Derlega & Margulis, 1983).

This study is unique and of interest for several reasons. First it suggests that ethnographically oriented inductive inquiry elicits information not typically available through conventional psychometric questionnaires of standardized behavior. Second, this naturalistic methodology is particularly suited to interpersonally complex, ecological phenomena and is likely to shed important light on child and adolescent self-disclosure content and process.

Third, this study highlights three particularly relevant social psychological constructs that may provide useful insights into the self-disclosure process. Based on the predictions of psychological reactance theory (Brehm, 1966; Brehm & Brehm, 1981), it is not surprising that therapists who bore down on the adolescent met with resistance. According to this theory, as soon as the adolescent began to feel that his or her control over disclosing information was being constrained, the adolescent would stop sharing information in order to regain control over the behavior. By pressing for more information, the therapist is increasing the adolescent's feelings of reactance, and thus will make his or her resolve to remain quiet even stronger.

When the adolescent did offer input, many times it was designed to bullshit the therapist or his or her parents. By presenting him- or herself in a particular light (i.e., impression management), the adolescent hoped to avoid being held responsible for any unpleasant consequences (Schlenker, 1982) his or her drug-taking behaviors may have caused. This bullshitting, along with trying to talk his or her parents out of following the therapist's suggestions, also permitted the adolescent to appear much more in control. In an attempt to cover personal insecurities, the adolescent employed a symbolic self-completion technique (Wicklund & Gollwitzer, 1982) to present him- or herself as more self-assured and complete than he or she really was. Thus, the disclosures that were offered during treatment were offered for self-presentation, rather than self-disclosure, reasons.

Measuring self-disclosure within the family

An understanding of self-disclosure within the family is likely to be enhanced through application of "whole family" assessment methods. While these tools do not specifically address self-disclosure, they do focus on communication, empathy, and related processes. Research approaches have ranged from microlevel observation of family interaction in the laboratory to the more commonly employed self-report inventories. Family observation scales attempt to assess family members' specific "minute-by-minute" behavior toward one another (Carlson & Grotevant, 1987). In this approach, family behavior while performing a shared task is videotaped and subsequently rated, or rated simultaneously from a video monitor or from behind a one-way mirror. The rating systems usually center around particular theoretical dimensions of family functioning such as separation-individuation (Beavers, 1982) or the relationship between the family and surrounding social context (Skinner & Steinhauer, 1986). While these rating systems may promise objectivity, a consistent limitation has been relatively poor interrater reliability (Carlson & Grotevant, 1987).

Of particular interest to those studying adolescent self-disclosure are self-report measures that assess the respondents' perception of family functioning. While these instruments do not specifically assess self-disclosure, studies with these tools have provided a valuable perspective on adolescents' views of family life. Many of these scales assess intrafamilial communication as well as more specific dimensions, such as empathy, conflict resolution, and emotional distance regulation.

One of the best known self-report scales, the Family Environment Scale (FES; Moos & Moos, 1986) is a 10-subscale instrument loosely grounded in Murray's personality theory that emphasizes the interaction between intrapsychic needs and perceived environmental pressure. Of interest to self-disclosure researchers is the expressiveness subscale that is part of the broader relationship dimension. As formulated by Moos and Moos (1986), the expressiveness items assess the extent to which family members are encouraged to act openly and to express their feelings directly. There are suggestions that expressiveness is an important dimension of adolescent adjustment and family health. In research with adolescent respondents, higher expressiveness has been found to be associated with lower levels of conflict among both intact and divorced African-American families (Dancy

& Handal, 1984). Kleinman, Handal, Enos, Searight, and Ross (1989) found expressiveness to be positively related to psychological distress among nonclinical male teenagers.

The Family Adaptability and Cohesion Evaluation Scales (Olson, Russell, & Sprenkle, 1980; Olson & Portner, 1983) were developed to assess families from the circumplex model of family functioning. The circumplex model centers around two basic dimensions – adaptability and cohesion – both of which are described as existing in moderate degrees in healthy families. *Adaptability* is defined as the ability of the family to change its organizational pattern under stress (Olson et al., 1980). Family factors that are likely to contribute to self-disclosure are reflected in the *cohesion* dimension, which is described as assessing the "emotional bonding members have with one another and the degree of individual autonomy a person experiences in the family system" (Olson, Sprenkle, & Russell, 1979, p. 5). Specific constructs within the cohesion dimension, such as boundaries, emotional bonding, coalitions, and friends, are likely to encompass aspects of self-disclosure within the family and between the family and outsiders.

Olson and Portner (1983) indicate that communication is an important determinant of the balance between adaptability and cohesion within the family. Barnes and Olson (1985) found that, for adolescents, low levels of communication were associated with the healthy, balanced family type, while higher degrees of communication were associated with the more dysfunctional, "extreme" family. Among parents, the opposite pattern emerged with higher levels of communication associated with greater family health. The findings may reflect the longitudinal pattern described earlier in which normal adolescent development includes a relative reduction in self-disclosure to parents with increased disclosure to peers. However, a more recent study found that self-reported parent–adolescent communication was associated with an optimal balance of cohesion and adaptability as well as with the adolescent's academic competence. Adolescents who were less communicative came from more extreme families and demonstrated less academic competence (Masselam, Marcus, & Stunkard, 1990).

An instrument that appears to have considerable promise for assessing adolescents' perceptions of family communication is the Family Assessment Measure III (FAM III; Skinner, Steinhauer, & Santa-Barbara, 1983). Theoretically, the FAM III is based on the Process Model of Family Functioning (PMFF: Steinhauer et al., 1984), which asserts that family members share common goals (e.g., biological, psychological, and social) without which the family would cease to exist. The primary goal of family functioning is to accomplish a variety of basic developmental tasks successfully. Of interest to self-disclosure investigators is that communication and affective expression are among the dimensions important for accomplishing these developmental tasks. The measure is comprised of 134 Likert Scale items constituting three subscales: a 50-item general scale, focusing on the overall level of family health or pathology; a 42-item dyadic relationships scale, measuring perceptions of the relationships of specific pairs of family members (e.g., husband–wife, father–son), and a 42-item self-rating scale, which examines each member's perception of his or her functioning within the family system. The FAM is considered appropriate for use with family members who are at least 10 to 12 years of age. The FAM III is unique in the area of family assessment in that it provides a quick, yet effective means of examining multiple levels of the family system (i.e., individual, dyadic, and whole; Grotevant & Carlson, 1989).

While the FAM III appears promising for simultaneously examining these distinct vantage points, there have been few studies with adolescents. Garfinkle et al. (1983) found that when compared with mothers of nonclinical adolescents, mothers of teenagers with anorexia nervosa exhibited differences with respect to the communication and affective expression subscales.

Three of the current authors (HRS, CMM, and TUK) have completed a number of studies involving the Family-of-Origins Scale (FOS; Hovestadt, Anderson, Piercy, Cochran, & Fine, 1985) with adolescents. The FOS is a 40-item, 10-subscale instrument that is founded on the two dimensions of autonomy and intimacy. The FOS is related to psychodynamic models of family functioning that emphasize the role of internalized representations of family relationships as important to psychological health (Framo, 1976; Gavin & Wamboldt, 1992). It is of interest that family observation studies have found strong associations between parent–adolescent communication, which simultaneous promotes both individuality and connectedness, and higher levels of adolescent ego development (Grotevant & Cooper, 1985; Leaper et al., 1989). Thus, psychological health among adolescents appears to be the result of a process of mutual redefinition of the parent–child relationship rather than the child simply severing ties (Grotevant & Cooper, 1985). From the perspective of self-disclosure, healthy development is a complex process of boundary regulation with alternatives of opening and closing boundaries between the adolescent and their parents (Derlega & Margulis, 1983).

The FOS subscales that appear most directly to assess dimensions relevant to self-disclosure include empathy, openness to others, range of feelings, clarity of expression, and mood and tone. In a study of African-American adolescents, FOS empathy, which assesses family members' interpersonal sensitivity, was found to be positively related to adjustment (Piatt, Ketterson, Skitka, Searight, Rogers, Reuterman, & Manley, 1993). In a recent study, the FOS was administered to a sample of 40 adolescents undergoing inpatient treatment for substance abuse. The scale was administered to the participants at the inpatient unit, and scores were compared with those of nonclinical adolescents. The substance-abusing group scored significantly lower on the total FOS and on five of the subscales. Three of these subscales are relevant to self-disclosure process within the family: clarity of expression (assessing clarity in communicating thoughts and feelings), range of feelings (measuring the latitude for emotional expression), and mood and tone (assessing the general emotional atmosphere) were found to differentiate adolescents in substance abuse treatment from nonclinical adolescents (Searight et al., 1991). In addition to these three scales, openness to others (assessing family members' receptiveness to a range of perspectives) was also found to differentiate nonclinical adolescents from those in inpatient psychiatric treatment (Searight, Niedermeier, Handal, Brown, & Manley, 1992). The FOS appears to have considerable promise of assessing family climates contributing to open and clear communication.

A common factor that appears to unite three of these assessment instruments – the Family-of-Origin Scale, Family Environment Scale, and Family Adaptability and Cohesion Evaluation Scales – is the construct of family intimacy. Our research suggests that when applied to adolescents, these three instruments converge on a shared construct that appears to reflect the dimensions of emotional closeness, warmth, receptiveness of family members' to one another, and support (Manley, Searight, Schudy, Skitka, & Russo, 1992). These elements also appear to be very salient aspects of interpersonal climates promoting self-disclosure (Jouard, 1971; Derlega & Margulis, 1983).

Conclusion

A number of sources, including theoretical writing about the family life cycle, empirical research in developmental psychology focusing on parent–child relationships, and family assessment, suggest that self-disclosure is an important dimension of parent–child and marital interaction. While patterns of self-disclosure with parents versus peers do appear to change as children move through adolescence, disclosures by young people about feelings as well as for purposes of opinion clarification and social validation are likely to be an important dimension of healthy family life. Parental factors associated with adolescent self-disclosure appear to be warmth, support, and clear limits coupled with a challenging "give and take" style of exchange around significant issues. An important dimension for future investigation is the relationship between child and adolescent self-disclosure in families characterized by dysfunctional patterns of enmeshment and disengagement. At present, it is unclear how these larger systemic patterns influence many microlevel communication processes including self-disclosure. The growing number of self-report family assessment instruments may be useful in this regard. In the therapeutic arena, improving self-disclosure appears to be an important component of healthier marital communication. However, with adolescents in family therapy, provoking disclosure around important developmental issues such as drug experimentation or sexuality may conflict with the individuation process. Qualitative methods, involving semistructured interviewing and participant observation, may be of more value than traditional structured behavioral observation and techniques and psychometric instruments in studying self-disclosure within the family environment (Moon, Dillon, & Sprenkle, 1990).

References

Adams, J. S. (1965). Inequity in social exchange. In L. Berkowitz (Ed.), *Advances in experimental social psychology* (Vol. 2, pp. 267–99). New York: Academic.

Barnes, G., Farell, M. P., & Windle, M. L. (1990). Parent–adolescent interactions in the development of alcohol abuse and other deviant behaviors. In B. K. Barber & B. C. Rolling (Eds.), *Parent–adolescent relationships* (pp. 121–40). New York: University Press of America.

Barnes, H. L., & Olson, O. H. (1985). Parent–adolescent communication. In O. H. Olson, H. I. McCubbin, H. Barnes, A. Larsen, M. Muxen, & M. Wilson (Eds.), *Family inventories: Inventories used in a national survey* (pp. 55–70). St. Paul: University of Minnesota.

Bateson, G. (1972). *Steps to an ecology of mind.* New York: Ballantine.

Baumrind, D. (1967). Childcare practices anteceding patterns of preschool behavior. *Genetic Psychology Monographs, 75,* 43–88.

Baumrind, D. (1978). Reciprocal rights and responsibilities in parent–child relations. *Journal of Social Issues, 34,* 179–196.

Baumrind, D. (1991). Effective parenting during the early adolescent transition. In P. A. Cowan & E. M. Hetherington (Eds.), *Family transitions* (pp. 219–44). Hillsdale, NJ: Erlbaum.

Beavers, W. R. (1976). A theoretical basis for family evaluation. In J. M. Lewis, W. R. Beavers, J. T. Gossett, & V. A. Phillips (Eds.), *No single thread: psychological health in family systems* (pp. 46–82). New York: Brunner/Mazel.

Bednar, K. L., Burlingame, G. M., & Masters, K. S. (1988). Systems of family treatment: Substance or semantics? *Annual Review of Psychology, 39,* 401–34.

Blechman (1991). Effective communication: Enabling multiproblem families to change. In P. A. Cowan & E. M. Hetherington (Eds.), *Family transitions* (pp. 219–44). Hillsdale, NJ: Erlbaum.

Borduin, C. M., & Henggeler, S. W. (1987). Post-divorce mother–son relations of delinquent and well-adjusted adolescents. *Journal of Applied Developmental Psychology, 8,* 273–88.

Brehm, J. W. (1966). *A theory of psychological reactance.* New York: Academic.

Brehm, S. S., & Brehm, J. W. (1981). *Psychological reactance: A theory of freedom and control.* New York: Academic.

Broffenbrenner, U. (1986). Ecology of the family as a context for human development. *Developmental Psychology, 22,* 723–42.

Brook, J. S., Whiteman, M., & Gordon, A. S. (1983). Stages of drug use in adolescence: Personality, peer, and family correlates. *Developmental Psychology, 19,* 269–77.

Buhrmester, N., & Furman, W. (1987). The development of companionship and intimacy. *Child Development, 58,* 1101–13.

Carlson, C. I., & Grotevant, H. D. (1987). A comparative review of family rating scales: Guidelines for clinicians and researchers. *Journal of Family Psychology, 1,* 23–47.

Carter, B., & McGoldrick, M. (1989). *The changing family life cycle* (2nd ed.). Boston: Allyn & Bacon.

Chelune, G. J. (Ed.). (1979). *Self-disclosure: Origins, patterns and implications of openness in interpersonal relationships.* San Francisco, CA: Jossey-Bass.

Cowan, P. A. (1991). Individual and family life transitions: A proposal for a new definition. In P. A. Cowan & E. M. Hetherington (Eds.), *Family transitions* (pp. 219–44). Hillsdale, NJ: Erlbaum.

Cozby, P. C. (1973). Self-disclosure: A literature review. *Psychological Bulletin, 2,* 73–91.

Csikszentmihalyi, M., & Larson, R. (1984). *Being adolescent.* New York: Basic.

Dalusio, V. E. (1972). *Self-disclosure and perception of that self-disclosure between parents and their teenage children.* Unpublished doctoral dissertation, United States International University.

Dancy, B. L., & Handal, P. J. (1984). Perceived family climate, psychological adjustment and peer relationships of black adolescents: A function of parental marital status or perceived family conflict. *Journal of Community Psychology, 12,* 222–29.

Derlega, V. J., & Margulis, S. T. (1983). Lonelieness and intimate communication. In D. Perlman & P. C. Cozby (Eds.), *Social psychology* (pp. 207–26). New York: C&S Publishing.

Elder, G. H., Jr. (1991). Family transitions, cycles, and social change. In P. A. Cowan & E. M. Hetherington (Eds.), *Family transitions* (pp. 219–44). Hillsdale, NJ: Erlbaum.

Framo, J. (1976). Family of origin as a therapeutic resource for adults in marital and family therapy: You can and should go home. *Family Process, 15,* 193–210.

Garfinkel, P. E., Garner, D. M., Rose, J., Darby, P. L., Brandes, J. S., O'Hanlon, J., & Walsh, N. (1983). A comparison of characteristics in the families of patients with anorexia nervosa and normal controls. *Psychological Medicine, 13,* 821–8.

Gavin, L. A., & Wamboldt, F. S. (1992). The Family-of-Origin Scale Revisited: What can be measured from whom and how? *Journal of Marital and Family Therapy, 18,* 179–88.

Greenberg, J., & Cohen, R. C. (1982). *Equity and justice in social behavior.* New York: Academic.

Grotevant, H. D., & Carlson, C. I. (1989). *Family assessment – A guide to methods and measures.* New York: Guilford.

Grotevant, H. K., & Cooper, C. R. (1985). Patterns of interaction in family relationships and the development of identity exploration in adolescence. *Child Development, 56,* 415–28.

Guerney, B. G. (1977). *Relationship enhancement.* San Francisco: Jossey-Bass.

Haley, J. (1976). *Problem-solving therapy.* San Francisco: Jossey-Bass.

Hauser, S. T., Powers, S. I., Noam, G., Jacobson, A. M., Weiss, B., & Follansbee, D. J. (1984). Familial contexts of adolescent ego development. *Child Development, 55,* 195–213.

Henggeler, S. W., & Borduin, C. M. (1990). *Family therapy and beyond.* Pacific Grove, CA: Brooks/Cole.

Hoffman, L. (1981). *Foundations of family therapy.* New York: Basic.

Hovestadt, A. J., Anderson, W. R., Piercy, F. P., Cochran, S. W., & Fine, M. (1985). A family-of-origin scale. *Journal of Marital and Family Therapy, 11,* 287–97.

Hunter, F. T., & Youniss, J. (1982). Changes in functions of three relationships during adolescence. *Developmental Psychology, 18,* 800–811.

Jackson, D. D. (1957). The question of family homeostasis. *Psychiatric Quarterly Supplement, 31,* 79–90.

Jouard, S. (1971). *The transparent self: Self-disclosure and well-being* (2nd ed.). New York: Van Nostrand-Reinhold.

Kleinman, S. L., Handal, P. J., Enos, D. M., Searight, H. R., & Ross, M. J. (1989). Relationship between perceived family climate and adolescent adjustment. *Journal of Clinical Child Psychology, 18,* 351–9.

Komarovsky, M. (1974). Patterns of self-disclosure of male undergraduates. *Journal of Marriage and the Family, 36,* 677–86.

Kramer, J. (1985). Family myth and homeostasis. *Archives of General Psychiatry, 9,* 457–63.

Leaper, C., Hanser, S. T., Kremen, A., Powers, S. I., Jacobson, A. M., Noam, G. G., Weiss-Perry, B., & Follansbee, D. (1989). Adolescent–parent interactions in relation to adolescents' gender and ego development pathway: A longitudinal study. *Journal of Early Adolescence, 9,* 335–61.

Levant, R. F. (1986). Client centered skills-training programs for the family. In R. F. Levant (Ed.), *Psychoeducational approaches to family counseling.* New York: Springer.

Manley, C. M., Searight, H. R., Schudy, K. L., Skitka, L. J., & Russo, J. R. (1992). The Family-of-Origin Scale with adolescents: Construct validity. Unpublished manuscript.

Mann, B. J., Borduin, C. M., Henggeler, S. W., & Blaske, D. M. (1990). An investigation of systemic conceptualizations of parent–child coalitions and symptom change. *Journal of Consulting and Clinical Psychology, 58,* 336–44.

Masselam, V. S., Marcus, R. S., & Stunkard, C. L. (1990). Parent–adolescent communication, family functioning, and school performance. *Adolescence, 24,* 724–37.

Minuchin, S. (1974). *Families and family therapy.* Cambridge, MA: Harvard University Press.

Minuchin, S., Rosman, B., & Baker, L. (1978). *Psychosomatic families: Anorexia nervosa in context.* Cambridge, MA: Harvard University Press.

Moon, S. M., Dillion, D. R., & Sprenkle, D. H. (1990). Family therapy and qualitative research. *Journal of Marital and Family Therapy, 16,* 357–73.

Moos, R. H., & Moos, B. (1986). *Family Environment Scale manual.* Palo Alto, CA: Consulting Psychologists Press.

Newfield, N. A., Kuehl, B. P., Joanning, H., & Quinn, W. H. (1987, October). A mini ethnography of the family therapy of adolescent drug abuse: The ambiguous experience. Paper presented at the 45th Annual Meeting of the American Association for Marriage and Family Therapy, Chicago.

Nichols, M. P. (1984). *Family therapy: Concepts and methods.* New York: Gardner.

Niedermeier, C., Handal, P. J., Brown, N. Y., Manley, C. M., & Searight, H. R. (1992, August). The relationship between family functioning and psychological distress among adolescent psychiatric inpatients. Paper presented at the American Psychological Association annual meeting, Washington, DC.

Norrell, J. E. (1984). Self-disclosure: Implications for the study of parent–adolescent interaction. *Journal of Youth and Adolescence, 13,* 163–78.

Olson, D. H., & Portner, J. (1983). Family adaptability and cohesion evaluation scales. In E. E. Filsinger (Ed.), *Marriage and family assessment* (pp. 299–316). Beverly Hills, CA: Sage.

Olson, D. H., Russell, C. S., & Sprenkle, D. H. (1980). Circumplex model of marital and family systems: Theoretical update. *Family Process, 22,* 69–83.

Olson, D. H., Sprenkle, D. H., & Russell, C. S. (1979). Circumplex model of marital and family systems: Cohesion and adaptability dimensions, family types, and clinical application. *Family Process, 18,* 3–28.

Piatte, A. L., Ketterson, T. U., Skitka, L. J., Searight, H. R., Rogers, B. J., Reuterman, N. A., & Manley, C. M. (1993). The relationship of psychological adjustment to perceived family functioning among African-American adolescents. *Adolescence, 23,* 674–84.

Quinn, W. H., Kuehl, B. P., Thomas, F. N., & Joanning, H. (1988). Families of adolescent drug abusers: Systemic interventions to attain drug-free behavior. *American Journal of Drug and Alcohol Abuse, 14,* 65–87.

Reiss, D. (1981). *The family's construction of reality.* Cambridge, MA: Harvard University Press.

Riskin, J. (1982). Research on "nonlabeled" families: A longitudinal study. In F. Walsh (Ed.), *Normal family processes* (pp. 67–93). New York: Guilford.

Rogers, C. (1951). Client-centered therapy: Its current practice, implications, and theory. Boston: Houghton-Mifflin.

Sameroff, A. J. (1983). Development systems: Contexts and evolution. In W. Kessen (Ed.), *Handbook of child psychology: Vol. 1. History, theories and methods* (pp. 238–94). New York: Wiley.

Sameroff, A. J. (1987). The social context of development. In N. Eisenberg (Ed.), *Contemporary topics in developmental psychology* (pp. 273–91). New York: Wiley.

Santrock, J. W. (1990). *Adolescence* (4th ed.). Dubuque, IA: Brown.

Schlenker, B. R. (1982). Translating actions into attitudes: An identity-analytic approach to the explanation of social conduct. In L. Berkowitz (Ed.), *Advances in experimental social psychology* (Vol. 15, pp. 193–247). New York: Academic.

Searight, H. R., Manley, C. M., Binder, A. F., Krohn, E., Rogers, B. J., & Russo, J. R. (1991). The families of origin of adolescent drug abusers: Perceived autonomy and intimacy. *Contemporary Family Therapy, 13,* 71–81.

Searight, H. R., Niedermeier, C., Handal, P. J., Brown, N. Y., & Manley, C. M. (1992, August). *The relationship between family function, and psychological distress among adolescent psychiatric inpatients.* Paper presented at the annual meeting of the American Psychological Association, Washington, DC.

Searight, H. R., & Openlander, P. (1986). Assessment and treatment of social contexts: Towards an interactional therapy. *Journal of Social and Personal Relationships, 3,* 71–87.

Selvini Palazzoli, M., Boscolo, L., Cecchin, G., & Prata, G. (1978). *Paradox and counterparadox.* New York: Aronson.

Skinner, H., & Steinhauer, P. D. (1986). *Family Assessment Measure Clinical Rating Scale*. Toronto. Addictions Research Foundation.

Skinner, H. A., Steinhauer, P. D., & Santa-Barbara, J. (1983). The family assessment measure. *Canadian Journal of Community Mental Health, 2,* 91–105.

Snoek, D., & Rothblum, E. (1979). Self-disclosure among adolescents in relation to parental affection and control patterns. *Adolescence, 14,* 333–40.

Sroufe, L. A. (1989). Relationships and relationship disturbances. In A. J. Sameroff & R. N. Emde (Eds.), *Relationship disturbances in early childhood: A developmental approach* (pp. 97–124). New York: Basic.

Steinhauer, P. D., Santa-Barbara, J., & Skinner, H. (1984). The process model of family functioning. *Canadian Journal of Psychiatry, 29,* 77–88.

Turner, R. A., Irwin, C. E., & Millstein, S. (1991). Family structure, family processes, and experimenting with substances during adolescence. *Journal of Research on Adolescence, 1,* 93–106.

Von Bertalanfy, L. (1969). General systems theory and psychiatry: An overview. In W. Gray, F. Duhl, & N. Rizzo (Eds.), *General systems theory and psychiatry* (pp. 33–46). Boston: Little, Brown.

West, L. W., & Zingle, H. W. (1969). A self-disclosure inventory for adolescents. *Psychological Reports, 24,* 439–55.

Wicklund, R. A., & Gollwitzer, P. M. (1982). *Symbolic self-completion*. Hillsdale, NJ: Erlbaum.

Younnis, J. (1983). Social construction of adolescence by adolescents and parents. In H. D. Grotevant & C. R. Cooper (Eds.), *Adolescent development in the family: New directions for child development* (pp. 93–103). San Francisco: Jossey-Bass.

Author index

Aboud, F. E., 66, 91
Abramovitch, R., 83
Adam-Tucker, C., 171
Adams, G., 37
Adams, J. S., 212
Adams, N. E., 185
Adams, R. G., 39, 46
Adelman, M. B., 38
Adelson, J., 43, 61
Ahn, R., 116, 117
Albrecht, T. L., 38
Allen, J. G., 81, 128
Allinsmith, W. A., 136
Alpert, R., 135, 136
Altman, I., 1, 2, 40, 42
Alvarez, M., 119
Aman, C., 166, 188, 189
Anchor, K. N., 105
Anderson, C. A., 100
Anderson, W. R., 219
Aquan-Assee, J., 84, 87
Archer, R. L., 2, 31, 116
Argyle, M., 82
Aries, E. J., 19
Asher, S., 100, 103, 104
Ausubel, D. P., 136
Autsen, J., 79
Avery, A. W., 82

Baddeley, A. D., 177
Bailey, G., 180
Bailey, R., 180
Baillet, S. D., 176
Baker, L., 213
Balk, D., 82
Balkwell, J. W., 15
Balswick, J. O., 15
Bandura, A., 169, 175, 178, 179, 180, 185
Bank, S. P., 81
Bardwich, J., 29

Barger, S. D., 193
Barnes, G., 213
Barnes, H. L., 218
Barnett, J. K., 58, 81, 114
Barnett, M. A., 120, 121
Bateson, G., 204, 205
Batson, C. D., 113, 115
Batten, P. G., 2, 100
Baumrind, D., 149, 151, 207, 211
Beardsall, L., 120
Beavers, W. R., 217
Bednar, K. L., 214
Beeghly, M., 86
Belk, S. S., 2, 63
Bell, N. J., 82
Belle, D., 197
Belletirie, G., 46
Berg, J. H., 2, 31
Berg-Cross, L., 15, 81
Bergout Austin, A. M., 81
Berliner, L., 169, 171, 181
Berndt, T. J., 3, 14, 59, 61, 62, 63, 65, 66,
    71, 72, 74, 83, 101
Berscheid, E., 59
Bierman, K. L., 62
Bigelow, B. J., 61
Bigelow, R., 14
Bixenstine, B. A., 145
Bixenstine, V. E., 145
Blaske, D. M., 212
Blechman, 207, 208
Blieszner, R., 46
Block, J. H., 113, 119
Blos, P., 41, 44
Blume, E. S., 173, 178
Blyth, D. A., 15, 27, 32
Bohannon, J. N., 176
Borduin, C. M., 205, 206, 212, 213
Boscolo, L., 214
Bottoms, B. L., 166, 177

227

Subject index

DATE DUE			
JUL 2 2 '96			
MAY 0 2 2000			